BREATHE

Living My Best Life With Chronic Lung Cancer

Jim Petzing

Paperback ISBN: 978-1-5356-1789-5
ePub ISBN: 978-1-5356-1790-1
Kindle ISBN: 978-1-5356-1791-8

This book is dedicated to the entire staff at OptumCare Cancer Care in Henderson, NV, especially Dr. Gollard and my oncology nurses (Marianne, Janet and Radka) who have taken care of me for over 2½ years.

Also, a very special thank you to Dr. Tahir for getting me started on the right track quickly.

And, finally, without Janice, my high school friend, I wouldn't be here today.

You all have provided me with the strength to keep on fighting.

OCT 17 2017

It's Back. Can't Believe I Have to Fight Cancer... Again!

Sometimes life just isn't fair! After being cancer-free for 2 1/2 years and feeling great, I got told today by my general practitioner that my recent CT scan shows cancer in my right lung.

Needless to say, I'm reeling from this news. Mostly, I'm angry. The thought of having to endure body-crushing sickness and pain all over again is overwhelming. I don't yet know how extensive or developed this new cancer is, but this will be confirmed by a PET scan that likely will be scheduled for tomorrow or Wednesday.

On a positive note, I'm not a novice anymore and know how the process works. I will be a force to be reckoned with, so my doctors better be ready for me and all of my questions.

My biggest concern is whether my health insurance (Health Plan of Nevada) will cover surgery and treatments outside of the State. I have not been impressed with my current network of providers and am very anxious about moving forward here.

Ironically, I was looking for a new project to work on, so now I have one..... ME. I want to believe our Higher Power only gives us what they believe we can truly handle. However, this is getting a little ridiculous. I already survived neck cancer and a plane crash in 2015. Now I have cancer again? Just having trouble making sense of it all.

Since writing about your sickness is therapeutically proven to aid in healing, I will continue to provide regular updates here on CaringBridge.org. Please keep me in your thoughts and prayers. They really do help!

OCT 18 2017

Just Getting Over the Shock...So Glad I Have Support

When I got the bad news yesterday on the phone from Dr. Tahir, I was playing in a poker tourney at the Venetian. I had a mini meltdown on the phone with him and then went back to the poker table to try to resume play with tears welling up in my eyes. I felt like everyone was staring at me, which I guess they were since an older woman in Seat 6 looked over at me in Seat 3 and asked me if I was alright. The words, "No, I'm not...I just got told I have fucking cancer again!" came rolling out of my mouth. I think my table mates were as shocked as I was at that point. The older woman got up, came over and wrapped her arms around me. She whispered in my ear, "You can fight this and will win, just like you do here." I half-smiled and said, "Thank you."

Right after that scene, I was moved to another table. I couldn't get my conversation with Dr. Tahir out of my head and didn't really want to be playing anymore, so I just shoved my chips in with Q6 on a Q32 flop and got busted by KQ. Off I went to my car in the parking garage, on the seventh floor, where I proceeded to call my family and friends to let them know my situation. It was deja vu from 2 1/2 years ago. These calls are not fun to make. I got my crying out of the way and tried to remain calm and collected when talking to everyone. I was so angry that this bullshit cancer was back in my body. Why me...again!?

After 90 minutes on the phone in my car, I left the Venetian and went home to hug my cats, Zing & Zang. They bring me great joy! Of course, they were really just interested in being fed the minute I walked in the door.

I microwaved two corn dogs on a stick and a chicken cordon bleu breast for dinner. Yes, comfort food. I know how bad that sounds from a fattening caloric standpoint, but boy they were good. When I was sick the last time, I ate my way up to 235 lbs. before the treatments started because I knew I'd be losing a lot of weight during the process. It ended up being about 40 lbs.

So I watched a few TV shows, including *The Voice* and *Anderson Cooper 360*, and then fell asleep on the couch from pure mental and physical exhaustion. I awoke at 1am, got up and threw myself into bed. Again, I awoke at 4:20am and couldn't get back to sleep. So I checked Facebook and saw all of the amazing messages of concern, caring and support coming in. I read every one of them. You have no idea how much it helps to know that you're out there thinking about and praying for me. I really do believe in the power of prayer!

My Mom is the only person I didn't call yesterday when I got the bad news. She's 84 and in a beautiful assisted living center in Connecticut where I grew up. She has a 12-hour aide every day in her apartment from 8am-8pm, and I didn't want her to be alone when I called her with my cancer diagnosis. We spoke around 8:30am her time this morning and, of course, she was quite upset and concerned. What's most difficult for her is, that due to her medical condition, she wasn't able to travel to come see me when I was fighting the battle the last time and won't be able to this time either. She feels quite bad about that.

I did most of my crying yesterday, but can't help getting teary-eyed every once in a while when I think about what's possibly in store for me. I met with Dr Tahir at 8am to get the official report from Friday's CT scan. In layman's terms, the scan showed two cancer spots in my right lung. One is at the top, near where the trachea and esophagus split the lungs, and the other is at the bottom of the lung. The bad news is that this is a spreading cancer and not isolated. Apparently, it's inoperable, which rules out surgery as an option for treatment. So it's looking like I'll be doing the chemo/radiation combo again.

Next steps are a full body PET scan, which will show how developed and extensive the cancer is and where else it might have traveled, plus a biopsy of the lower cancerous node to determine the cell type we're dealing with.

Hopefully, this will happen by the end of the week. The doctor is concerned about my anxiety level and potential inability to sleep, so he prescribed Xanax. I've never taken it before, so we'll see how that works.

I think the most important thing for me right now is to keep busy so I don't become preoccupied with the situation. So, I went to The Venetian and played the $200 NLH tourney placing 44th of 247 players, but not good enough to win any money this time. Before the tourney, I had breakfast with my good friend, Louise, who also played the tourney and cashed in 12th place. You go, Weezie!! She, along with so many of my other poker and dealer friends, were there today giving me lots of hugs of caring and support. It felt good to know that I have so many people in my corner.

I know I'll need all of you as I enter this battle once again.

OCT 19 2017

The Frustration Begins

Yesterday was more than frustrating. I received a call from the scheduling department at the facility I'm assigned to for my upcoming PET scan. My doctor had put a stat (rush) on the order, so I expected to be going for it in a day or two.

Here's how my conversation went:

> Me: Yes, this is James.
>
> Her: Hi, we are calling to schedule your PET scan as ordered by Dr. Tahir.
>
> Me: Great, I hope we can do it today or tomorrow.
>
> Her: (Chuckle) Sir, the earliest we can get you in is Friday, October 27th at 4pm.
>
> Me: Are you kidding me? My doctor ordered a stat on it. This is unacceptable!
>
> Her: We are completely booked until them. We have no openings.

Me: (Loud and Firm) Well you need to find one, honey! Do you understand that I have two cancerous spots in my right lung and it could be spreading through my body as we speak? I'm not going to wait for ten more days to get this PET scan. Stat means "now," "immediately," "ASAP." Do you understand that?

Her: I'll get my supervisor on the phone

Me: (Sarcastically) GOOD IDEA!

Supervisor: Mr. Petzing, I understand you're upset?

Me: (Laughing) Uh....I'd say irate!

Supervisor: What can I do to help you?

Me: Tell me that you can get me in today or tomorrow for my PET scan!

Supervisor: That likely won't be possible, but let me see what I can do. I need to put you on a brief hold.

Me: Fine. (Wait two minutes)

Supervisor: Thank you for waiting. We just had one opening become available this Friday, October 20th at 2pm. Does that work for you?

Me: YES! Book it!

And so she did.

This is just one example of how "sick" people like me are treated by the health care system. It's absurd. I'm so thankful that I'm an assertive, unafraid, direct and "get it done" type of guy. NO ONE will ever mess with me when it comes to my health and my life. Just think of all the people (maybe even yourself) that don't even challenge what they're told. They just play along because they think they have to. Well let me tell you, you don't have to succumb to it. When you have cancer or any debilitating illness that may be a life or death situation, you MUST stand up for yourself and not let anyone F**K with you...ever!

It makes me very concerned and sad to think that there are many older folks and passive personality types that just fall in line and do what their told, even when it can negatively affect them. They accept the status quo without even questioning it! Well let me tell you, don't ever do that when it comes to your health and well-being. You need to be your own best advocate. Fight for yourself because no one else will.

The medical community (especially here in Las Vegas) is a full-fledged, profit hungry, politically entangled, manufacturing type industry. They just "process" the next poor soul waiting in line. There is no sense of urgency and virtually no empathy or caring exhibited. So YES, I'm very frustrated and I'm sure there is much more to come. I'm so passionate about this right now, that I'm thinking of taking on this issue as a project. I will escalate this as far as I can. No one, especially someone who is sick and possibly dying, deserves to be caught up in this bureaucratic bullshit.

So after dealing with that crap all morning, I pulled myself together and went and played poker. I busted the noon tourney and ran very deep in the 7pm tourney placing 7th out of 40, but out of the money. I got home at 2:15am, took a Xanax and slept like a baby for a change.

OCT 20 2017

In Turmoil

I got up at 9am today, which is very late for me. Usually Zing & Zang are in my face, purring and rubbing up against me around 7am so that I get up to feed them. They must have known I needed the sleep.

I spent most of the morning on the phone with yet another scheduler -- this time for my biopsy. Dr. Tahir's order for the PET scan and biopsy was a bit unclear, so there was confusion over whether the biopsy and PET scan could be scheduled at the same place on the same day. After two hours of back and forth, and the scheduler speaking directly with Dr. Tahir, it was determined that I need to have the PET scan first to see where else the cancer may have spread. If it has, there may be more than one biopsy required. At this point, the cancer spot in my lower right lung is definitely going to be biopsied, hopefully next week. I'm praying that no other cancer is found in my body during the PET scan tomorrow.

I played poker again today, but my head really wasn't into it. I busted 59th of 130 players and felt weepy the entire day at the table. I think the emotional turmoil I'm in has caught up with me. I'm a great at compartmentalizing my feelings, but sometimes they just escape out of their boxes. That happened today. Instead of hanging around playing penny slots and waiting for the 7pm tourney, I drove home, got in bed and slept for two hours. I guess I needed it. I'm a little anxious about my PET scan tomorrow...not for the test itself (done it before), but for the impending results. Hoping for the best.

OCT 21 2017

PET Scan Done...Touched by a Tribute to Me!

I woke up this morning in a funk, anxious about getting my PET scan and the results that will be coming on Monday. After making some eggs and sausage for breakfast, I laid on my living room couch with Zing & Zang and called my Dad, Cheryl (Stepmom) and Mom. They are all very concerned and feel a bit helpless, like I do. Everything is out of our control right now. All we can do is wait for more information and then take action based on it. I'm trying to remain calm, but it's hard. Today was a sad, weepy one for me. Hopefully, tomorrow will be better. It will be a tough weekend wondering about whether my cancer has spread and if it's even treatable, but I'll try to stay positive and keep occupied playing poker.

My PET scan was at 2pm. After filling out the traditional paperwork, I was weighed and injected with a radioactive sugar solution. Then I was given the choice of vanilla or mocha-flavored Barium and sucked down 14oz of the vanilla "shake." It was kind of nasty. I had my own TV room to hang out in for 45 minutes and decided to watch *Ellen* while the cancer cells lurking in my body feasted on the infused sugar. The radiation will light up those cells and be very evident on the PET scan. I changed into a stylish open-backed gown, left my black socks on, and got on the sheeted PET scan table. I asked the assistant to take a few photos for posterity sake, which she kindly obliged. I posted them on Facebook and got many comments on my "nice" legs and fashion mishap (black socks with green gown). I'm very glad that Fashion Police has been cancelled.

The PET scan itself lasted 30 minutes. The table I was lying on moved back and forth through a long dark tunnel. They scanned from my eyebrows to my thighs. Hopefully, all they saw was the two cancer spots I already know I have in my right lung from the CT scan I had last week. When we finished, I changed back into my street clothes and called Dr. Tahir on his direct line. He was out of the office today and told me to call him first thing on Monday morning for the results. When I met with him this past Tuesday to discuss the CT scan results and the debacle I went through with his staff, he gave me his personal cell phone number to call so I can avoid getting caught up in the mess at his office. We really bonded in that meeting. I learned that he has a very ill 23-year-old son that has been hooked up to tubes and receiving 24 hour care at home since he was 2, when he was only given 6 months to live. I was really moved by his story. I'm so hoping that he will be my advocate and help me get to the Mayo Clinic in Arizona, where I want to be treated.

After leaving the PET scan facility, I drove to the Venetian, had a sweet pork quesadilla, played penny slots and won $50. Then I played the 7pm re-buy tourney and busted out at 10:30pm when my AJ was sucked out on by JT after I shoved pre-flop and the player who called spiked a T on the flop. I'll try again tomorrow.

On an amazing note today, the folks at the "Run It Up Reno" poker series paid tribute to my plight with a group photo and mass wish for me to "run good" in my cancer battle. I was supposed to be there this past week playing in their tournaments, but I cancelled my trip last Saturday when I knew in my heart that I would be getting bad news about my cancer coming back. Unfortunately, I was right. If you'd like to see this beautiful tribute, just go to RunItUpReno.com.

And, finally, a poker friend of mine, who is playing today in the Main Event of "Run It Up Reno" has dedicated his play in the event to ME, since I could not be there myself. He called and told me on Wednesday that he is donating 50% of his winnings in the Main Event to help me pay for some of the out-of-pocket costs that I'm incurring in this new cancer fight. I can't even begin to express in words how touched I am by this incredible act of generosity and support. He wishes to remain anonymous, but he'll always hold a special place as one of my angels in this journey.

OCT 22 2017

I'm an Emotional Wreck this Morning

It's true. I just can't stop crying this morning.

Last night when I got home from playing poker around 12:30am, I did something that I told people in my book NOT to do. I went online and researched anything I could find about lung cancer. When I did this the last time prior to getting the results from my neck cancer PET scan, I made myself crazy with fear and anxiety. Everything I read was dire. But, I just couldn't help myself this time. Tomorrow morning, I get the results of my PET scan, and I want to be prepared with as much information as possible. I want to be able to speak intelligently with my doctor and ask the right questions about my status, stage, upcoming biopsy and prognosis for the future.

I think I've been in denial about just how bad lung cancer is. Since I've never been a smoker, I naively thought that it was something "foreign" that could never happen to me. Guess I was wrong about that.

Apparently, there are two types of lung cancer: small cell and non-small cell. Small cell is really bad. With treatment, folks generally can live 12-24 months, but only 2 to 4 months without it. Based upon what I read, I'm "hoping" I have non-small cell (can't believe I said that.) This is a little better, relatively speaking.

If I'm in Stage 1A or B, it looks like 60% of people who undergo treatment are still alive after 5 years. As the stages go up to 2, 3, and 4, the survival rates decrease considerably. You can do the research yourself. I can't even go there with you right now. I'm wanting to believe that I'm in Stage 1 with a squamous cell carcinoma. That's the type of neck cancer cell I had the last time. It's my best hope. Disturbingly, it is treatable, but not curable. It will always be there. Lurking. Waiting to attack. The PET scan and upcoming biopsy later this week should reveal where exactly I stand.

After taking a Xanax and being online until 3am, I finally fell asleep. When I woke up this morning, I had a text from Elizabeth, one of my best girlfriends and "angels," who cared for me when I battled neck cancer in Michigan. She drove me 40 miles each way to most of my radiation treatments and sat with me,providing comfort during all seven of my four-hour chemo infusions. She sent me a very meaningful biblical passage that I'm still processing and trying to embrace. I'll share it with you another time. Elizabeth is like the sister I never had. She was and continues to be my key spiritual support.

Ironically, Elizabeth moved to Scottsdale, AZ a couple of weeks ago and lives only seven minutes from my ex-wife, Charlene, who I also have a great relationship with. They met for the first time this past Wednesday and really hit it off. I'm so glad. Additionally, Charlene's and my best couple friends, Steve & Cory, also live in Scottsdale. I know it's my Higher Power's plan for me to go to AZ to have my treatments at either the Mayo Clinic or the Cancer Treatment Center of America. This is my goal. It's no coincidence.

After my emotional call with Elizabeth, I called my boyfriend, Chris, in Michigan. I couldn't stop crying. I told him about the research I had done, and he already knew the information because he had done the same. We've been physically apart for two years, but have been able to see each other every four to six weeks during that entire time. It has been difficult, but we've managed. And now this. He's there and I'm here. I know how badly he feels that he isn't here with me right now, but I've told him to save his vacation days so he can support me in person when I really need him. We both feel quite helpless right now. I'm very stressed and sad about it.

So rather than sit around the house today and dwell on what tomorrow's results will bring, I'm heading out the door to go play poker at the Venetian. All I can say is CANCER SUCKS and I will do my very best to fight the fight and win again! I'm not going down. It's not my time. It can't be.

OCT 24 2017

Bad News...I Have Lung Cancer

It's hard to believe that I have the Big C....again! This time it's in my right lung and likely spreading.

I woke up this morning scared to face the day. Last Friday, Dr. Tahir told me to call his direct cell line at 8am to get my PET scan results. When he answered, he was still on his way into the office and told me to call him back at 9am, which I did. Our call didn't last long. All he said was, "Jim, I need you to come see me to review these results, so we can discuss the options you have. I've already gone downstairs to share them with an oncologist friend of mine, so I'll let you know what he thinks, too."

His words felt like a gut punch, and my mind started racing. I immediately called my bestie, Louise. She was already on her way to be with me and took me to my quickly scheduled 11am appointment with Dr. Tahir.. By this point, friends and family were texting and calling me to see what my results were, because I thought I'd have them by 9am. I avoided those calls and texts -- except for Dad's. When I answered his call, I could barely speak. I was upset and crying uncontrollably. I told him I was sorry I couldn't talk right then and that I was going to see Dr. Tahir at 11am to get my results. He understood and, like everyone, told me he was praying hard for good results and that he loved me.

Louise and I went for a quick breakfast and put a list of questions together to ask Dr. Tahir. I tend to get very emotional and blank out in these "bad news" meetings, so I'm glad Louise could join me to take notes and provide support. We were ushered into his office immediately.

Dr. Tahir came in with a concerned look on his face and got right down to delivering the information we needed, but didn't want to hear.

Basically, my PET scan results confirmed that I have lung cancer (likely Stage 2). There is one large tumor in the hilar region of my upper right lung crossing over my trachea, a smaller one in my lower lobe and two floating nodules in the esophageal region. Next step is a bronchoscopy to obtain a tissue sample so that the specific type of cancer cell can be identified. This will help determine the best options for a treatment plan. The PET scan also revealed a suspicious spot in my lumbar area, which requires a bone scan. So, there are still a lot of unknowns and unanswered questions. I'll be getting assigned a lung specialist and oncologist shortly.

Louise drove me back to my place and we debriefed our meeting with Dr. Tahir. After she left, I started making the tough calls to my family and close friends to update them on the day's events. By 2:15pm, I was emotionally exhausted and got in bed to take a much needed nap with Zing & Zang by my side.

I got up at 5pm, made a few more calls, answered texts, and decided to order a pizza for delivery. I took another Xanax to reduce my anxiety and have had a pleasant evening watching The Voice and catching up with the day's news on CNN.

Ironically, three years ago yesterday was my last chemo and radiation treatment for neck cancer. It's so hard to comprehend and understand why this is happening all over again. I beat it once. I will beat it again! I'm going to kick cancer's ass. Count on it.

OCT 28 2017

A Bad Week

It's 4:15am and I can't sleep.

It hasn't been a good week. On Monday night, I had a really bad night with shortness of breath, ongoing dry cough, a severe headache and lots of anxiety. On Tuesday morning, I drove myself to the ER at Sunrise Hospital here in Vegas at 8am. I was lucky that there was only one other family in the waiting area, so I was whisked through the system (which never happens) and ended up in an ER "room" with a curtain. This ER is the same one that took in and treated 250 of the victims from the recent October 1 Las Vegas Massacre concert shootings.

I brought with me all of my test results that I've been collecting over the past month or so: chest x-ray, CT scan, PET scan and pulmonary tests. I went through the usual Q&A about my current situation and cancer history, and then got the routine blood pressure/blood tests and a breathing mask. One of the doctors wanted me to have another chest x-ray. Based on what he saw (my large 5 1/2" tumor in my right lung and a couple of smaller ones), they decided that I'd be transferred to Dignity Health-San Martin Hospital for a bronchoscopy. Unfortunately, my Health Plan of Nevada HMO insurance, that I pay $475/month for, wasn't accepted at Sunrise Hospital for that particular procedure. My transfer by ambulance couldn't happen until 7pm, so my friends, Louise and Ardys, came to be with me for a few hours in the ER so I wouldn't be alone.

As the day progressed, the ER became overloaded with patients. They needed my "room," so I was moved into the hallway at 4:15pm right in front of the entrance where all of the ambulances were dropping off patients. I felt like I was watching an episode of the television show, *ER*. I saw a little bit of everything from folks with drug overdoses to a guy who fell off of a 6' ft ladder that ended up piercing him. It was sad to experience all of this, but it did make the time go by faster as did a surprise visit from my friend, Jackie.

Around 7:30pm, the ambulance came to transfer me to Dignity Health-San Martin. While riding over in the back of the vehicle, the EMT told me that they were taking me to the nicest hospital of 17 in the Vegas area. I was surprised to learn this as I've come to realize that I have really shitty insurance that keeps me from going out of state and dictates exactly where I go and who I go to for everything. I will never sign on with an HMO insurance policy again.

I got really lucky. San Martin Hospital was a newer facility, beautiful, and not crowded. Because I was transferred by Sunrise Hospital, all of the paperwork had been taken care of so I was immediately taken to my room and given the usual tests. I met Dr. Singh at midnight, who would be my internist during my stay. He told me I'd see him again in the morning and that I'd likely be having a bronchoscopy. I was given a breathing treatment, Ativan, an IV, and other meds, which helped me to have a very restful sleep.

On Tuesday morning at 7am, Dr. Singh arrived and told me that Dr. Oh would be doing a less invasive tissue biopsy via needle through my lung instead of the originally planned bronchoscopy. However, it was decided that I'd need another CT scan before that decision would be final. So I was wheeled down to radiology. But, upon reviewing the CT scan results, there was a change in plans. Dr. Oh felt that it was too dangerous to do the needle biopsy because there was so much lung to get through first before reaching my tumor. Apparently, the large tumor in my right lung is intertwined with my trachea, heart vessels/arteries and other tissues, so they would need to try something different. It looked like I would be getting a bronchoscopy instead, but they'd need a lung surgeon versus a radiologist for that procedure.

I was wheeled back up to my room. I hadn't even gotten settled when another doctor and his assistant walked in. He asked if we could turn off the television because we needed to talk. His name was Dr. Osman, a heart and lung surgeon. He told me that he had reviewed all of my paperwork, along with the recent CT scan, and wondered if I had family in the area. I said, "No, but I have a great network of friends here." He asked me a few other questions about my background, work experience, etc., and I knew he was trying to get a sense for how smart I was and how much information I could handle and process.

Dr. Osman said, "Your situation doesn't look good, Jim. You have multiple tumors, including an exceptionally large one on your right lung that is obstructing your trachea, and at least four lymph nodes showing up in your scans. Given your previous bout with neck cancer, it's highly likely that you are in Stage 3AB or 4 of lung cancer, but we won't know for sure until we do a biopsy and test your nodes."

This was information I DID NOT expect to hear. I thought I might be in Stage 2, at the worst. I'm not sure I heard much else Dr. Osman said, other than he would be doing a mediastinoscopy and bronchoscopy on Wednesday afternoon to biopsy the lymph nodes in question. This would identify the type of cancer cell I had, and if it was related or not to my neck cancer. He told me to pray hard that his educated guess was wrong. I liked Dr. Osman a lot and told him to be a straight shooter with me, but I couldn't believe what I had just heard. He left the room and said I'd see him in the morning.

Just as he walked out, Louise, walked in. I burst into tears and sobbed uncontrollably. I felt like I was falling apart. How could this be? It just didn't make sense. How could this be happening to me...again? How could it be so dire? I still don't have those answers, but I'm trying to be strong and embrace the situation. Right now, the only thing I have control of is my attitude, so I'm trying to remain optimistic and positive. However, there are still so many unknowns and that is frightening.

Louise was so sweet and tried to calm me down. My immediate reaction was that I needed to call Dad and Cheryl and let them know what was going on. I knew they were concerned and would want an update. I think Cheryl answered the phone. I was a blubbering mess, crying so hard that it set off my heart monitor. I let them know what Dr. Osman had told me and they were crying, too. It was awful.

The nurses brought in some sedatives -- Ativan, I think -- and that calmed me down a little. Later I texted and called my boyfriend Chris, Elizabeth, my "angel", and other people I felt needed to know what was going on with me at that moment. Louise stayed into the afternoon/early evening, providing much needed love and support. Then Ardys, another close girlfriend, came by later in the evening. I felt like I was living one of my actual nightmares. In fact, I was.

I slept okay that night from all of the drugs they pumped into me. On Thursday morning, the nurses told me that my procedure had been moved up from 2pm to 11:30am. At 11:20am, the gurney attendants came to my room and wheeled me away. I was parked in the hallway outside the surgery room. Dr. Osman came out, greeted me and told me what he would be doing.

I was taken into the surgery room and the last thing I remember was being put on the operating table before waking up in anesthesia recovery.

The surgery lasted longer than expected and I was back in my room at 4:30pm. A large bandage was taped below my Adam's apple, covering the 2" incision made during the mediastinoscopy. The back of my neck and head were really stiff and hurting, likely from the surgeon contorting my neck to get to the area he needed to biopsy. My throat was sore from the bronchoscopy, but nothing like I experienced during my radiation treatments for neck cancer.

The biggest, unwelcome surprise came later in the early evening. I wasn't aware that they had catheterized me during the surgery, so when I went to urinate, I almost had a heart attack. It was the most painful pee I've ever had. It felt like shards of glass were coming out my penis. I've been told it's similar to the pain women have with a bladder infection. All I can say is that I did a lot of yelling and swearing. The nurses got me a medication to take to address that issue, but it didn't start working until the third time I had to pee. Good Lord! Just awful.

My friend, Jackie, came by in the evening to check on me. I was so hungry from not eating for two days that I ate the gross orange chicken breast and brown rice with veggies that was served for dinner. It settled well until I got one of my coughing attacks. Then, out of nowhere, my entire dinner came up and out without warning all over the bed. I tried to stop it with my hands, but that didn't work so well.

"Nurse!" Jackie ran into the hall. She then came back and folded up the bed spread that was covered in vomit. Thank you, Jackie! They cleaned me up, changed my bedding and I got re-settled in bed.

I had a horrible night's sleep on Thursday night. It felt like I was looking at the clock every 20 minutes. I was drugged up with morphine and Xanax but was in a lot of a pain mostly with an extremely stiff neck and pounding headache. The nurses were in and out all night monitoring me, taking blood, checking my pressure and giving me breathing treatments. Breakfast came at 8am and I ate it.

Dr. Singh popped in around 11:30am and said that I would be released at 1pm. After signing many discharge papers and getting instructions for my medications and follow up appointments, I was put in a wheelchair and taken downstairs. Ardys went to get her car. As I was being taken through the main lobby, I started feeling nauseous and asked the volunteer for a barf bag. She clearly didn't have one. In the distance, I saw a big waste receptacle by the front door and flew out of the wheelchair toward it. I made it just in time and had a violent vomiting attack. Anything and everything in my body came out. I was totally taken by surprise. The pain was intense. I stood over the receptacle waiting for someone to help me. The volunteer freaked out and went running back upstairs. The person at the front desk just sat there. Ardys came back in and got me paper towels to clean myself up. I was wheeled back upstairs to my room. They gave me an anti-nausea medication and another drug for pain. The doctor chalked it up to a combo of the anesthesia after-effects, drugs and the stress I was under. I ended up staying in bed until 3:30pm and then was discharged...again. Mission accomplished this time. Ardys drove me home.

I was so tired from not sleeping last night that I immediately got in bed for a nap. Ardys decided to stay overnight with me to be sure that I would be okay. I slept for about two hours. It felt so good to be in my own bed. Ardys made me a cream cheese, garlic and sausage omelet for dinner. Yummy! We chatted for a couple of hours, then went to bed around 11pm. It was really nice having her here.

I slept well until 4:15am and have been up since then. I'm feeling a bit achy and lethargic today, but was able to feed the cats, clean their box, make the bed and vacuum. I'm determined not to lay around feeling sorry for myself. So, I'm going across the street for breakfast after I shower. This afternoon, I think Ardys and I will go for a manicure/pedicure and then a movie. Maybe tomorrow I can get back to the poker tables.

OCT 29 2017

Felt Good Today

Today is my brother Ed's birthday. I'll give him a call later to see how he's doing, since I wasn't able to get a card out to him this past week. He has been so concerned about me and wants to help out in any way possible. But, right now, there's really nothing anyone can do until I get my results on Tuesday/Wednesday and put a plan together.

I'm very anxious and concerned about what I'm going to hear given what Dr. Osman has already surmised. I'm trying to mentally prepare myself for the worst. It's a little overwhelming.

Yesterday I hung low. I had a pretty good night's sleep. I decided that I needed to get outside for some fresh air, so I walked across the street to the Tuscany Suites hotel and had breakfast at Marilyn's Cafe. My friend, Lynnore, turned me on to it last Spring and now it has become a regular spot for me. It's very diner-like with good food and reasonable prices. After walking back home, I was exhausted. Sounds crazy because it's only a quarter mile away.

I got on the couch, watched some college football and then took a 2 1/2 hour nap. I'm still catching up on sleep from my hospital stay last week. For dinner, I had a burger and applesauce and watched Dateline and 48 Hours, while playing poker online...unsuccessfully. Before getting in bed, I took off the gauze patch covering the incision made at the base of my neck during the mediastinoscopy. It's bigger than I thought -- about two inches long. It should heal fine, but I'll have a small scar there.

Today, I'm committed to getting back to normal. I'm going to play the noon $200 No Limit Holdem Re-Buy tourney at the Venetian. Sitting around worrying about my results isn't healthy, so getting back on the felt will help occupy my mind.

Since my car is still at Sunrise Hospital, where I went to the ER on Tuesday morning, I'll take an Uber to go pick it up. I hope I can remember where I parked. Mission accomplished. I found it without a problem and headed over to Sam's Barber Salon for a much-needed haircut.

I busted out of the Venetian tourney in 11th of 84 players after 9+ hours of play. Unfortunately, only the top nine made money, so I bubbled again. I was totally card dead in the last few levels and that was my demise. It felt good to get back on the felt after a week away. It also kept my mind occupied.

It's now 11:30pm. I'm going to read up more on lung cancer in preparation for getting my results. I want to be able to ask all the right questions and actively participate in determining the best possible treatment options. Needless to say, I'm quite anxious and just want to get things rolling. Hope I'm able to sleep tonight.

OCT 31 2017

Persistence Pays Off

I'm so over customer service. The lack of empathy they show on a regular basis is as exhausting as it is frustrating.

If you recall, I met my soon-to-be oncologist, Dr. Gollard in my hospital room last week. He had been contacted by my lung surgeon, Dr. Osman. Apparently, Dr. Osman recommended Dr. Gollard and wanted him to meet me BEFORE my results come in tomorrow or Wednesday. During our brief encounter, Dr. Gollard told me that he was a practitioner in my insurance network and that I should call his office immediately to set up an appointment as soon as possible.

So, I started calling late Thursday afternoon last week. Not once, in seven tries over three days, did I ever reach Dr. Gollard's office directly. I was always routed to a call center where I spoke to four different people on the seven occasions I called. The only one who was remotely helpful was a woman named Denise.

Thankfully, I got Denise again on my seventh try today and was even more relieved when she remembered speaking to me.

"I'm feeling frustrated and very angry because I never got a return call," I told Denise. "I don't understand how someone with Stage 3 Cancer or worse could be treated like that."

She apologized profusely and said, "Dr. Gollard's staff never answers their phone, so EVERYONE who calls their office always gets routed to us at the call center."

Oh really!? Well I certainly *will* be addressing this issue with Dr. Gollard shortly.

Denise felt my pain and decided to help address my plight. She finally reached Vanessa, Dr. Gollard's scheduler. Denise communicated my negative experience to date and, low and behold, I finally had an appointment scheduled with Dr. Gollard: Wednesday, November 1 at 1:45pm. It's a miracle!

At the same time, though, why did it have to take so long? Why couldn't Vanessa have called me directly after one of the six previous calls? I'd left my name, number and a clear message that Dr. Gollard requested that I call immediately for an appointment.

Denise told me that, while I was on hold and she was working on things, Vanessa said she never received a referral order from Health Plan of Nevada. So, in Vanessa's mind, she had no reason to call me back since my insurance wouldn't pay for the appointment anyway.

WAIT....WHAAAAAT!? Are you kidding me?

I told Denise to tell Vanessa that I would pay for the $250 appointment directly out of my pocket and submit their charge to the insurance company later.

That seemed to work!

What is wrong with these robots who work in customer service and end up causing unnecessary agony for their current and future clients? Management is clearly asleep at the wheel! It's so very very wrong.

Thank you from the bottom of my heart, Denise. I clearly could not have done it without you!

Persistence appears to work wonders! AND....If I had not done so or pleaded for help, I'd be waiting another week to get my biopsy results. So, don't give up. Be your own advocate! Make people want to assist you by baring your soul and expressing the gravity of your situation. I feel like every day I'm not starting my treatments is a day of life I'm losing. So, take matters into your own hands and do what you have to do to make things happen for you!

NOV 1 2017

It's An Anxious Time

I slept in this morning after a bad night's sleep. I woke up at about 3am coughing and hacking. No matter what I did, I couldn't stop it. This happens every now and again, but this time it lasted for almost an hour. I started getting a little panicky, so I tried to calm myself down. Finally, after propping myself up with three pillows and meditating a bit, the coughing stopped. Fortunately, nothing was coming up...no blood, no mucous, no food. It was just dry deep hacking.

When I finally dragged myself out of bed, I fed the cats, started a load of laundry, cleaned the house, paid some bills and watched CNN. I also tried to set up an additional appointment with another oncologist in my insurance network, so I'd have at least two opinions by the end of this week. Unfortunately, but not surprisingly, I got the usual message from Health Care Partners -- the scheduling service for everything -- that "someone" will get back to me in 48 hours. Yeah, right. It took them over seven days to call me the first time. There is never a sense of urgency. They honestly just don't give a damn. I am at their mercy.

My friends, Jackie & Vi, wanted to meet for lunch, so I walked across the street to Marilyn's Cafe and joined them at 12:40pm. I thought I was doing a good job holding up emotionally, but I just couldn't stop the tears from welling up in my eyes when we began chatting.

My whole life, I've been able to compartmentalize my feelings. Box them up. Keep them on their respective shelves. It's a great coping mechanism, but not a healthy way to live. When I finally admitted to myself and others at age 41 that I was gay, I decided that I wouldn't hide my feelings about anything anymore. I would either say how I was feeling about something or demonstrate it through concern, laughter, questions or crying. I like it much better this way, but it's not always easy to control involuntary emotional reactions. That's what happened at lunch today. I think everything I've been going through over the past few weeks has built up to a point where it has become slightly overwhelming for me. Jackie & Vi were great lunch dates. They got my mind working on other things, and even made me laugh a little.

This afternoon, I spent most of my time exploring alternative insurance options. One of my key findings was that only individual policy insurance obtained via HMO's participating in Obamacare/Affordable Care Act (ACA) protects the individual who has a pre-existing condition from being discriminated against. That's the good news. The bad news is that the HMO networks lock you solely into their doctors, specialists and hospitals only in the state where you live.

If I was in a PPO through a group insurance program sponsored by a company where I worked, I also couldn't be discriminated against for having a pre-existing condition. They would automatically cover me. However, when I tried to obtain an individual PPO policy with Blue Cross Blue Shield and United Health Care, I was turned down as a retiree living in Nevada with a pre-existing condition (former and current cancer patient). However, I believe that if I was the domestic partner of someone covered by their company's group insurance program, I would still be able to get coverage even with having a pre-existing condition. Unfortunately, that's not my situation.

So the bottom line is that individuals, who are independently employed, unemployed, or not working for a company that sponsors a group insurance program, are only able to access individual insurance today through an HMO. For example, currently I pay $459/month for HMO insurance and have a $6,000 out of pocket deductible. Next year my same insurance is going to be 36% more! As I mentioned already, I'm only able to go to doctors, hospitals, and specialists in Nevada. This is a problem for me because my goal is to get to the Cancer Treatment Center of America or Mayo Clinic in Arizona for my treatments.

Blue Cross Blue Shield did refer me to the Healthcare.gov website to explore the possibility of some other/better options given my situation. I'll research them tomorrow, but I'm not holding my breath.

On a "positive" note, I did get a full body bone scan scheduled today for November 9th. My recent PET scan showed a "lit up" area in my lumbar, so the doctors want to check all the bones in my body for the possible spreading of the lung cancer.

Tomorrow afternoon at 1:45pm, I meet with Dr. Gollard to get my tissue biopsy results and pathology report. His office called today to confirm and Ronnie (his admin) and I bonded on the phone. I told her how frustrated I've been with the whole insurance mess and she understood. I think I was a little high strung and emotional with her, so she set me up to meet with a social worker in their office tomorrow, too. Slowly, but surely, I'm making progress.

Louise is taking me to my appointment tomorrow. I don't want to hear the news alone. I don't mean to sound pessimistic, but I already know the news will be bad and that the best-case scenario I can hope for is Stage 3A non-small cell lung cancer. This is actually what I want to hear. Not of the other worse options. Louise will take notes and possibly record the meeting so we can go back and review exactly what Dr. Gollard says. I'm sure I won't be at my best once I hear the news, so having Louise there will be a huge benefit.

Since I know that I won't be in any shape to call my family and closest friends immediately after my session with Dr. Gollard, I'm going to have Louise and Jackie contact them tomorrow evening with the basic outline of what we hear. That will give me overnight to pull myself together and call them myself on Thursday morning/afternoon. I think this will work best for me.

NOV 2 2017

The News is Bad, But it Could Have Been Worse...I've Got This!

Louise picked me at 1pm to drive me to see Dr. Gollard. Today was the day I've been waiting for...and not waiting for. The pathology results to be shared with me would confirm what kind of lung cancer I have, how bad it is, and if there's any chance for treatment. I had done a lot of online research and, based on my findings and knowledge of my current state, I've mentally prepared myself the best I can.

When we arrived at the office, I had pages of paperwork to fill out. The office staff could not have been nicer. I got to meet Ronnie, who I had spoken with the previous day. She came over to where we were sitting in the waiting room and introduced herself. She grabbed some of the papers from me and said, "Oh, don't you worry about this. All I need you to do is sign here, here and here, and I'll fill out the rest for you!?"

WAIT..WHAT? How awesome was that? Now we're talking!

Soon we were taken into a typical doctor's office room. My blood pressure was taken, then a social worker named Cathy came in. She cheerfully explained that she was there to assist me with any non-medical concerns.

And, energetically added that she was a new member of the team and happy to be there.

Dr. Gollard arrived at long last. I squeezed the rosary I had in my left hand. Louise had let me borrow it for support and protection. It was one of four of her Dad's special rosaries. I held my breath.

Dr. Gollard sat down and we exchanged a few pleasantries. He shuffled a few papers before looking at me. "Okay, you have non-small cell Stage 3 -- likely 3B -- lung cancer."

I couldn't help but exhale a sigh of relief. My self-diagnosis had been right. This was the second-best news I could have heard today. Stage 3A, of course, would have been better, but that was alright. I took a deep breath and remained calm, focused and ready to discuss Dr. Gollard's thoughts on treatment options.

What I liked most about Dr. Gollard was his ability to explain a complex situation in a simple way. He indicated that the most important goal we should have is to get the cancer out of my body. To do that, he recommended we start with an intensive chemotherapy program of three different cancer meds, including a newer immunotherapy drug. This, in turn, should help shrink the very large tumor in my right lung, the smaller one in the lower lobe, and kill the cancerous lymph nodes currently housed in the middle of my chest.

The larger tumor posed the biggest problem, since it is connected to tissues and vessels leading to other key organs -- like my heart -- and crossing over my trachea. Because of this, surgery is not an option at this time. However, it could be IF the chemotherapy program works in shrinking down the size of the tumor and disconnecting it.

This all seemed rationale and reasonable to me. Louise was shaking her head in agreement, too. I went into the meeting thinking that I'd immediately go get a second opinion, but Dr. Gollard had a good treatment plan in place. Clearly, chemotherapy was the correct approach.

I asked him why he wasn't recommending radiation in combination with chemo, like I had with my neck cancer treatments. Interestingly, he explained that a surgeon wouldn't even consider operating on the lung if it was radiated because it would be too risky. I'd have to wait at least three to four months for the radiation to be out of my body. Additionally, radiation works best when targeted against smaller areas/tumors/nodes, not large ones like mine.

So, I'm moving forward with Dr. Gollard's recommended plan. I mentioned that I wanted to take a cruise over Thanksgiving and would prefer to do that before getting really sick from the treatments. He chuckled.

I asked, "When do you think we should start this?"

He said, "Next week. You have a serious situation that we need to start attacking now."

Okay then. Next week it is!

My first chemotherapy session is scheduled for next Wednesday, November 8. I have experience with chemo from battling neck cancer, so I know what to expect. I will be getting a drip from multiple bags (five or six) for an average of five hours each time. I'll be getting chemo eight times over the next 12 weeks with check-ins on my off weeks. This will take me through the end of January or so when I will get another PET scan to see if the tumors have shrunk or the cancerous lymph nodes have gone. At that point, we will be at a fork in the road with new decisions to make and plans to develop. I'm good with this.

Louise and I met two of the chemo nurses who explained the three different cancer meds I'll be getting: Cisplatin (Platinol), Necitumumab (Portrazza), and Gemcitabine (Gemzar). Each have their own side effects, which I won't get into now.

The chemo bar will be serving me a cocktail of old standards, along with a "new kid on the block." The staff indicated that I should be fairly functional on most days during the treatment; but, from experience, I know that over time I will feel sicker and sicker. So, when I feel okay, I can assure you that I'll be at the poker tables!

Louise asked Dr. Gollard if could travel. He didn't think that was a good idea, but said he may make an exception for Thanksgiving as that is my off-week – pending how I feel and do after my Tuesday, November 22 treatment, of course.

I'd really like to go to see my Dad and Cheryl for Thanksgiving with Chris, who lives in Michigan. Especially, since I probably won't be able to go on a cruise and doubt I'll feel well enough to travel at Christmas. We'll see. I need to take one day at a time.

Dr. Gollard also thinks that it's critical for me get an MRI of my brain and spine and a full body bone scan. These tests will tell us if the cancer has spread undetected anywhere else. I like his thoroughness. I have the bone scan set up for next Thursday, the day after my first chemo treatment. Likely, the brain and spine MRIs will happen at the same time sometime next week, too.

My appointment lasted almost two hours. After Louise dropped me off, I immediately got on the phone and called my Dad & Cheryl, Mom, Chris and Elizabeth with my news. I asked my Dad to call Ed (my brother) and Louise to call Jackie, Ardys and my ex-wife, Charlene. I think everyone is breathing a little easier because I'm feeling "good" about the situation and have a plan now.

So, yes, I have Stage 3B non-small cell lung cancer. I never smoked. The doctors aren't certain how I got this but are in agreement that it is independent of my neck cancer, even though they are both squamous cell-derived cancers.

I've had my sad, angry and fearful moments. Now I'm putting my arsenal together to fight the fight. It will be a long battle, but I am more than ready for it...spiritually, mentally and physically.

I am not going down to this bastard called Cancer. FUCK Cancer! I will be #PetzingStrong and win. I HATE to lose. I BELIEVE IN ME!

NOV 3 2017

Feeling #PetzingStrong!

What a difference a day makes! I'm feeling so relieved and mentally sound today. I met Louise and Ardys for breakfast at Grand Luxe in the Venetian and both of them commented on how much better I looked and sounded. I felt so much more relaxed and centered for the first time in weeks. Step 1 of my plan is now underway, and next Wednesday I'll be in the chemo chair for my first treatment. I never thought in my wildest dreams I'd be getting started this quickly. My guess was December 1st at best.

I'm glad I was wrong.

After breakfast, all of us went to play the Survivor Tournament in the Venetian Poker Room. For those not familiar, the goal in a survivor tourney is to be one of the last 10% of the remaining players with any amount of chips...even one. So, if you "survive" the field and get to the end (last 10%) with chips, you win $3400! 12 folks out of 117 players did that today. Unfortunately, Louise, Ardys and I weren't in that group.

During one of the breaks, Lisa, a good poker friend of mine playing in the tournament, came over to my table to see me. She had a surprise gift and explained that the company it came from employs people transitioning out of homelessness. Out of her pocketbook, came a very small off-white bag with black imprinting and a pull string. Then, out of the bag, came a key, the size of a house key. Lisa told me that The Giving Keys company, out of Los Angeles, imprints a special word on the key that would be meaningful to the person you're giving it to. The gift recipient is supposed to embrace this word and then pay the key forward to a person they feel needs the message more than they do.

On MY key was the word STRENGTH. The key was on a simple silver chain. I was so touched by Lisa's thoughtfulness. I put the chain over my head, hung it off my neck and tucked it under my shirt. The key fell right in the middle of my chest where, ironically, there are a number of cancerous lymph nodes. We hugged and I thanked Lisa for her awesome gift. She graciously offered to help me in any way possible. I definitely will take her up on that as I get further along in my treatments.

It was really nice that a few other players and dealers came by to see how I was doing, too. It's very reassuring to know that they, and all of you, are in my corner together as one. This abundance of amazing energy fills me with even more STRENGTH everyday as I prepare for my upcoming battle.

Come on, Cancer. Just try underestimating me. That will be fun! #PetzingStrong!

NOV 5 2017

My Heart Is Broken. I Will Miss You, Scott.

I received shocking and devastating news this morning. One of my best friends from Douglas, MI, Scott Eilbes, passed away suddenly yesterday after developing a heart complication following a surgical procedure on his stomach. Scott, was not only my restaurant and martini lounge manager for five years at Zing, but was also one of the four "angels" who supported and watched over me throughout my battle with neck cancer in late 2014/early 2015.

Scott had a really tough life ever since he was shot in the face and stomach during a street assault and robbery attempt in little Saugatuck, MI around ten years ago. The perpetrator was found guilty and is currently serving jail time. But Scott lost everything -- including two Bed & Breakfasts due to all of the astronomical medical bills and his lack of insurance coverage. He had to endure a number of surgeries and a fake eye replacement. Scott never gave up and didn't let his dire situation bring him down. He jumped from job to job until he began working for me in February 2011. In 2012, he became the manager of my restaurant, Zing, and did an awesome job! He treated Zing as if it were his own baby. We shared an office in the studio apartment above the restaurant and spent many hours together, working hard and laughing a lot. He had an amazing, sarcastic wit and was fun to be around.

Scott was always there for me throughout the good times and bad. When I was sick, he often took me to my daily radiation treatments. When I couldn't work, he covered for me without ever complaining. If I needed him to go above and beyond, he did it with a smile. Scott was dedicated, loyal, caring and giving. If you needed help, he happily offered it. Scott lived simply and was not into anything fancy. However, he did have a love for nice dress shirts. Scott never did anything halfway because that was never good enough. He was a perfectionist, sometimes to a fault. His self-taught, creative design talent was off the hook. Without him, I could not have brought my vision for Zing to life.

Scott was like a brother to me. I'll never forget the Caribbean cruise we went on to celebrate his 50th birthday and the completion of my neck cancer treatments. I still wasn't feeling well, but was determined to prove to everyone, including myself, that I could do it. A week before the cruise, I had my feeding tube removed. I was still not drinking or eating properly because my throat hurt so badly, and I didn't have much of an appetite. During the entire cruise, Scott made sure I stayed hydrated and ate appropriately. He was an outstanding cruise partner.

Happily, three weeks ago, I was able to see and spend quality time with Scott while he was here in Vegas with his family. The nice breakfast we had at Grand Luxe will be my last memory of Scott and an ongoing reminder of all the good times we enjoyed together.

How quickly things change. This is why life cannot be taken lightly. It must be lived fully each day. You just don't know if you'll be here tomorrow, the next day, in a month or in a year.

Scott consistently exuded positive attitude and energy, despite his daily struggles with health, financial, and personal relationship issues. He always tried to do better and improve his situation, regardless of his circumstances. He never gave up.

Scott, your battles are over. Finally, you are comfortable and safe...fully embraced by God's arms. Rest in peace, dear friend. You were my "angel" on earth and now you are truly an angel in heaven. Please watch over me. I will miss you.

NOV 7 2017

Playing the Hand You're Dealt

For the past few days, I've immersed myself in playing poker to keep myself distracted. The poker table is, and always has been, a happy place for me. I know that may sound a bit strange to many of you who don't play, but the game of poker has so many components that intrigue and motivate me: risk/reward, analysis, strategy, psychology, human behavior and competition. Just like the song says, "You gotta know when to hold 'em, know when to fold 'em." Poker is about making informed decisions. Importantly, you also must learn how to play the cards you're dealt because, more often than not, your starting hands in poker will be sub-optimal. You just can't sit around and fold every time. Sometimes you've got to get creative and figure out how to get in the game with bad cards.

Interestingly, poker has similarities to life. For instance, both have "bad beats." These are situations where statistically you should definitely win a given hand and a corresponding big pot. But, unfortunately, you don't because another player gets lucky. As a result, your bad luck turns into the need to battle back from a chip deficit. It doesn't necessarily mean you've been outplayed, but now significant work is required to get back into the game.

Tournament poker -- my specialty -- requires intense focus, flexibility, agility and endurance. You've got to be able to change up your game based upon the hands you're dealt, overall table dynamics (e.g passive, aggressive, tight, loose, etc.), the players at your table, the size of your chip stack versus other players' stacks and where you are in the tournament (e.g. early, middle, late, final table, etc.) Honing these skills over the past eight years has been especially helpful in preparing me to deal with whatever challenges life throws in my path.

Life has sure dealt me some pretty shitty cards recently, as you well know. Being diagnosed with cancer – AGAIN – and losing my best friend is unbearable. But, it's time to embrace it. Not feel sorry for myself. It's time to figure out how to work with what I've got. I can't let cancer defeat me. I need to stay positive and WIN! Losing is NOT a viable option.

And I will WIN -- just as I have over the past few days at the poker table. #PetzingStrong

I received another unique gift this past Saturday via UPS. It came from my friend, Silvio, who I met a little over a year ago playing poker in Los Angeles. Silvio is a documentary film producer and has taken an interest in my story. He's quite talented and very thoughtful. Silvio and his brother, Luigi, sent me a gorgeous, 6" high black stone sculpture in the shape of a "Spade" (the suit in cards, not the gardening/farming tool.) It was carved by a friend of theirs. When they saw it among his many works of art, they immediately thought of me and my battle.

Silvio and Luigi sent a nice card with the Spade. On it they wrote, "We are with you in this trying time. We pray that this rock will help protect and heal you on this part of your journey." Also included was the following passage from 1 Corinthians 10:4: "*And all drank from the same spiritual drink, for they were drinking from a spiritual rock which followed them, and the rock was Christ.*"

The Spade now sits on the side dresser next to my bed where I see it when I get up in the morning and go to bed at night. For me, it represents STRENGTH and ENDURANCE. I will need both of these to win my long fight against lung cancer!

Thank you, Silvio and Luigi! I'm very thankful and touched by your gift.

NOV 8 2017

And it All Starts Again Tomorrow

There's good news and bad news tonight. The good news is that I start chemotherapy treatments tomorrow morning, much sooner than I originally anticipated. The bad news is I know how sick I'm going to get over the next few weeks. Been there. Done that. It's hard to believe, after being cancer-free for 2 1/2 years, that I will be once again relying on chemotherapy to shrink the tumors in my right lung and eliminate the cancerous nodes in the middle of my chest.

Interestingly, lung cancer is rarely seen in someone under 65 years old who has never smoked. That's me. At 57, I've never smoked a cigarette. Ever! The doctors still aren't sure how I got this cancer, but they seem fairly confident that it's not related to my previous neck cancer, even though both cancers grew from squamous cells.

My appointment is at 11am and I've been told that the infusion should last between five and six hours. I plan to bring a few magazines, a book, a laptop and my cell phone. If history repeats itself, I'll fall asleep for at least 90 to 120 minutes during the drip.

In preparation for tomorrow, my oncologist ordered anti-nausea medication, which I've been taking every eight hours. I really hope I don't feel nauseous after the treatments. It's such a horrible feeling. However, from the reading I've done on the different cancer meds I'll be receiving, it's common to get flu-like symptoms such as body aches, fever, chills and nausea.

A bad skin rash is also not unheard of. But maybe I'll be one of the lucky ones and avoid these issues.

Jackie is picking me up at 10:30am and taking me to Dr. Gollard's office. She'll get me settled in, and then pick me up at 5pm to bring me home. I'll need to rely on my friends here for transportation to and from treatments, especially as I get sicker. I'll be having eight treatments over the next 12 weeks, structured as a two weeks on and one week off cycle.

I'm excited that Chris will be coming to see me on the Friday after Thanksgiving through the following Tuesday, and my Dad & Cheryl will be visiting in early December for five days. Hopefully, I'll feel well enough to get out of my apartment once in a while to play some poker or go to a movie. I'll just have to wait and see.

I received a card from my friend, Ryan, the other day with four words on it.

Faith. Strength. Patience. Hope.

A great reminder of what I need to focus on right now.

Faith in my Higher Power that he is watching over me during this challenging time, along with Faith in Dr. Gollard and his chemotherapy plan for me.

Strength to do this all over again and to endure the poisoning of my body.

Patience to accept that this is going to be a long process. The chemotherapy plan is just the first step in battling this ugly disease. After 12 weeks, we'll need to determine the appropriate next steps based on my PET scan results.

Finally, Hope. I must believe that I can beat the odds and WIN! I will work hard to research other treatment options that may be available to me and, in turn, will have a Plan B in my back pocket.

I will not lose Hope...ever.

#PetzingStrong

NOV 9 2017

Drip, Drip and More Drip

My first chemo is in the books. Frankly, it was uneventful. Since I'm familiar with the process already, I wasn't too anxious today. Jackie picked me up at 10:30am and we arrived a little ahead of my appointment time. They were ready for me.

Drip...Drip...Drip...

That's all that happened for 5 1/2 hours today in a group room. I was meant to be in my oncologist's new renovated space across the hall, but it isn't ready yet. So, I was dripping along with six other folks in the same small room. Luckily, I got one of the three recliners since I was going to be there the longest. I felt bad for the folks that got the straight back chairs. Not cool. Jackie stayed for the first 90 minutes, then came back to get me at the end of day. She's so organized and is going to coordinate my transportation to/from treatments and schedule "help" coverage with friends for the next few months. I'm supposed to report in to her every morning with a rating of 1 (Awesome) to 5 (Horrible) based on how I'm feeling when I get up. We'll see how that goes.

In my meeting with the chemo nurses last week, I had requested a private room. From my past experience getting chemo for neck cancer, I knew this would be the most helpful for me. They immediately addressed the "small room" group situation when I got there, were quite apologetic and made me feel as comfortable as possible. If I'm being totally honest, the real reason why I didn't want to drip with others is because I know that at least half of us won't make it. Some of us will die within the next few months, or within in a year or two, and some of us won't. It's an odd, disturbing and eerie feeling that is extremely hard to divorce yourself from when everyone around you is sick and doing what they need to do to live.

Anyway, I didn't have a choice today, so I made the best of it. I reached out in conversation to Suzannah, a pleasant blonde woman in her mid-60's suffering from metastatic breast cancer, and Frank, an older retired "salt of the earth," type man. He's battling bladder cancer and was there for the third treatment in his series. Both of them were really nice and we shared small talk.

My infusion went through my left wrist. The first bag was saline to clear out my veins. This was followed by an anti-nausea bag. The third bag was Benadryl with steroids. Radka, my sweet-as-can-be Bulgarian chemo nurse, affectionately calls these three preliminary bags "the appetizers." The beauty of Bag #3 is that it puts me to sleep for a nice 90-minute nap. The steroids in it, too, always give me an artificial "high" for two or three days following the treatment.

Bag #4, my immunotherapy medicine, was Necitumumab. I can't even begin to say it correctly, so the trade name is Portrazza, which is so much easier to pronounce. After the Portrazza, I received a bag of Gemzar. So far so good.

The big bag of the day was Bag #6, Cisplatin (trade name Platinol.) When Radka pushed the buttons to let the flow begin into my IV, I yelped aloud. The initial sting felt like a bolt of lightning or an electrical shock. She stopped it and we tried again. Same reaction. After the third failed attempt, we moved the IV line to the vein in my elbow and all was fine. Radka indicated that this is sometimes a problem for some folks. It wasn't a big deal, but it was an unpleasant surprise. Both Suzanne and Frank empathetically winced with me.

Bag #7, the final one, was more saline to wash out the veins. At 4:45pm, it was time to hit the road.

I got out of the chair feeling good. I'm used to sitting long periods of time playing poker, so I didn't find it difficult. Plus, I was reclined most of the time. I had to get up and pee twice during the infusion, yet the overall process of getting chemo isn't that bad all. It's the side effects of it on the body, as time goes along, that becomes brutal to handle. Radka said that I should feel pretty decent until Monday when I might start experiencing some aches, pains, nausea and tiredness. We'll have to wait and see. At least I can get some poker in this weekend!

On the way home, Jackie stopped at CVS so I could pick up a new prescription to fight off my coughing and hacking spasms. These have progressively gotten worse, waking me up last night on three different occasions. Nothing comes up when I cough, but the coughs keep coming and coming and coming. Some cough attacks last for five minutes or more.

As this is happening, I get panicky and start breathing hard, which I can't do well to begin with. Then, I worry I won't be able to stop and have to talk myself down. It's not pleasant. I took my first dose before dinner tonight and haven't coughed once. I'll take another before I go to bed. I'm looking forward to a good night's sleep – finally.

Tomorrow, Ardys is picking me up at 12:15pm to take me for my full body bone scan. Then, on Friday, I go back to Dr. Gollard's for hydration. On Monday, I'm off to Quest Diagnostics for blood work prior to next Wednesday's chemo treatment. I'm also going to be meeting with a pulmonary specialist and having both a brain and spinal MRI done sometime soon. So, all in all, lots of doctor appointments in the near future.

Overall, a good start today!

NOV 10 2017

Hope Springs Eternal

I'm feeling great today (a 1 out of 5 on Jackie's wellness scale.) This is not unusual, given my previous experience receiving chemotherapy and with the effects of bag #3 coursing through me.

Bag #3 is also called the "fun bag." The steroids and Benadryl help offset any and all immediate negative reactions to the poisonous chemo medicines. The artificial high isn't too bad either. It gives me a nice burst of energy for two or three days.

Until day four.

This is when the steroids wear off and the poison takes over, causing flu-like symptoms and a general feeling of lousiness. That's where my hydration appointment comes in. It will help reduce this uncomfortable side effect, along with the two anti-nausea pills I take daily.

Keeping my fingers crossed that I don't get as sick as expected. I'd like to have a few weeks of feeling well enough to live a "normal life" instead of being curled up in bed or on my couch. I'm planning to fight through the sick feelings and will not let them get me down.

My day started off with Jackie and Vi and a nice breakfast in the Tuscany Suites Hotel. Afterwards, I played a few slot machines -- breaking even -- and made a football bet on tonight's Arizona vs Seattle game.

Ardys picked me up at noon and took me to Steinberg Medical Associates for my full body bone scan. After checking in, I received a shot of radioactive solution. It needed two hours to assimilate into my body, so Ardys and I went to a nearby nail salon and had mani/pedis. It was fun to chat and get my mind off things. We headed back to Steinberg a little before 3pm. When I arrived, I was immediately whisked away for my scan.

It was a relatively simple procedure. I took off my sweater jacket and belt and emptied all of my pockets. I got on the very narrow table (width of my body) on my back and then had a large wide band wrapped around my arms at my elbows to keep them in place during the scan. I was told that the scanner would come very close to my face and body but would not touch me. So, I decided to close my eyes and meditate during the 40-minute procedure. Basically, the table moved slowly through the scanner in one direction, capturing all of my bones from head to toe.

I was required to do this scan because my PET scan showed an abnormal spot in my lumbar. The doctors want to be sure that my cancer hasn't spread there or to any other bones, so this scan will identify if there are any other problems we need to know about. The hope is that it's just a preliminary indicator of a degenerative situation beginning, and not cancer. Results should be in by late tomorrow or Monday morning. I'm not too worried about this.

Ardys dropped me off at home around 4:30pm and I called my Dad & Cheryl and Ed, my brother, to coordinate their December trips to see me. I'm really looking forward to having them here before I get too sick to enjoy their visits. The cumulative effect of the chemo treatments will have me feeling very sick by mid-December through the end of January.

I also talked with Chris tonight. We've been together over three years. I miss him so much. He lives in Michigan with his four girls, ages 10-18 (the oldest is at Central Michigan University), and has very limited vacation time to see me. I'm excited that he's coming to Vegas for five days after Thanksgiving. He always makes me feel so good.

Yesterday, Chris sent me a beautiful text message that really made my day. I read it just as I was headed to my first chemo treatment. I want to share it with you.

He writes, "Baby, on this cold November morning I saw a symbol of Hope. It's a red rose in my Michigan garden fighting against the odds of the cold days ahead. It made me think of you today as you start this difficult journey again. While the rose will go dormant, it will blossom bigger and bolder in the Spring. Just like you!! I love you."

I believe in symbols and I can relate to that rose. My body is going to die a bit over the next few Fall and Winter months, but with the purpose of shrinking the tumor in my right lung and killing the cancerous lymph nodes in the middle of my chest. Hopefully, then, I can have surgery to remove the tumor and/or part or all of my lung.

When Spring comes, the cancer will be gone, and I can blossom again into an even better me!

#PetzingStrong

NOV 11 2017

Care Package Friday!

I got up early yesterday as I needed to be at Dr. Gollard's office by 9am for an infusion of anti-nausea meds and extra hydration. I really like how proactive he is in addressing the expected side effects of my chemo treatments before they take hold and kick my butt. This drip only lasted 1hr 45mins and I was on my way to the Venetian to play in their Monster Stack tourney at noon.

Unfortunately, I didn't make the money in that one or the 7pm Rebuy tourney, so I headed home. When I checked my mailbox, the postman had placed a key in it for me to access some larger packages from another box. To my surprise, there were three different care packages from my friends, Ann, Krista and Eric.

Ann is a good high school friend. When I opened her care package, it made me laugh out loud. There were a lot of fun items packed into it, but the best part was the *F**K Cancer Adult Coloring Book* with colored pencils. It will definitely help keep me entertained during my Wednesday chemo treatments.

Krista is a poker friend of mine here in Vegas. Her care package came in a tote bag inscribed with "Like A Boss." It had a little bit of everything... from a blanket, eye mask, neck supporter and ear plugs to use during my chemo sessions to socks, Aveno bath products and Lipton Noodle Soup.

And, finally, Eric is a friend from Douglas, MI where I lived for five years before moving to Vegas in January 2016. His care package had ginger candy and a peppermint tea stirrer.

Thanks for your thoughtful gestures and making my day special!

NOV 12 2017

My First Book is Helping Others!

I believe most of you know that I wrote a book, "From Feeding Tube to Final Table: A Cancer Survivor's Story," about my previous battle with neck cancer in 2014/2015. It was published and released on Amazon.com back in mid-May of this year. The book is full of hope and inspiration for the cancer patient and their loved ones. It's selling well and been getting 5-Star reviews. However, what's most important and meaningful to me is that I know it's helping others with their cancer fight as I continue to get Facebook messages, texts and calls telling me so.

NOTE: Unfortunately, my first book is no longer available for purchase due to low demand during 2019/2020.

Here's an example of a Facebook Messenger post I received the other day:

"Hello, my name is Kathy M. and your book was given to my husband by his cousin, Bob J., who is also a poker player like you. I wanted to let you know how helpful it has been in my husband's ability to face radiation. They plan 35 hits of it for head and neck cancer that now has grown from his left side and extended behind his esophagus. I have recommended your book to his radiologist to help patients who are finding it difficult to face."

"I am also wondering if your esophagus was radiated when you had treatment. Our current concern is not only eradicating the cancer, but being able to retain the ability to swallow. Any insight from your experience is helpful. We will try to have him practice swallowing daily (if he can) so that he retains memory on that, but don't know if the muscle will be affected. Again, thank you for keeping your journal and sharing your story."

Here was my response to Kathy:

"Hi Kathy, so sorry to hear about your husband's battle. He can do it, but it will be very uncomfortable. I highly recommend that he get a feeding tube if the docs are recommending it. I wasn't even able to swallow a pill, let alone eat or drink anything. It's so important that he get extra nutrition and calories as they will be needed to help him stay strong and heal properly. All of my meds went through the tube. Liquid morphine was the best! As for my esophagus, it was indirectly affected. I did very little swallowing while going through treatment. It was too painful. I had no trouble getting that reflex back. When my throat healed inside, it did narrow my passageway, so swallowing big pills is tough, but no other issues."

"If you or your husband want to chat directly, I'm happy to do so. I should let you know that I just got diagnosed with Stage 3B non-small cell lung cancer. I've never smoked. As you can imagine, it came as quite the surprise. I started chemo to shrink my tumors so surgery might become an option for me down the road. I've started my second book on my blog at CaringBridge.org under Jim Petzing. This one starts on October 17. You can register for free and you may want to also set up a site for your husband. Prayers for all of us!"

Kathy's daughter, Gina, then responded to me saying:

"My dad does often mention it to people how you recommended the feeding tube right out of the gate! It really isn't a big deal to have it now, but at the time it sounded so horrific. You have really helped him already!"

I just can't begin to tell you how good this makes me feel! It's so nice to know that I am making a little bit of a difference in other peoples' lives, as many have done for me.

While finishing this entry, I just received a Facebook Messenger post from Laurie V, a member of the Douglas United Church of Christ in Douglas, MI where I used to attend services. She writes:

"Thinking of you and holding you to the light, Jim. We lit a candle for you this morning. Peace be with you."

I so miss my church family and Pastor Sal. They were pivotal in supporting me in my battle with neck cancer and I know they're still behind me in my new fight against lung cancer. It means so much that they still include me in their thoughts and prayers, even though I'm so far away here in Vegas.

I'm feeling #PetzingStrong today!

NOV 15 2017

Chemo #2 In the Bag

I got up just before 7am after a very restful seven hours of sleep. My doctor has me on Xanax. I take it, as needed, usually before bedtime. It functions a lot like a sleeping pill and I wake up totally refreshed and ready to embark on my day. Of course, Zing & Zang (my cats) were right there on the bed with me and kind of in my face, so I dragged myself out of bed to feed them. They are the sweetest guys.

I turned on the TV to ABC's "Good Morning America." I really like George, Robin, Mike, Ginger and the gang and converted to their morning show when I was sick the last time. NBC's "Today Show" just doesn't do it for me anymore.

As usual, the news today was filled with stories about Trump, Trump Jr., Russian meddling in the election, student deaths from fraternity hazing, men and women sexually assaulted by deviants in power positions, psycho shooter rampages and Blake Shelton being named as *PEOPLE* Magazine's Sexiest Man Alive!

Really?! Huh? Nothing against Blake, but I think there were some better choices!

For breakfast, I had a Jimmy Dean's sausage, egg and cheese croissant and some of my friend Sherry's amazing banana bread, along with a strong cup of coffee. My appetite is generally pretty good in the morning, but wanes as the day progresses. I usually don't eat lunch, so I have a later dinner just to get something in my system. I've already dropped 8 lbs. in about two weeks.

After showering and throwing on some clothes, I headed out to Dr. Gollard's office for my consult with him and my Wednesday chemo treatment. I drove myself today because I've been feeling so good and didn't want to inconvenience any of my friends. I'll definitely need rides, help and more support down the road. I'll be sure to reach out to them.

I arrived at 8:45am for my 9am appointment with Dr. Gollard, but he was delayed doing rounds at the hospital. Radka, my amazing chemo nurse, thought we should get the chemo infusion going since it will be another 5 1/2 hour session.

The entire office has moved across the hall into their new space and it's beautiful. It's an open floor plan concept with 12 half-wall cubicle stations for chemo dripping. There is a ton of light, so it feels bright, airy and "happy," relatively speaking. The chairs are all comfortable leather recliners and there is a full complement of pillows, blankets and snacks, water soda, etc.

It looks like Dr. Gollard and I will get together later today after I'm finished with my infusion. I've been keeping a running list of questions for him on my cell phone:

> * What are the results from my bone scan I had last week?
>
> * When is one considered to be officially constipated and what can be done for it? (I've been a little light on bowel movements this past week.)
>
> * Is it odd that the wheezing in my chest cavity has returned? (This was a symptom of the walking pneumonia I had back in late July through September.)

*Is the plan still to have chemo treatments 8x over 12 weeks and then get a PET scan to see if the tumors have shrunk and cancerous lymph nodes are gone?

*Do I still need to get a brain and spine MRI based on the bone scan results?

*Should I be wearing a mask when I'm in the casino playing poker?

*Is there a special diet I should be following?

*When will I start experiencing flu-like symptoms and feeling lousy?

So, as you can see, we have a lot to discuss

It's now 1:25pm and we're over four hours into my drip. I had an awesome 90-minute nap after the "fun" bag and am now wide awake and full of energy. I love the artificial high I get!

If I'm still feeling energized later this afternoon and into the early evening, I'll probably go play a 7pm poker tourney tonight. I've been on the felt the past few days, but no cashes to report. Hopefully that will change soon!

Tomorrow morning, I'll be going to see Dr. Tahir, my general practitioner. I haven't been there since I got the bad news from him a few weeks ago. It will be good to re-connect and update him with where I am in the process. I'm planning to give him my first book, "From Feeding Tube to Final Table: A Cancer Survivor's Story," to read and pass along to some of his other cancer patients who may be facing this awful dilemma for the first time. I wish I had read a book like it before going through it all. It would have been so helpful in providing guidance and setting appropriate expectations.

Last night, Chris took a dozen of my books to a Gilda's Club meeting in Lowell, MI, where he and three of his girls are part of a cancer support group. There are separate programs for cancer patients and their loved ones, along with adult and kid groups. They've been twice now and are finding it helpful. Chris told me that he gave my book to two cancer patients who asked if they could read it. I get great pleasure in knowing that it will benefit others.

It's now 2pm. Only 45 minutes to go with my drip. The day has progressed quickly, so that's good. I'm looking forward to meeting with Dr. Gollard a little bit later. I'll be sure to give you an update on what I learn in my next entry.

#PetzingStrong

NOV 16 2017

Doing The Right Thing

Yesterday's chemotherapy infusion lasted 6 1/2 hours. It's the longest one I've ever had. Fortunately, I napped for about 2 1/2 hours of it, so the time went by fairly quickly. When I finished dripping, I met with Dr. Gollard to discuss my status and get several of my questions answered. So, here's what I learned:

> *We are still on the original plan of having 8 chemo sessions over a 12 week period, taking us through the end of January. At that point, I will get a PET scan to see if the cancerous lymph nodes in the middle of my chest are gone, as well as to determine if the large and smaller tumors in my right lung have shrunk enough to allow surgery to become an option. Dr. Gollard is hopefully optimistic.
>
> *My bone scan results indicated an abnormality in the lumbar area, like the PET scan did. Both Dr. Gollard and Dr. Tahir think that this may be a harbinger of the metastatic spread of my cancer, which would not be good. To get a closer look at the tissue surrounding the lumbar area in question, I will undergo a spinal MRI, and likely a spinal biopsy, at the end of the month. And, just to be sure the

cancer hasn't spread to my brain, I'll be getting a brain MRI in conjunction with the spinal MRI.

*Since heavy wheezing has returned in my chest cavity, Dr. Gollard has put me on a high powered antibiotic for two weeks to kick it out of my system. And, to address my constipation issue, I've also been put on Colace.

*I don't need to wear a mask while playing poker in the casino, especially because I play in smoke-free rooms and second-hand smoke is a cumulative longer term issue that builds up over years of daily exposure.

*I will start feeling really sick shortly after this weekend, on or around Day 12 to 15 of the treatment cycle. Today is Day 9. I should expect to have flu-like symptoms, along with general fatigue and body aches. This pattern is similar to the last time I had chemo and got bashed with the side effects around Day 13. The good news, however, is that I can go in for a hydration and anti-nausea drip anytime I want.

*I don't need to be on any kind of special diet, especially since I'll be losing my appetite. Dr. Gollard said to eat what I want and try to keep the weight on. I've already lost about eight pounds since treatment began.

*Since my immune system is being compromised, I shouldn't be traveling long distances, especially in an airplane, or putting unnecessary stress on my body.

Overall, after my chat with Dr. Gollard, I feel like I'm doing the right thing at the right time and that all is moving along as it should be. I'm trying very hard to stay in the moment and not jump ahead to the end of January and the "What if?" scenarios I may be faced with then.

Given that this coming week I will not be having chemo, Dr. Gollard wanted me to have a Neulasta Onpro patch applied. You may have seen this advertised on TV. Neulasta is a prescription medicine used to help reduce the chance of infection due to a low white blood cell count caused by chemotherapy.

The Neulasta Onpro is applied on the same day chemotherapy is administered and is designed to automatically inject Neulasta the next day, approximately 27 hours after application. Dr. Gollard's nurse, Janet, applied the patch to my abdomen. Moments later it beeped and then pricked me with its tiny needle. When the Neulasta gets into my system, it will stimulate my bone marrow to produce more white blood cells to replace the ones being killed off by the chemotherapy.

I left Dr. Gollard's office around 4:45pm, and drove over to Green Valley to meet Jackie for dinner at The Cheesecake Factory. It was nice to just decompress and catch up with her. Jackie invited me to enjoy Thanksgiving at her home, so I plan to do that it if I'm feeling up to it!

NOV 19 2017

Kicking Ass in Poker

I got up early today and headed to Dr. Gollard's for my second hydration and anti-nausea treatment at 9am. Since I was one of the first patients to arrive, I was ushered right in. Radka was ready for me and got the drip going.

Surprisingly, I haven't really started feeling sick yet. Clearly, Dr. Gollard's proactive approach to battling the side effects of the chemo is working and I'm so grateful for that. Once those flu-like symptoms start, they don't go away and general misery sets in.

Today's treatment only lasted a couple of hours, so I went to the Venetian to play the noon $250 No Limit Hold'em tourney. I got fairly deep but ended up busting out around 5pm not making the money. It was about then when the steroids from my hydration drip kicked in and I suddenly had all kinds of energy. So, I hung out, played some slots and won $230. As 7pm rolled around, I decided to play the $200 NLH $25K Guarantee Rebuy tourney. There were 96 total players in the tournament and, after 10 hours of play, including breaks, I found myself in the Final 4. We were all fairly close in chip stack counts, so we decided to chop the remaining prize money. Although I was in 4th place, I got better than 3rd place money and took home a net win of $4,229. It felt really good to know that, even while fighting the Big C, I can still kick ass in poker! Unfortunately, as the chemo side effects start to take hold later next week, I just won't have the endurance to play these lengthy tournaments any longer.

I got home around 5:15am (on Saturday morning) and laid down on my bed fully clothed to catch 2 1/2 hours of sleep before meeting my good friends, Steve & Cory, for breakfast at Marilyn's Cafe. They were in town from Scottsdale, AZ for a funeral and wanted to see me and catch up. It had been at least three years since we last saw each other, but it seemed like yesterday. It's so nice when friendships are like that! They both looked great and are doing well. If I have the option for lung surgery down the road, I'm hoping to go to the Mayo Clinic or Cancer Treatment Center of America in Phoenix. Having Steve & Cory close by would be awesome.

NOV 20 2017

Just Another Day

I got up at 5:25am to get to Quest for my blood draw before it got too crowded. As a walk-in, you are taken in between standing appointments. I was fortunate again today to only have to wait 35 minutes before my name was called at about 6:20am. My every Monday blood draw is fairly routine and provides Dr. Gollard with a look at how the chemo treatments are affecting things like my magnesium levels, white blood cell counts, etc. He then adjusts my treatments accordingly.

Quest is just a couple miles away, so I was home by 6:40am and went back to bed for 3 hours. When I awoke, I had a bad headache, felt queasy and was a bit dizzy. Not surprisingly, these are common side effects of the chemotherapy, so I was expecting that they'd be arriving soon.

I received a text message from Jackie. She had made chicken noodle soup for me and wondered if I could meet her for an early lunch to pick it up. I hadn't eaten since 7pm the previous night, so I told her that I needed to grab some breakfast. Since her office is in the backyard of my apartment complex, I drove over to meet her there to pick up the soup. I had it for dinner tonight. YUM!

After breakfast, I headed over to the Venetian to play the noon $400 NLH SuperStack poker tournament. It didn't go so well today. I busted around 4pm. I played some slots afterwards to pass the time and then headed home, where I proceeded to get in bed for a nap after watching the *ABC Nightly News* and chatting with Chris on the phone.

I got up at 7:45pm, made a quick dinner, watched *The Voice* (one of my favorites), and played some online poker. It was a nice, relaxing evening. I also opened up a care package that was sent to me from a childhood friend, Lori. It was full of homemade chocolate chip cookies. I enjoyed a few of them tonight for dessert.

I'm going to give myself a break tomorrow from poker, as I'm starting to feel a bit fatigued. I will go grocery shopping to pick up food and other necessities for the weekend. Chris arrives on Friday morning. I can't wait! I haven't seen Chris since September 25 and really miss him. I have a surprise planned for Saturday night, which I think we'll both enjoy.

Time for bed now.

NOV 22 2017

I Am Thankful

With Thanksgiving upon us tomorrow, I've been thinking a lot lately about what I have to be thankful for. Sometimes this is hard given I have the Big C again, but I still do feel blessed for the many good things in my life.

Here is what I'm thankful for:

> *My family (Mom, Dad & Cheryl, Brother Ed and his wife Sharon) who cares so very much about me. We may be small, but we're #PetzingStrong!
>
> *My boyfriend, Chris, who is one of my angels on this earth. He stuck with me through my first cancer battle and is in my corner again. I can't wait to see him on Friday.
>
> *My BFF's (Elizabeth, Charlene (ex-wife), Jackie, Louise, Ardys, Lynnore, and April) who are always there for me providing friendship, laughter and support
>
> *My church family (Pastor Sal & the entire congregation) at the Douglas UCC in Douglas, MI who continually pray for me

*My wonderful group of high school friends, who I've reconnected with on Facebook, that send me daily words of encouragement and inspiration

*All of you, who follow me here on CaringBridge, that continue to fill me positive energy

*My doctors (Dr. Gollard and Dr. Tahir) and care team (Radka and staff), who treat me as a priority with kindness and empathy

*The technological advancements in cancer treatment that give folks like me a better opportunity to win our fight today versus yesterday

*The ability to be retired at an early age and do what I love to do everyday

*Living in Las Vegas in a beautiful condo with my two awesome cats, Zing & Zang, who give me nothing but love and great joy!

*Knowing that I've had more opportunities than most to see and experience the world, traveling to over 90 countries in my lifetime

*Not having to worry about anything, except getting myself better and beating this bastard called Cancer!

Of course, I'm just thankful to be alive and have the chance to keep on living. I've never taken life for granted and have always lived it to its fullest. Life is just too precious not to maximize every day!

Here's wishing you, your family and loved ones, a very Happy Thanksgiving!

NOV 25 2017

Mind Over Matter

It's 2:30am on the Saturday after Thanksgiving. Chris arrived from Michigan yesterday at 9:30am. We had a full day of activities: going out for breakfast at Grand Luxe, redeeming my accumulated slot points at the Venetian for Grazie Gifts (2- $50 Albertson Gift Cards and entries into a slot credit drawing), taking a nap, going to see the movie *Bad Moms*, cooking dinner, watching some college football and enjoying the original TV version of *Frosty The Snowman*. Given the three-hour time difference for him, Chris faded fast and we were in bed by 8:30pm last night. After six hours of good shut eye, I awoke and was unable to fall back asleep. So, here I am with an update on my past few days.

After writing my previous journal entry, "I Am Thankful," I had breakfast with my friend, Lynnore, and then we played the noon $400 No Limit Hold'em SuperStack tourney at the Venetian. At 7:45pm, almost eight hours later, I found myself at the final two tables of the event and managed to min cash placing 15th of 143 players for $831. I was feeling really good, had a lot of energy, and knew I wouldn't being playing poker again until next week after Chris leaves, so I decided to late register for the 7pm $200 NLH Rebuy tournament.

In order to start off with 24K in chips versus 12K in chips, I paid an extra $100 and did the rebuy. Well, I'm very excited to say that I actually won the tournament 9 hours and 15 minutes later at 5:15am, outlasting 76 other players to win $7,513! That's a big pay day for a $300 investment.

Frankly, I don't know how I managed to play poker that day for over 17 hours, but I did. It's amazing what an adrenaline rush can do and I'm guessing there must have been some leftover steroids from my recent hydration drip that kept me going, too. Or, perhaps it's mind over matter?! Needless to say, it was a great start to my Thanksgiving Day!

I got home Thanksgiving morning around 6:30am, crawled into bed and couldn't fall asleep until 8am because I was so wound up. Fortunately, I did get a good 3 hours in, hit the shower by 11:15am and was on the road to Jackie's house at 12:15pm for Thanksgiving dinner. Jackie and her husband, Mike, live in a neighboring suburb – Henderson -- and are two of the most gracious people I know. They had a gang of about 30 family members and close friends for their Thanksgiving celebration. That's a lot of work, but they do it every year and provide so much joy for all of us lucky enough to attend!

At just before 3pm, I left Jackie & Mike's and headed over to Susannah & Joe's, who also live in Henderson. They are a very nice couple from Connecticut who I met playing poker. They, too, had a large gathering of around 20 or so folks in their gorgeous home. Fortunately, their sit down was around 3:45pm, so I got to enjoy two Thanksgiving dinners. Given that my appetite is light, I did a "tapas" Thanksgiving and just put small slices of turkey and brisket and little spoonfuls of all the other side dishes on my plate at both parties. It worked out well and I wasn't overstuffed.

I got home about 7pm, laid on my couch and fell asleep. I woke up about 8:30pm, dragged myself into bed, and slept until 6:30am on Friday morning. I really needed that 10 hours of sleep. Before I knew it, I was on the way to airport to pick up Chris. I'm so glad he's here for the next few days and that

I'm feeling really well. It's been two months since we've seen each other and that's the longest we've been apart in over 3 1/2 years.

Speaking of feeling well, I'm shocked that the chemo side effects haven't hit me yet. Dr. Gollard was sure that I'd be struggling this past week, but the worst I felt was a 1.5 out of 5. When I had chemo during my neck cancer battle, I started getting very sick at about Day 13 of my treatment cycle. Today is Day 18! Maybe my body has built up a high tolerance for chemo? Could it be that I may not feel sick at all during the next nine weeks of treatment? That would be such a blessing! I already feel so lucky that the "chemo coma" has been delayed, allowing me to fully enjoy the Thanksgiving holiday and my time with Chris.

It's funny. For the past few days, the song from the old Heinz ketchup television commercial, "Anticipation," has been streaming through my head. Anticipation keeps making you wait. And that's where I find myself now. Waiting for the chemo whammy to hit. Dr. Gollard and his staff are going to be very surprised when I see them on Wednesday for Chemo #3 and tell them how good I've been feeling!

#PetzingStrong

NOV 26 2017

Why are Some So Mean?

I try very hard to be upbeat and positive in my journal posts. However, for a few days now, I've been debating about sharing a negative situation that occurred earlier this past week. So, to be balanced and honest about everything that I've been experiencing, I'm going to let you know what happened.

On Wednesday morning, I received a disturbing phone call from my realtor in Douglas, MI. Kevin has the listing for my former restaurant, which has been on the market for almost two years now. When I answered the phone, he breathed a big sigh of relief... thankful that I was still alive!

Apparently, a number of people in the tiny towns of Saugatuck (pop. 800) and Douglas (pop. 1200) are finding great pleasure in spreading a rumor that I have died. This, of course, coming after one of my best friends and angels from the same area, Scott, was laid to rest just four days earlier.

I lived in Douglas, MI for five years, where I had a steak and seafood house called Zing Eat Drink. We were a four-star restaurant on Trip Advisor and three and half stars on Yelp. I was also the President of the Saugatuck Douglas

Area Business Association and a weekly columnist in *The Local Observer* newspaper.

Saugatuck and Douglas are seasonal resort towns in Southwest Michigan on the lake. They haven't changed in twenty years because people don't want them to. It is lively in the Summer and sleepy the rest of the year, making it very difficult for business owners to be successful. Additionally, with travel trends showing folks taking three- or four-day weekend trips versus week long vacations, the area has continued to suffer... however, few are willing to admit this.

To help bring about needed change to this bucolic community living in the past, I ran for Douglas City Council in 2015 against two incumbents, a past council member and two new candidates. Three of the six of us would be elected. I came in fourth, losing by twenty votes. It was very clear that the community did not want to evolve from being a seasonal resort area to a year-round destination. This due, in a large part, to the fact that Saugatuck-Douglas has the oldest average age population of any Michigan town/city (64 years of age), given its propensity for being a popular retirement and second home area for many.

Since I was very outspoken in my weekly columns about the issues that needed to be addressed in town AND was quite controversial in my campaign platform, people either loved me or hated me. The haters were so bad that they created an actual four color, multi-page newspaper mocking me and my position on various issues. They even printed and distributed this newspaper in selected PO Boxes at our local Douglas Post Office prior to the election. Obviously, these folks had way too much time on their hands and were very afraid of change.

I share this with you because there is a group of evil, insecure, vindictive, uncaring, and soulless people in Saugatuck-Douglas who have nothing better to do with their miserable selves other than to spread hurtful rumors and falsehoods.

So, after hearing about the rumor that I had died, I went to Facebook and posted the following out of anger:

"For those of you getting off on spreading information about me that is not true, please keep me out of your idiotic, small town rumor mill. I may have cancer, but I'm fighting hard and will persevere again! You can count on that...much to your dismay. Just leave me alone and find something more constructive to do with your time, like repenting for all of your sins during this holiday season. Shame on you."

I received over 125 "likes" and many comments of support from other residents there, who understand the "Mean Girl" syndrome that exists in the community. One of my favorite responses was:

"Unfortunately, every village has an idiot. Sounds like we are breeding more than our fair share here in Douglas."

Not only did my realtor share this horrific rumor with me, but another business owner also contacted me on Facebook Messenger with the following:

"I have to tell you, when I heard that you had died, I freaked out for a bit and went to your CaringBridge.org site and other places to see if it was true. I read every single one of your posts on Facebook and on CaringBridge and I kept thinking, 'this is not true.' I heard it from my neighbor who goes to a coffee group with a bunch of blowhards every morning, so I'm not sure exactly who he heard it from. All I have to say is that I was SO glad when you finally made a post that it was just a RUMOR. This town is so full of shit bags who love controversy, as you know. I try to avoid all the political crap in this town. You shouldn't have to deal with this stress with what you are going through, and I will stand up for you until the end of time. Keep your positive attitude and fuck these people in this trivial little town… xoxoxo."

So, yes, there are some good people in Saugatuck-Douglas, who truly understand the sad situation there. And, when I was living there sick with neck cancer, there were many amazing people who prayed for and supported me.

I guess what I don't understand is why people have to be so mean and can't let things go? Obviously, there are just some horrible folks out there who aren't happy unless they can find a way to try to hurt others. It is just so hard to comprehend!

#PetzingStrong

NOV 28 2017

Can't Get into the Christmas Spirit

Chris flew back to Michigan today. We had an awesome time during his visit. Even though we hadn't seen each other for two months, we were back in step immediately. I'm so grateful that I felt as well as I did while he was here. It enabled us to really enjoy the long Thanksgiving weekend!

Not only did we get to see Donnie & Marie's entertaining show at the Flamingo on Saturday night (a bucket list item for Chris), but we also were able to get together with so many of my friends here, including: Liina & Lynnore for breakfast on Sunday, Jackie & Sam for breakfast on Monday, and Ardys & Jimmy and Louise & Darryl for dinner on Monday night. Chris and I also saw the movie, *A Bad Moms Christmas*. It was okay, but a bit over the top. After that, we had fun watching the *Miss Universe Pageant* on Sunday night. Miss South Africa was an excellent choice!

Since I've been a bit more tired than usual, we also took a lot of naps and tried to sleep in on most mornings. I just got a text message from Chris that he landed safely in Grand Rapids tonight. It was fairly smooth sailing for him today, as he avoided the crazy Monday after Thanksgiving travel day.

Chris and I have been doing the long-distance relationship thing for almost two years now, ever since I moved to Vegas from Michigan in late January 2016 to pursue a professional poker career. It's been tough being physically apart, but we've been able to see each other almost once a month and are doing our best. Fortunately, we were also able to spend 2 1/2 weeks together in Michigan this past September. Our emotional bond is very strong, and it always feels so good to be with him.

With Christmas approaching, I've been a little disconnected lately. It has never been a favorite holiday of mine, because I feel the true meaning of the holiday has been lost in the stress-inducing, hustle and bustle of gift buying and giving. With so much emphasis placed on that, the importance of the birth of Christ has almost been forgotten.

Don't get me wrong, I do enjoy the spirit of Christmas and have always enjoyed having a Christmas tree, but this season I just haven't felt it (yet). Likely, it's due to my recent cancer diagnosis and just not feeling like myself. As a result, my motivation for "doing" Christmas has been almost non-existent and I find myself in kind of a funky, "Bah Humbug" state.

To help me snap out of it, Chris surprised me last night by stringing pretty white lights and hanging mini ornaments on on my fake, plastic 7 ft. house plant. It looks really nice and put a smile on my face. This past weekend, I also got confirmation from my bestie and "angel," Elizabeth, that she is coming to spend Christmas with me from December 23-26. I'm excited about that! Elizabeth moved from Saugatuck, MI to Scottsdale, AZ a couple of months of ago and is loving it. She was always by my side during my previous battle with neck cancer.

Yesterday, Chris and I met with my oncologist, Dr. Gollard, for a check-in meeting. He was surprised that I've been doing so well and didn't get really sick this past week as projected. He attributed much of it to my positive attitude and fighter mentality. He now also thinks that I might be able to get through the next two months of chemo treatments without having too many issues. Knock on wood... that would be amazing!

Today, I had my brain and spinal MRIs. I have never had an MRI before and was shocked at how noisy the machine was. Even with headphones on and listening to smooth jazz, the buzzing and beeping that went on for an hour was just ridiculous. I even commented to the technician how surprised I was, that with today's technological advancements, there wasn't a quieter, less intrusive machine. She didn't really like that and said, "It is what it is."

Hopefully, the MRI results will show that my lung cancer hasn't spread to my brain or spine. There has been some concern about a spot that has shown up in my lower lumbar area in both my recent CT and PET scans. Fingers crossed that all is clear. I should know something by Friday.

Tomorrow I'm back at Dr. Gollard's for chemo treatment #3 of 8. It will be another long day.

#PetzingStrong

DEC 1 2017

Cupcakes at Chemo!

I was back at Dr. Gollard's for Chemo #3 on Wednesday. My drip lasted 6 hours and all went well. It was really nice that Louise came by around 3:15pm to hang with me. We chatted about poker, insurance, relationships and life in general. More importantly, she made me laugh. When you're sick with cancer, you don't feel like laughing, or even smiling, that much. So when someone can bring that out of me, it feels great!

While Louise and I were visiting, the nurses asked if we would like to indulge in some cupcakes that one of their drug reps had brought into the office. Well, we jumped at that generous offer and each picked out one.

I chose the traditional "Birthday Cake" cupcake. Marble cake, rich vanilla and chocolate icing and colorful sprinkles – so good! Louise picked the "Decadent Mint Chocolate" cupcake, which had double chocolate cake and a mint fudge icing. She had a small piece of both cupcakes and I ate the rest. They were delicious!

We were like little kids at a birthday party. Louise took a picture of me with my fingers and face covered in chocolate frosting. I posted it to my Facebook page with the heading, "Cupcakes at Chemo!"

Well, this post certainly caused some debate. One of my Canadian friends, who used to own a vitamin store, wrote the following: "WOW, it boggles my mind that your doctor would allow you to have sugar, as sugar feeds cancer. If I were you, I'd give them a big miss on this, Jim. Don't mean to be mean, but it's a fact."

Interestingly, Chris and I had just had a conversation with Dr. Gollard earlier in the week about cancer & sugar. His position, which is held by most western medicine oncologists and doctors, is that this is an "old wives' tale" that has been exacerbated by alternative medicine aficionados. Dr. Gollard shared a number of stories and research studies with us that confirmed the falsehood of this belief. Additionally, I went online myself and saw that leading cancer treatment centers like Mayo Clinic and MD Anderson, along with other major research organizations, refute the notion that sugar causes and/or accelerates cancer.

A doctor friend of mine on Facebook responded: "Very simply, sugar is glucose, which is the main fuel of the body. The brain, in fact, only functions on glucose, therefore easy to find confounding bias with a simple sugar diet. Cancer cells grow abnormally, so use more glucose, but you can't get around that because you (your brain) need it, too."

When his dad was going through chemotherapy, he told him, "Eat what sounds good, because calories are gold no matter how you spend them! Just make sure you're getting proper nutrition overall."

This is exactly what Dr. Gollard told me, too. It's important that I keep my caloric intake up to help me fight the cancer and heal from the treatments. I've already lost 11 lbs. due to a decreased appetite, so Dr. Gollard told me to eat anything and everything I want while undergoing treatment. Except, of course, no alcohol because that would make me quite sick.

I was in fighter mode, so one of my Facebook retorts was: "I have lung cancer and NEVER smoked a fucking cigarette in my life. I doubt that a cupcake or two is going to do a whole lot of damage!"

Another good friend wrote: "Jim, I honestly believe that beating cancer is a combination of medical and attitude. And, a cupcake improves my attitude! So I say keep doing what you're doing, because you look strong and happy during a crappy circumstance."

Yes, this became my own version of "Cupcake Wars" and now I have a few friends calling me, "Cupcake," which I'm not too excited about.

After Louise dropped me off at home, I had all kinds of energy from the steroids that were mixed into my chemo cocktail, so I decided to play the 7pm Rebuy poker tournament at the Venetian. I outlasted more than half of the field but didn't cash in this one.

On Thursday morning, I got up early for my 8:45am appointment with my new pulmonologist, Dr. Tavares. He spent over 30 minutes with me, discussing different options I might have pending the effectiveness and outcome of my chemotherapy treatment. They range from the goal of being able to surgically remove the tumor, lung, and/or part of the lung, to inserting a stent with a balloon in the bronchial tube, to exploring clinical trials. I feel like I'll be in good hands when we have our next set of key decisions to make at the end of January/early February.

Today, I'm back again for my "Bags 'O Fun" hydration treatment, which hopefully will keep me feeling well until next Wednesday's chemo infusion. Overall, it's truly a miracle how well I've been doing. I haven't felt that sick at all, so we're going to keep the current plan in place as long as we can.

My other good news is that it looks like the brain and spinal MRIs came back negative for cancer. This is awesome! Radka took a look at the results and said that they're may be some degenerative things going on, but nothing too serious. I'll discuss them further with Dr. Gollard when I meet with him next week. Thankfully, I can rest easy this weekend and work on winning the $250K Guarantee $600 NLH Poker Tourney at the Wynn!

DEC 4 2017

Feeling Inspired By Thoughtful Cards

I'm still feeling really Good. It's hard to believe that I'm doing so well at close to the halfway point of my chemotherapy treatments. Believe me... I'M not complaining. I am so grateful!

I had a weekend full of playing poker and was excited to cash in 24th of 775 players in the Wynn $600 NLH December Classic event. It was a $2,762 win, so that will help pay for some of my $6K insurance deductible. It's just crazy how much everything costs!

I've been collecting "get well" cards that have been sent to me. I look forward to receiving them and read every word. They really do inspire me! When I'm feeling down, I go back and look at them again. There are two that really stand out. One is from my ex-wife, Charlene, and the other comes from Joel and David, a wonderful couple from Missouri. I'd like to share them both with you.

The cover of Charlene's card says: "To Someone Truly Incredible." On the inside, it says the following:

"Dearest Jim, Sometimes I find myself thinking of you -- of your strength and motivation and the amazing way you manage to keep it all together. I see how others look at you, and I know that they think these same things about you, too. But for as many times as these thoughts surround you, I wonder if you even know how truly wonderful you are and how much you are admired by those who are lucky enough to be part of your life... Today I wanted to make sure you know. You can do this! #PetzingStrong. Love you, Charlene."

This makes me so happy! I really am trying to be strong and motivated, not just for myself, but for everyone that cares about me. Clearly, I'm dealing with a lot and it's very tough, but I'm doing my absolute best to stay positive and live "normally" day to day as I can.

Joel and David's card is completely handwritten, except for the sentiment on the front, which says, "Geez." On the inside, they write:

"James, I won't waste space with empty platitudes, verses or pithy quotes. I don't believe in magic words. But what I can offer you is my heart-felt love and support from afar. I hope you can feel my BIG HUG from Missouri. David and I know that these are pretty shitty times for you. Let's be honest, sometimes life really sucks! But you have the amazing skill of finding beauty, even in the shit. You are a beautiful and inspiring man. May you be filled with all the beauty you deserve! You're amazing! We love you and are so happy our paths crossed long ago. You bring us joy just by being YOU! Love, Joel & David"

I was really touched by this sentiment and really do believe that out of something bad will come something good. It's quite difficult to embrace this concept while fighting a life-threatening disease, but my first book, "From Feeding Tube to Final Table: A Cancer Survivor's Story," did come out of my first battle with cancer and I know it has been helping others. Again, I need to embrace the cards I've been dealt and make them work for Me. I CAN and I WILL! Because this is who I am.

DEC 6 2017

Why are Men so Stubborn?

So I'm back at Dr. Gollard's for Chemo #4 of 8. After spending almost seven hours here today, I'll be halfway through my chemotherapy treatments with my final one scheduled for Wednesday, January 17. Then, I will undergo another PET scan to see if the large and small tumors in my right lung have shrunk and if the cancerous nodes in the middle of my chest have been eradicated.

Honestly, this is all I want for Christmas...along with continuing to feel good for the next five plus weeks as I finish out Phase 1 of this process.

Ardys is coming by in an hour or so to hang with me at chemo. Early this evening, we're going to grab some dinner and see the movie, "Three Billboards Outside Ebbing, Missouri." I'm looking forward to it!

On Friday, Ed, and his wife, Sharon, are flying in from Maryland for a long weekend! It will be so good to see them. I wish we weren't so far apart geographically. They love Vegas and we always have fun when they're here. I have a surprise planned for them on Saturday night that I know we'll all enjoy!

Unfortunately, my Dad and Cheryl couldn't come visit this week as originally planned. Dad got diverticulitis and Cheryl came down with a horrible bout of shingles on her face by the right eye and on top of her head. Just horrible. I'm glad they stayed home to recover, so they can be 100% healthy when they go on their Christmas cruise in a couple of weeks. It looks like they'll reschedule their trip here for mid to late January.

So, I've been thinking a lot lately about how bad men are at going to the doctor when they are sick. I guess it's a "guy" thing to tough things out, not show vulnerability and not ask for help. When it comes to making sure you are healthy, these are not good qualities.

If you are a man reading this journal entry, please take notice! If you are someone with a man in your life who is stubborn about going to the doctor to get things checked out, you need to take notice, too! You and/or your guy could be facing a life-threatening disease or illness and not even know it. So, if something doesn't seem right, or is just a bit off with your overall state of health, don't put off going to see your doctor about it.

I can speak from personal experience about this! When I found a lump on the left side of my neck in the summer of 2014, I was in Vegas playing in the Main Event of the World Series of Poker. I woke up one morning, started shaving, and noticed it. It hadn't been there the day before, so I chalked it up to an infected hair follicle or lymph node and decided that I'd get it looked at when I got home to Michigan...if it was still there. Interestingly, it didn't hurt and I felt great! It never occurred to me that I could have a problem.

When I got back to Michigan, the lump had increased slightly in size, but didn't hurt when I pushed on it. I thought about letting the lump run its course, but decided I better get it looked at. I thank my Mom for that!

While growing up, she was adamant about me seeing a doctor if I felt sick or something just didn't seem right relative to my body. So, I went to my local general practitioner and was put on antibiotics for 10 days. They didn't work and I called her back. She became concerned and had me go see an ENT doctor, who scoped my throat, saw some redness, and did a needle biopsy of the lump in my neck. Four days later, I was diagnosed with neck cancer. It had already started spreading from the left side of my neck across to the right side where, when I pressed on my neck, I could feel smaller lumps under my skin.

Before I could start my treatment plan of 35 consecutive days of radiation (Monday through Friday) and seven weekly chemo infusions, I had to visit a "cancer" dentist and get his seal approval that everything in my mouth was perfect...no gum disease, broken/chipped teeth, cavities, etc. This, I learned, was because the radiation that would be going into my mouth to reach my cancer origination point in the back of my throat, can cause a deadly disease in the mouth if it gets into the bloodstream and goes to the wrong places.

While I was in the dentist's chair undergoing his thorough evaluation, he told me about the many other men like me who had been in his chair with neck, throat, tongue, or mouth cancer and got there too late to be "saved". Most of these men were big smokers and/or drinkers. They were already in late stage cancer with a dire long term prognosis, because they didn't act soon enough when they had early stage symptoms that they "blew off."

Again, thanks to my Mom, my oral hygiene skills have always been good, so I passed the dental exam with flying colors. The dentist told me how lucky I was that he didn't have to fix anything before moving on to radiation and that I caught my problem early.

So, gentlemen, don't be too proud to get to the doctor is something is wrong with you!

Interestingly, a similar set of circumstances happened this time around, too. I hadn't been feeling well for almost two months this past summer. I had an ongoing dry cough, wheezing, and a little shortness of breath. I chalked it up to a case of "Vegas Fever." I wasn't sick enough to stay at home in bed, so I continued to function as usual. When I flew back to Michigan for three weeks in December, I decided to go see my doctor there to get checked out.

Something didn't seem right, as I couldn't kick the cough. Dr. Myers ordered a chest x-ray and the results showed that I had walking pneumonia and didn't even know it. He also noticed an "odd obstruction" in the right lung. He was concerned about it and told me to get a CT scan when I got back to Vegas, which I did do promptly upon my return.

Four days later, I was diagnosed with Stage 3B lung cancer. The docs say it has been growing in my body for at least six months. I would have never known I was sick again with cancer had I not gone to the doctor and got the chest x-ray. I feel lucky for the second time and hopefully have caught this cancer early enough to beat it, too.

Again, if you or a loved one aren't feeling right or sense that something may be wrong with your health, don't delay. Get to a doctor and get checked out! It very well could be a matter of life or death.

#PetzingStrong

DEC 8 2017

Two Special Gifts in a Box

When I got home from playing poker last night, there was a small package waiting for me in my mailbox. It was from my Dad & Cheryl. They had planned to be here visiting me the past few days but had to cancel their trip due to Cheryl's bout with shingles. We don't exchange Christmas gifts, so I was curious what they had sent.

I opened the box and there was an envelope that said, "Please Read. Love you, Dad & Cheryl."

Inside there was a letter:

> "Dear Jim, these are not Christmas gifts. Rather, Love gifts, which include our desire to provide you with the signs of our complete and total love for you and our desire to give you items we saw that we hope will soothe you during your fight to beat the dreaded 'C.' We had planned to bring these to you on our visit this week, but since that is not possible we are sending them to you instead. We hope you find these items helpful during your battle and will know that we are with you 24/7 in our prayers, thoughts, words and deeds.

> *Jesus Calling* was given to us by our dear friend Heather, "my Consort", who is a longtime widow friend of ours from my Club Managers time on their Board of Directors. I found this so uplifting that we wanted you to have it. So, we ordered it online, as we did the bracelet. We hope you will enjoy these. Dad & Cheryl"

Jesus Calling, Enjoying Peace in His Presence by Sarah Young, is a beautiful, small leather-bound book of devotions for everyday of the year. My bestie, Elizabeth, has a similar book that she reads from each day, and I know it has helped her immensely in providing comfort and helping her live in the moment. I look forward to reading from this book each morning before I start my day. I'm sure there will be many passages that give me hope, strength and inspiration to keep fighting my battle.

The other gift in the box was a gorgeous, individually hand-crafted, braided black leather and solid stainless steel bracelet with a genuine black sapphire gemstone, magnetic closure and engraved sentiment that says, "My Dear Son, May God always protect you and give you strength." I love it! I put it on today at Dr. Gollard's before I started my hydration treatment. I'll call Dad & Cheryl later this morning to thank them for these lovely, thoughtful gifts.

As I write, Ed and Sharon are on a flight from Maryland to Vegas to come visit me for the weekend. I'll pick them up from the airport after I finish with my infusion. I'm excited to see them, as we don't get to do it often enough. We'll do some gambling, dining out and catching up. It will be really nice to spend quality time with them.

Fortunately, I'm still feeling quite well and should have the energy to keep up with Ed and Sharon. However, I may need to catch a nap or two as I've only had 4 hours of sleep each of the past two nights due to the side effects from the steroids in my chemo "fun bag." Once I finish the antibiotic I'm on, I can go back to taking Xanax at night before I go to bed. It really helps me sleep like a baby.

Hope you all have a wonderful weekend!

DEC 9 2017

So Glad Family is Here!

After my 90-minute hydration infusion yesterday, I drove over to McCarran Airport to pick up Ed and Sharon. They flew in from Baltimore for a long weekend visit. It has been well over a year since we've seen each other, so I've been excited to spend some quality time with them.

We were all hungry, so we headed over to the Venetian for a long lunch at Grand Luxe. It was so good catching up. Sometimes I just don't realize how important family is, especially when you come from a very small one. I'm fortunate that my Mom (84), Dad (85), Cheryl (75), and Charlene (70, ex-wife) are all still living. Ed (54) is my full brother and he has three children, my two nieces (Alise and Tania) and nephew (Seth). I have a half-brother, Mark (43), but he has chosen to remove himself and his family from ours. It's a sad situation and one I don't understand or agree with, but is his decision to live with forever. I also have one Aunt (Jacque) and Uncle (Lou), and three cousins (Kim, Stacey and Erik.) That's it!

Even though Ed and I don't see each other often enough, we are pretty good at staying in touch by phone. However, it's just not the same as being one on one in person. I really miss that interaction and am so grateful that he and

Sharon have taken the time out of their busy schedules to come check in on me during my current cancer battle. It means a lot!

After lunch, they dropped me off at home, took my car and checked into their hotel while I took a much needed three-hour nap. Ed and Sharon popped back over to my place around 7:15pm and we continued our chat from lunch. Before we knew it, it was 9pm (midnight their time), so we headed across the street to the Tuscany Casino and played some craps and slots... unsuccessfully. Ed, however, found a lucky seat at a blackjack table and won $40.

We all were a bit hungry, so we dropped into PUB 365 at the hotel to grab a bite. I've never eaten there before, but knew that they were known for their incredible selection of 365 different beers, micro beers, specialty beers, etc. Surprisingly, for a Friday night, they were not crowded at all. We ordered wings, mac and cheese, and chicken sandwiches. Ed had a beer, too. Sooooo good! Really hit the spot. We finished up just past midnight and I was home around 12:30am.

My body clock continues to be messed up from the chemo and hydration steroids I received this week, so I ended up watching *CNN* late night and *The Voice* on On Demand. Finally, I fell asleep around 2:30am and was up at 7:15am this morning. I'll definitely need another nap this afternoon before we go out tonight.

The last time Ed and Sharon were here, we found a local doughnut shop that has the most amazing treats ever! So last night, we decided that they'll pick up a dozen of those beauties for breakfast at my place this morning. Can't wait!

We don't have specific plans for the afternoon, but tonight we'll be going to see Masters of Illusion at Bally's. It's supposed to be an awesome show with five very talented illusionists. We love that stuff! I'm sure we'll also squeeze in some gambling and a late dinner. Should be another fun day!

So glad they're here!

DEC 13 2017

Feeling More Informed

Since I finished my antibiotic a couple of days ago, I'm now able to take Xanax at night before I go to bed. It helps me sleep like a baby and provides me with a good seven to nine hours. Thankfully, today I felt more refreshed and energized than I have since last Thursday...and I didn't need to take a nap!

I was up fairly early, did some paperwork and left for Dr. Tavares' office around 8:30am. He's my pulmonologist and today was my follow-up session with him. During our last appointment, he was concerned about my continued wheezing and extended me on an antibiotic for another week. He also put me on Symbicort, an inhaler.

I had a lot of "what if" questions for Dr. Tavares. Here's what I learned:

> * The large tumor in the middle of my right lung is infringing upon and putting pressure on my right bronchial tube causing shortness of breath. It's also intertwined with and connected to a number of pulmonary arteries and blood vessels. If the chemotherapy I'm receiving does the job it's supposed to, it's hoped that the tumor will shrink enough to become disconnected and operable. Likely, two-thirds

of my right lung will be removed (the upper and middle lobes) and there's a possibility that the entire lung may have to be removed if the smaller tumor in the lower lobe is not eradicated.

* It is possible to live fully without a lung. The recovery time for this surgery would be somewhere between one and four weeks, with a one week stay in the hospital. Follow-up chemo and/or radiation may be necessary. Dr. Tavares has recommended a local thoracic surgeon, who is affiliated with Stanford University. He is also open to helping me get into MD Anderson in Houston, TX, given the complexity of my situation, my previous history with neck cancer, and their expertise in treating late stage lung cancer.

* If the chemotherapy does not shrink the large and small tumors enough or if it does not remove the cancerous lymph nodes in the middle of my chest, chemotherapy may continue. Or, Dr. Tavares may insert a stent in my right bronchial tube. This would be a surgery where he uses a long, small wire to insert a balloon in the bronchial tube to keep the passageway open. Unfortunately, this would only be a temporary fix and ultimately, over the next two to three years, the tumor would continue to grow and collapse the lung. The prognosis for living beyond that timeframe is not good.

* Concurrent with the stent option, if chemotherapy doesn't work, would be an exploration of alternative medicine approaches and/or clinical trials. Dr. Tavares has a couple of doctors in mind if we need to pursue this route.

Needless to say, I'm praying every day that the chemotherapy I'm receiving is working! My shortness of breath has improved, so I'm feeling optimistic that the large tumor is shrinking and putting less pressure on my bronchial tube.

Unfortunately, I'm only halfway through my treatments and won't be getting a PET scan until the third or fourth week of January. It will show the status of my situation and decisions will be made from there.

I left Dr. Tavares' office feeling very informed and better about lung surgery. I'm not afraid and know that I can handle it. I just hope that the chemo does its job and I get the opportunity to be a surgical candidate. Fingers crossed.

After my appointment, I headed over to the Venetian to play in the $150 No Limit Hold'em poker tournament. For the last four hours of this grueling 10-hour event, I was a short stack just trying to climb the money ladder. Fortunately, all the big stacks eliminated each other, and I suddenly found myself in 3rd place of 113 players with a nice payday of $1,747!

Overall, it was a really good day!

#PetzingStrong

DEC 15 2017

Time for the Chest Port

I had my check-in with Dr. Gollard on Wednesday morning. He's very pleased with how the chemotherapy plan is going at the halfway point, especially since I no longer have a bad cough or shortness of breath, my blood work has been consistently good, and I haven't become really sick as previously expected.

The fact that my cough is gone is a great sign that the chemo is working and likely shrinking the large tumor in my right lung as hoped. This tumor had been pressing against the bronchial tube causing the cough, but apparently has "backed off." I'm very optimistic. Every day, I also try to visualize that the tumor is disconnecting from my pulmonary arteries and getting smaller and smaller so that it can be operable.

I shared with Dr. Gollard that the only issues I'm consistently having now are fatigue, constipation and a soreness on the underside of my lower left arm where I've developed a painful rash. It looks like it may be a result of some of the chemo meds leaking from the vein. Dr. Gollard put me on a new antibiotic which seems to be clearing up the problem.

Given how well things are going, we're continuing with the current plan through mid-January. The only change is that I need to have a chest port installed because my veins in both arms and the top of my hands are hardening from the harshness of the chemo meds I've been receiving, plus those I had infused three years ago when I was treated for neck cancer. Dr. Gollard put in a stat request for the port placement and I had the outpatient surgery done today. My appointment was at 7:30am, so Chris and I left my condo at 6:45am to give us plenty of time to get there during rush hour.

The procedure was fairly easy to endure. I was given some "relaxation" drugs via an IV but did not fall asleep during the placement of the port under the skin in my upper left chest. Once I got on the operating table, the procedure itself took about 30 minutes. The worst part was the ten different injections of numbing medication the surgeon gave me at the start. This was necessary so I wouldn't feel anything. I'm very used to needle pricks and insertions these days, so it really wasn't too bad. All went smoothly. I wasn't too drugged out, but I still needed Chris to drive us to breakfast and home.

It's so great having Chris here! He flew in from Grand Rapids, MI yesterday morning. We went for a Mexican lunch and then watched the last episode of Season 1 and the first two episodes of Season 2 of "Stranger Things" on Netflix before napping for a couple of hours. For dinner, we went across the street to PUB 365 at the Tuscany Suites and had fish 'n chips (Chris) and a patty melt (me). We were both tired after dinner, so called it quits and retired early.

This afternoon, after my regular nap, we went to see the movie, *Murder on the Orient Express*, with a surprising all-star cast including folks like: Johnny Depp, Kenneth Branagh, Penelope Cruz, Michelle Pfeiffer, Willem Dafoe, Daisy Ridley and Dame Judi Dench to name just a few. I had never seen the original, so was very engaged and entertained by this "who dunnit?" The cinematography was amazing and the film quite enjoyable. I recommend it!

I'm feeling a little "blah" tonight from today's procedure and have been popping a lot of Tylenol to kill the pain. I also don't have an appetite this evening, so I'm skipping dinner. Since I had a big breakfast, it's not that big of a problem. I'll get back on track tomorrow.

That's it for now. Enjoy your weekend!

DEC 20 2017

Keeping the Faith

Chris and I had an awesome time while he was here. I drove him to the airport early Monday morning at 4:15am for his 6am flight. He owes me! It's always hard to see him go, but he'll be back in mid-January when I finish my chemo treatments.

Well, I finally feel like I'm getting into the Christmas spirit a bit. Chris and I found a unique Christmas store while we got lost looking for the movie theater on Sunday. Clearly, we're both quite directionally challenged. I bought a few decorations to make my place a little more festive since Elizabeth is coming to see me this weekend for Christmas. Zing & Zang have sniffed and checked all of them out and have provided their seal of approval. So, we're good to go!

I can't wait for Elizabeth to arrive on Saturday. We haven't seen each other for six months. She took amazing care of me the last time I was sick with the Big C: driving me to radiation treatments almost every day (35 in total), sitting with me during each of my seven chemo sessions and keeping up my spirits on a daily basis. I just love her so much and have got some fun things planned for us this weekend. More on that in a future journal entry.

I'm really enjoying my *Jesus Calling* book of daily devotions that my Dad & Cheryl gave me. One of my favorite passages so far is the following:

"I am taking care of you. Feel the warmth and security of being enveloped in My loving Presence. Every detail of your life is under My control. Moreover, everything fits into a pattern for good, to those who love Me and are called according to My design and purpose.

"Because the world is in an abnormal, fallen condition, people tend to think that chance governs the universe. Events may seem to occur randomly, with little or no meaning. People who view the world this way have overlooked one basic fact: the limitations of human understanding. What you know of the world you inhabit is only the tip of the iceberg. Submerged beneath the surface of the visible world are mysteries too vast for you to comprehend. If you could only see how close I am to you and how constantly I work on your behalf, you would never again doubt that I am wonderfully caring for you. This is why YOU MUST LIVE BY FAITH, not by sight; trusting in My mysterious majestic Presence." Romans 8:28 (AMP); Job 42:1-3, 1 Peter 5-7 and 2 Corinthians 5:7

I have never been a very religious person; however, I am quite spiritual. I regained my spirituality when I started attending the United Church of Christ in Douglas, MI, back in 2015. Pastor Sal's homily each Sunday inspired me. It's his special gift! I definitely need to find a similar one here in Vegas. It's one of my 2018 resolutions.

Coming out of my renewed spirituality has been both a richer appreciation for living life fully each day, along with much more faith in my Higher Power. I believe that we're all on a pre-determined path, call it Destiny if you like. Along that path are detours, barriers, forks in the road and many choices we have the opportunity to make for ourselves.

But, ultimately, we will experience what He wants for us and end up where we're supposed to be. So, I don't believe that things in our life happen by chance. He is watching over us as we advance along our path. I know my

Higher Power was watching over me during my battle with neck cancer and I'm sure He is here with me now as I fight lung cancer. I continue to believe in Him, as my faith gets stronger every day.

So you might be asking yourself, "Why do bad things happen to good people then?" It's a great question. I often ask myself, "How is it that I have the Big C....AGAIN?!" This is very hard to accept. However, I believe He is challenging me to persevere and conquer this life-threatening barrier, so I can spread the learning and help others. I know it's part of a much bigger plan that He has for me. #PetzingStrong

DEC 23 2017

Unexpected Spiritual Healing

I had my fifth of eight chemotherapy infusions this past Wednesday. This time, however, instead of a receiving it via an IV in my arm or on the top of my hand, I got it through my new chest port. Radka was really excited that she no longer had to deal with trying to find a "good" vein, since so many of mine have hardened from all of the chemo.

Another nice benefit of the chest port is that the chemo infusion goes faster. Instead of taking six to seven hours, it was completed in only 4 1/2 hours and I was hands and arms-free the entire time. No more bruising, too!

Jackie came by to keep me company for the last 90 minutes of my infusion. I always love catching up with her. It really made the time fly by. When I finished, we went to The Cheesecake Factory for a late lunch/early dinner and completely gorged ourselves. Interestingly, I'm always ravenous after chemo. I think it's driven by the steroids I receive in the "fun" bag of drugs.

I was going to play poker that evening but fell asleep on the couch around 5pm from the food-induced coma. Clearly, I was too tired and my body was telling me to stay at home. So, I did.

On Thursday, I played the noon poker tourney at Venetian and ran fairly deep in it. However, I busted out seven hours later and didn't cash. The 7pm $200 NLH Bounty tournament with $50 bounties for each person you knock out had just started, so I jumped into that one since I still had tons of energy and wasn't ready to go home.

At the beginning of this tourney, a poker acquaintance of mine, Gino, came over to me to relay a message. I had met Gino and his wife, Dilek, at a party this past Summer at Jackie's house. Sadly, Dilek was battling cancer and was in an experimental alternative treatment program because traditional therapies were not working for her. I happened to have my book, "From Feeding Tube to Final Table: A Cancer Survivor's Story," with me. It's full of hope and inspiration for the cancer patient and their loved ones, so I thought that she might benefit from reading it. I signed a copy and gave it to her as a gift. I never saw Dilek again after Jackie's party. Then on Facebook, about a month ago, I saw a post from Gino that Dilek had passed on... as so many do from this ugly, debilitating, nasty and horrific disease. Of course, this sad news hit me quite hard, because ultimately, I could be called to Heaven in the same way. I just don't believe it's my time.

I got up from poker table when Gino came over to see me. We hugged and I expressed my condolences. He had tears in his eyes and wanted me to know that Dilek had told him that I was one of two people who really inspired her to keep on fighting her cancer with a positive outlook and attitude, even when she had received a terminal diagnosis. She loved my book. I was so touched. I thanked Gino for telling me and we hugged again. I felt Dilek was there with us.

Fast forward to 4am Friday morning (nine hours later), and I am one of three players left in the 7pm bounty tournament from an original field of 76. We were all fairly close in chip count, so the chip leader asked if we wanted to chop the prize money evenly. I was happy to do so and came away with $1920 (better than second place money) plus $200 in bounties for a total cash out of $2120. It felt good! I was still a bit wired from the excitement, so I decided to play my favorite Willie Wonka slot machine and won an additional $200 before heading home at 5:15am.

I got in bed at 5:40am. A quick 100 minutes later my phone alarm rang at 7:20am. I jumped out of bed, threw on some clothes, got in my car and drove it to Service King for my 8:15am appointment with the State Farm insurance adjuster. I have some front left bumper damage that needs to be fixed and for State Farm to cover it, they require their own evaluation of it. I had already had my Nissan dealer do a repair estimate, so I was hoping they'd be close. And they were! I walked out with a check for $868 toward the $1368 I'll have to pay the auto body shop. The difference is my $500 deductible.

While at Service King, I had the most unusual, unexpected, surprising, emotional and spiritually uplifting experience I've ever had, which I now must share with you.

My adjuster's name was Joyce. We had "bonded" via text the day before when she confirmed our appointment and I responded back saying, "I'll be there!" She texted back a "Thank you, no one ever says that!"

I got to Service King around 8am and Joyce rolled in around 8:20am. She introduced herself and told me that she would go out to my car, spend 20-25 minutes evaluating the damage, write up a repair estimate, and cut me a check on the spot for what State Farm would pay. I waited patiently in the lobby, had a coffee, checked Facebook and hoped that I'd get the money I was hoping for.

About 30 minutes later, Joyce called me into her office. She was a talker and we suddenly found ourselves in a personal conversation. I learned that she was from the South Side of Chicago, where she grew up with gangs, guns, drugs, and police brutality. Her stepson was murdered, and her ex-husband ended up in jail for gang-related crimes. Joyce had a very tough life and, in turn, became "tough" herself to survive. She went to school at 17 to learn about cars and how to repair them and has been in the "car" business for 34 years, 29 years with State Farm. She was proud to tell me that she was the first black woman at State Farm to achieve the status she had reached in her area of expertise.

Joyce went on to tell me about her second husband, who she loves to death and is 17 years younger than her. I shared with her that my ex-wife was 13 years older than me and that we lived in Chicago for many years, and are still best of friends. Joyce then got emotional and talked about how she's concerned that she has some polyps that need to be evaluated but is afraid of what she may learn. I shared with her that I'm in my second cancer battle and that she must go get checked out. She owes it to herself and to her husband.

It was at this point where Joyce excitedly began talking about her church, pastor and faith in the Lord. She told me that she was having an "out of the ordinary, out of body experience" driven by my presence and energy. Joyce exclaimed that she had never felt anything like this before as tears rolled down her face. She removed her glasses to wipe them away.

I was a bit stunned and fascinated at the same time. What was going on here? Is Joyce sending me a message? Is she channeling my Higher Power? Does she have a "gift" for me that I need to be open to receiving at this moment? It was a bit overwhelming.

Joyce picked up her cell phone and went to her Holy Bible app. She started reading out loud. It was from Romans Chapter 5 versus 3-5:

"Not only that, but we rejoice in our sufferings, knowing that suffering produces endurance, and endurance produces character, and character produces hope, and hope does not put us to shame, because God's love has been poured into our hearts through the Holy Spirit who has been given to us."

What was happening here? I just came to Service King to get my car repair estimate and a check. Now I'm having this intense experience with a complete stranger in her office with the door closed. It felt wrong, but right at the same time. I let myself open up to it even more.

Joyce asked if she could say a prayer of healing for me.

I said, "Of course!"

She got up from behind her desk, came over to me and stood behind my chair. She leaned over, wrapped her arms around me and, with her right hand, began gently rubbing my right chest in a circular motion over my cancer-ridden lung. In a low whispering voice, she began her prayer of healing. I shut my eyes and listened to every word. It was amazing! I felt like I was being healed.

Suddenly, there was a knock at Joyce's office door. We both jumped. She quickly opened the door and it was her assistant telling her that her 9am appointment had been waiting for fifteen minutes. Joyce said we were just finishing up. She went back to her desk, printed my check, handed it to me and with a big smile said, "Merry Christmas!" I thanked her and went out to my car.

What had just happened? I think it was an early Christmas present from my Higher Power. Perhaps Joyce is an angel on this great earth channeling him to and/or through me? Regardless, I feel so blessed to have had this experience. So unexpected. So surreal.

I felt compelled later in the day to reach out to Joyce. I texted her and said, "Thank You, Joyce! Merry Christmas!" She wrote back, "The blessing was truly mine."

DEC 25 2017

Helping the Homeless

Merry Christmas to all! I'm so blessed to be able to enjoy the holidays without feeling sick. Other than being cancer-free, it is truly the best gift I could receive this Christmas.

Elizabeth drove in from Scottsdale, AZ on Saturday afternoon with her dog, Cabo. I picked her up at the Mirage hotel at 6:30pm and we walked across the street to the Venetian for our evening of celebration. Our first stop was Human Nature's Jukebox show in the Sands Theater. I'm so glad I got tickets for this because we thoroughly enjoyed it. Human Nature is an Australian guy group that has performed in Vegas now for eight years or so but have been together for 22 years! They were the #1 Boy Band in Australia back in the 90's and are known for their Motown sound, incredible harmonies, and appreciation for the Oldies. As an extra bonus, they added a number of Holiday songs into their performance making it an extra special night. Their energy was contagious, and we left on a natural high. I found out later that Elizabeth had never been to a Vegas show before, so was excited that we were able to check that off her bucket list.

We had a late dinner at Chica, a newer Latin cuisine restaurant in the Venetian. It was decent, but not amazing. It was so good to catch up on various happenings in our lives over the past six months, since we last saw each other in Michigan this past Summer. When I was battling neck cancer while living in Douglas, MI in late 2014/early 2015, Elizabeth took such great care of me. I couldn't have beat it without her!

Elizabeth has always wanted to watch me play poker, so we headed to the poker room after dinner and I signed up for a \$1/\$2 No Limit Hold'em cash game. After I was seated, I pulled up an extra chair behind me for Elizabeth. On the very first hand, I ended up shoving all-in post-flop with a straight and flush draw. I was up against two callers and surprisingly hit my card on the turn to win \$345 right off the bat. It certainly was a great start! Elizabeth is my lucky charm. Ninety minutes later, we left the table \$132 ahead and found my favorite Willie Wonka slot machine where we were not as successful, but still had fun. It was now 1:30am and time for bed.

On Sunday morning, Elizabeth drove over to my place and we headed across the street to the Tuscany Suites and Marilyn's Cafe to reserve a breakfast table for seven us at 10:30am. It was our starting point for "Helping the Homeless."

A couple of weeks ago, I thought it would be nice if Elizabeth and I could spend some time on Christmas Eve distributing clothes to the homeless here in Vegas, especially because it's the season of giving and so many people are less fortunate than us. I told Jackie about our plan. She wanted to participate, too, so she got more folks involved. Then I found out that my friend, Suzannah and her husband, Joe, had a similar idea, so we all joined together as one group of 11 adults and 2 kids to help the homeless.

After breakfast, we met the other half of the group at "Tent City" on the very north end of Las Vegas Boulevard beyond downtown. Vi had targeted this location as a place where we'd find many homeless people struggling to live day to day. It was truly eye-opening. There were small pup tents, cardboard "shelters," grocery carts and homeless folks everywhere. At the corner of Las Vegas Blvd and Ogden Ave, there was a large, vacant rundown parking lot with a hot dog stand in the middle of it and a long line of people waiting to get a free hot dog.

We decided to make this our first stop for our five-car caravan and pulled over to the side lining our cars up next to each other. We flipped open our trunks and started setting up. Jackie had brought two six-foot tables, so we had one for men's clothes and the other for women's items. We also had blankets, pillows, gloves, hats, socks, shoes, belts, etc. I didn't exactly know what to expect. Soon we had a long line of almost 50 folks coming to visit us. Word spread and the line got bigger. Within 20 minutes, we had given away almost everything we had brought with us. It was incredible! Everyone was so well-mannered and appreciative. Many "Merry Christmases" were exchanged. I was excited to give my jeans, shoes, hoodies and sneakers to taller/bigger guys who have a really hard time finding free clothes that fit them. I think we were all moved by the experience.

We also had 35 bag lunches, 50 bags of Wendy's burgers & fries, Lynnore's homemade Christmas cookies, and cases of water to distribute, so we drove over to another spot near a group of homeless shelters and the immigration building. Again, just like that, everything was distributed within 20 minutes. Everyone was so thankful! We had helped almost 200 people in total and, perhaps, made Christmas just a little more special for them. I was so proud of our Helping the Homeless team!

Later that evening, Suzannah and Joe had a Jewish Christmas Eve gathering at their home. It was very casual and a great way to end the day. And, of course, we had Chinese food, while we reminisced about our day. We all decided that our "Helping the Homeless" effort MUST continue, so now we will be doing "Christmas in July" AND making our December initiative even bigger and better next year!

I was back at home by 8:30pm and in bed at 8:40pm completely exhausted. I got a full 11+ hours of sleep and am ready to enjoy a wonderful Christmas lunch with Elizabeth at Jackie and Mike's house. For Christmas dinner, Elizabeth is making me Shrimp Newburgh at my place tonight. I'm so looking forward to another great day!

DEC 27 2017

Tired But Positive!

I'm not a big fan of the Holidays, but I really enjoyed Christmas this year. Having Elizabeth here with me was awesome. We had so much fun and I'm especially glad she got to meet some of my friends. Now she knows that I'm being well taken care of during my cancer battle.

On Christmas Day, we went to Jackie & Mike's for Christmas lunch at 1pm. Their daughters, Sam and Nicki, were there, along with their good friends, Gary, Vi and Marika. It was the perfect group of nine. Mike fried a turkey and it was amazing...so incredibly juicy. And, of course, Jackie had made a ham and all the yummy side dishes, including a sweet potato casserole (begged for by Sam) that was to die for! After a much-needed walk around the block, we indulged in Sam's incredible pecan pie and a pumpkin pie.

And, then, the presents appeared. This was so unexpected! Jackie & Mike had gifts for all of us. They are such good people and so generous. They even got Zing & Zang kitty toys, which they've been enjoying at home.

My gift from Jackie & Mike made me tear up. It was a customized, wooden cutting board with "PETZING STRONG" engraved on it. It came with a stand, too, and now it's prominently displayed on my kitchen counter. I see it first thing every morning and at night before I go to bed. This gift was so very thoughtful. It serves as a constant reminder that I am strong and will beat this bastard called, Cancer.

Elizabeth and I left Jackie & Mike's around 5pm. I was exhausted, not to mention quite full from all the food I ate. I only had one plate, but I think I over did it. I'm just not able to process that much food these days. Elizabeth was going to make me Shrimp Newburgh for dinner later that night, but we both agreed that wasn't a good idea. I just needed to sleep. So, I dropped Elizabeth off at The Mirage, where she was staying with her dog, Cabo, and drove home. By 5:45pm, I was sound asleep for my daily two to three-hour nap. I got up around 8:30pm, turned on my "Xmas Tree" lights, made a PB&J sandwich accompanied by Cheetos and a glass of milk, wrapped myself in a cozy blanket, and happily ate my "Christmas Dinner" while watching the movie, *How The Grinch Stole Christmas*. It was just what the doctor ordered.

Elizabeth drove back to Scottsdale, AZ after we had breakfast at the Peppermill. It's a Vegas icon and 24-hour diner known for its throwback 70's atmosphere and huge portions. I decided to play a $250 NLH poker tournament at the Venetian, but that didn't go so well. And, not surprisingly, I was back in bed at 4:30pm and slept until 7:30pm. For dinner, I had leftovers from Jackie & Mike's Christmas lunch. Still so good!

DEC 28 2017

Problems are Opportunities

Today, I'm at Chemo #6 of 8. Louise will be stopping by early this afternoon to hang with me after my nap. Having a friend here makes the time pass so much faster.

The chest port is making a world of difference compared to the IV approach we were doing the first few weeks. Now my insurance will pay for me to get my blood drawn and tested at Dr. Gollard's versus having to make a special trip to Quest Diagnostics each week. Additionally, the whole chemo infusion process has been reduced by about 1hr 45mins and I'm hands and arms free! No more bruising, too.

At the end of chemo today, I will have the Neulasta Onpro "patch" installed on my stomach. I get these every two weeks prior to my week off from chemo. It injects a serum. Twenty-seven hours after it's installed, my bone marrow produces much needed white blood cells to replace the ones being killed off by the chemotherapy, and helps reduce the possibility of infection.

I'd like to end today's journal entry with a reading from my *Jesus Calling* book of daily devotions. This particular devotion has been sticking with me for a week or so now. It talks about problems being opportunities, IF we maintain a positive attitude and keep ourselves open to learning from them:

"When you are plagued by a persistent problem--one that goes on and on--view it as a rich opportunity. An ongoing problem is like a tutor who is always by your side. The learning possibilities are limited only by your willingness to be teachable. In faith, thank Me for your problem. Ask Me to open your eyes and your heart to all that I am accomplishing through this difficulty. Once you have become grateful for a problem, it loses its power to drag you down. On the contrary, your thankful attitude will lift you up into heavenly places with Me. From this perspective, your difficulty can be seen as a slight, temporary distress that is producing for you a transcendent Glory never to cease!"

Isaiah 30:20-21; 2 Corinthians 4:17 (AMP)

I truly believe that a positive attitude makes all the difference. It kept me going and fighting the last time, and now I'm doing it again! This cancer problem of mine is only temporary. I still have so many things to learn and people to help! I know there is a greater calling for me. #PetzingStrong

DEC 29 2017

Trust in Him

I try not to complain much, but I've been really tired for a week now. The chemotherapy treatments are starting to wear me down and I just don't have my normal high energy anymore. It's frustrating, but expected. Basically, my body is requesting a "time out" on a more regular basis. This is resulting in my need for a 2 1/2 to 3-hour nap every day and up to 10 hours of sleep each night. Sleep is good. It helps in the healing process.

I did have enough energy to play in Day 1b of the $400 No Limit Hold'em $250K Guarantee tourney at the Venetian yesterday, but it was difficult. After 10+ hours of play, including a few breaks, I qualified for Day 2 on Saturday with 53 other players from the original starting field of 344 players. We will join Wednesday's 32 qualifiers and today's set of qualifiers to play for the big money on Saturday. I have a decent chip stack of 156K, which is a little below the average of 195K and gives me 19.5 big blinds. I can work with that! We started at noon and finished at 10:30pm. I was exhausted, but felt good about my performance.

As I write, I'm receiving my hydration infusion on Happy Hydration Friday. It's a "Fun Bag" of goodies that helps reduce nausea and pumps steroids into me to lessen the negative impact of all the poison that is circulating throughout my body from Chemo Wednesdays. It makes such a huge, positive difference in how I feel and gets me through the weekend beautifully. It only takes about 90 minutes, so I should be out of here shortly and will play a one day poker tourney at the Wynn this afternoon.

My daily reading today from *Jesus Calling* is about having Trust in your Higher Power and knowing that he is watching out for you in both good and bad times. I have had so many experiences where I know this to be true. Additionally, he has placed angels on this earth and in heaven for me. They, too, are doing his work...guiding me, protecting me, supporting me, and providing me with the strength I need to fight through each day with a positive, can-do attitude. I couldn't do it without them.

I'd like to share this meaningful passage with you:

"Trust me with every fiber of your being! What I can accomplish in and through you is proportional to how much you depend on Me. One aspect of this is the degree to which you Trust me in a crisis or major decision. Some people fail miserably here, while others are at their best in tough times. Another aspect is even more telling: the constancy of your Trust in Me. People who rely on me in the midst of adversity may forget about Me when life is flowing smoothly. Difficult times can jolt you into awareness of your need for Me, whereas smooth sailing can lull you into the stupor of self-sufficiency.

I care as much about your tiny trust steps through daily life as about your dramatic leaps of faith. You may think that no one notices, but the One who is always beside you sees everything--and rejoices. Consistently trusting in Me is vital to flourishing in My Presence."

Psalm 40:4; Psalm 56:3-4; Psalm 62:8; Isaiah 26:3-4

DEC 30 2017

Poker Makes Me Strong

My hydration treatment yesterday was a breeze. I had good energy afterwards, so decided to play the Wynn $200 NLH poker tournament at noon. After 9+ hours, I found myself in the Final 4 from a starting field of 78 players. We were all fairly close in chip stacks, so we decided to do a proportional chip chop and split the remaining prize money, accordingly. I was in third place at the time, but got better than third place money by agreeing to the chop, so I was very happy walking away with a net win of $2,700 for a $300 investment.

Today, I play in Day 2 of the $400 NLH Venetian $250K Guarantee that I qualified for on Thursday. I'm a little below average in chips, but still have a good stack and hope to do as well as I did yesterday. First place should pay out close to $65K. It certainly would be nice to end 2017 with a BIG poker win!

I know this may sound strange to many of you, but I'm so glad and fortunate to have poker in my life. It is a passion that I love! It keeps my mind sharp and focused. It has opened up a social network for me, where I have made some incredible friends who are now my loving support network while I battle the Big C. Poker also keeps me occupied daily so that I don't have time or the opportunity to feel sorry for myself or stress and obsess over my health situation.

Poker players don't like to lose. We fight against the odds to win. We're competitive and never give up, even if we only have one chip in front of us. Good poker players always believe they can win! We strive to be the best at our craft and work at improving our skills every day. My doctors love that I play poker because the traits I've mentioned above are so very much needed when fighting for your life... like I am now. Believing in yourself makes all the difference!

On Facebook today, a friend of mine who is facing some of her own struggles proposed two questions to her followers that I really had to think about:

1. What endings are you facing this year?

2. What are you ready to let go of?

I'm usually quite quick on my feet and usually have an immediate answer ready to share, but not this time. I found these questions quite challenging. After about ten minutes of self-processing, here's how I responded:

"I'm not sure I believe in "endings" per se, as they tend to be so Final. For me, it's more about continuations and how you plan to approach them differently. For example, rather than outright ending a friendship or relationship that is bringing you down or is full of unnecessary stressful drama, address your issues with that person and work on modifying the relationship so it works better for you. More often than not, you must make the effort first. If it doesn't feel right after you do so, then end it."

"As for letting go, I believe in letting go of those things that you just can't control and in putting my trust and faith in my Higher Power and angels to support, guide and help me through difficult times and situations. For sure, I will work very hard to stay positive and happy, even while fighting my cancer battle. I will continue to let go of all negativity and bad/sad things that have happened to me in the past because there is absolutely nothing I can do about those things now. I'm only looking forward, focusing on a bright future...as you should be, too!"

In 2018, I will be stronger, braver, kinder, and unstoppable. Here's hoping the new year brings much good health, happiness, and love to all of us!

DEC 31 2017

Live Fully

It was nice to have back-to-back poker tourney cashes to end the year. Yesterday, I placed 95th of 1,115 players in Day 2 of the Venetian's $400 No Limit Hold'em $250K Guarantee for a min cash of $822. I took a risk on an open-ended straight draw and missed. Sometimes you just have to go for it, knowing that it may not always work out.

I finally got a good night's sleep last night, snoozing for nine hours. After pulling myself out of bed at 7am, I cleaned the house, did two loads of laundry, changed my bed, and headed across the street to have breakfast and make some football bets on today's pro games. On my way over to Albertson's to grab a few grocery items, I came to a stop light and suddenly had to throw up. I quickly put a hand over my mouth to catch what I could and with my other hand I opened the car door, leaned over and finished puking on the street.

I'm sorry if I just grossed you out, but it's something I've been dealing with lately. It also happened twice on Christmas Day. I think all the poison in my body from the chemo I've been receiving is starting to take its toll. I have a lot less energy than I used to and I easily get tired from doing simple things like making my bed, cleaning the cat box, or folding laundry. I've also been a little light-headed lately and clearly not feeling 100%. Unfortunately, all of these side effects come with the territory of being treated for cancer.

Well, here we are on New Year's Eve, the last day of 2017! It certainly has been a crazy and stressful year, in so many ways for so many people. 2017 had been moving along quite well for me until my lung cancer diagnosis in October. Sadly, we just never know when we're going to be faced with a life-threatening issue. It can happen anytime, anyplace and to anyone. No one is immune. This should give us all a swift kick in the butt and a much needed wake up call to live life fully today and every day, because tomorrow could be very different or may not come at all.

I saw this posting on Facebook the other day. It really struck me because it's so very true:

> "We are all just a car crash, a diagnosis, an unexpected phone call, a newfound love, or a broken heart away from becoming a completely different person. How beautifully fragile are we that so many things can take but a moment to alter who we are forever?" Samuel Decker Thompson

So as you inwardly reflect on your 2017 and how you'd like to enhance your 2018, please give some very serious thought to making necessary changes in your life that will enable you to be your best you! Don't put it off any longer. Take control. Life is too short to not maximize every moment you have to live it fully each day. Don't waste this precious commodity you've been given. It's God's gift...the gift of Life!

JAN 3 2018

My Healing Journey

I had a very nice and quiet New Year's Eve. Spent with it with Ardys and her husband, Jim, at their home. Ardys made a wonderful shrimp and pasta dish, and the three of us had great dinner conversation. After we finished, Jim went to a party at a friend's while Ardys and I sat and talked about life's challenges and opportunities as 2017 came to a close. We decided to watch the movie, *Mother!*, with Jennifer Lawrence, Javier Bardem, Ed Harris and Michelle Pfeiffer. We were both very sorry we did. It was just awful. I was asleep on the couch for about half of it, but every time I woke up the same gross, bizarre stuff was happening. Think of this movie as *Rosemary's Baby* gone even madder. I like twisted movies, but this was just too over the top with no redeeming qualities.

In general, I wasn't feeling great on New Year's Eve day, so I was in bed at Ardys' by 10:30pm and missed all the Pomp and Circumstance of Mariah Carey's re-do, Andy and Anderson's bantering about nothing, all the crazy people freezing their butts off and, of course, the ball dropping in Times Square. But, I'm totally fine with that! I find New Year's Eve to be such a forced holiday. It has never been my thing.

Jim made the three of us breakfast on New Year's morning, and then Ardys and I played in a poker tournament at the Venetian, but neither of us cashed. We played again yesterday and Ardys got through 11+ hours to qualify for Day 2 today with a nice healthy chip stack! I hope she takes it down.

I really haven't been feeling too great lately. I think all the poison from the six chemotherapy infusions has saturated my entire body. I'm always tired, even after a decent night of sleep. My head is full of mucous and my hacking cough has also returned, which I'm a bit concerned about and will address with Dr. Gollard next Wednesday when I meet with him. I've thrown up four times in the past ten days and I find myself in a constant state of "blah." However, I shouldn't complain. I'm handling these treatments so much better than the last time I received radiation and chemo during my battle with neck cancer.

This week is my "off" week from chemo and two weeks from today (January 17), I will finish this cycle of treatments. Hopefully, they have been shrinking the tumors in my right lung so that I can be operable in February. I'm guessing that Dr. Gollard will schedule a PET scan for me the last week of January. The results will provide my doctors with the necessary information to determine the appropriate next steps.

I've been trying so hard to stay in the moment and believe that my Higher Power and angels are watching over and helping me through this tough time. Pastor Sal, from the Douglas United Church of Christ in Douglas, MI, where I used to attend services, sent me a pamphlet a couple of months ago titled, "Your Healing Journey." There are so many useful and inspirational prayers, passages and stories within it.

Today, I have gratitude for two of the "Healing Prayers From Silent Unity":

"Perfect life is flowing through my entire body right now, doing its mighty work--cleansing, energizing, and strengthening every cell. The wisdom of God is present and working through every medical professional as they support my healing journey."

“The doctors and staff who care for me are divinely guided in their thoughts, words and actions. The all-powerful presence of divine love expresses through each of them. I am safe and secure.”

I feel so blessed to have an amazing team of doctors and nurses working on my behalf. I know they are helping to heal me, and I’ve placed all of my trust in them and my Higher Power. I am not afraid!

#PetzingStrong

JAN 5 2018

That's What Friends Are For

This has been a tough week for me as I've been feeling like shit.

I had to literally drag myself out of bed yesterday, even after getting a good night of sleep. My head has been clogged up for a week now with bloody yellow mucous pouring out every time I blow my nose. My nasty cough is persistent, I'm wheezing again and I get short of breath even after changing the cat box. I'm more tired than I've been in the past two months. The "Energizer Bunny" energy I had prior to starting chemo has disappeared and I'm constantly in a lethargic daze, generally feeling disconnected. And, thankfully, I finally had a bowel movement after six long days, but it was bloody.

I wasn't scheduled for a hydration treatment, because it's my chemo "off week." However, I know I need one and don't want to feel like this until next Wednesday when I'm back in for my next chemo infusion. So, I called Dr. Gollard's office early in the morning to see if I could come in for a "Fun Bag" and get checked out, as I fear my walking pneumonia has returned. This is a common occurrence for those suffering with lung cancer, especially when the immune system has been so violated, and can become a really big problem if it's not addressed. Later in the afternoon, I was finally able to speak with Radka and we set up an appointment for today at 8:45am. I'm breathing a little sigh of relief.

Interestingly, so many of my good friends just happened to check in on me yesterday. It's as if they knew I was hurting and needed their support:

Chris texts almost every morning to see how I'm doing. He really pushed me to call the doctor and to get an appointment to see him today.

Ed left a voice mail to say "hi" and give me some encouragement to keep fighting through the end of my chemo.

April, my good friend in Vancouver, Canada, whose Dad is suffering from prostate cancer, called to see how I was doing. She makes me laugh and we had a great chat catching up.

Nancy, one of my very first poker friends who I met almost ten years ago, also left a voice mail to check in on me. She's with her elderly Dad in New Jersey who is struggling with some serious medical issues. I'm praying for them.

Jackie texts me every morning for an update on how I'm feeling. I know I can count on her for anything I might need.

Elizabeth also texted from Cabo San Lucas, where she has been celebrating our entry into 2018 soaking up the sun with her daughter and a group of friends. Wish I was there!

Suzannah heard from Lynnore that I wasn't feeling well, so she texted to check in with me to see if there was anything she could do to help me out.

And, finally, Louise offered to take me to my hydration appointment today, but I think I'm fine getting there on my own. I know that she, too, is always there for me if I need her.

I can't tell you how blessed I feel knowing that I have so many amazing friends in my life that really care about me. This rang so true yesterday and was so comforting.

Perhaps you're familiar with Dionne Warwick's oldie, but goodie, hit song, "That's What Friends Are For?" Its lyrics have been going through my head a lot lately and really hit home:

"Keep smiling, keep shining. Knowing you can always count on me, for sure. That's what friends are for. For good times and bad times, I'll be on your side forever more. That's what friends are for!"

Yes, I know my friends are here for me in good times and bad times! And, I'm so very thankful for them.

JAN 6 2018

Making A Difference When You Least Expect It

It's 5:45am. I can't sleep. But, boy, do I feel like a "million dollars" today!

I am so glad that Chris pushed me to go to Dr. Gollard's yesterday. I arrived at 8:45am and Radka was ready for me. Since I had mentioned on the phone when making the appointment that I thought I might have walking pneumonia again, she had a private room waiting to keep me isolated from the other patients getting treatment that morning. We chatted about all the various ailments I've had over the past ten days since my last chemo treatment and how bad I've been feeling. She got right to it and took some blood to test.

My white blood cell count was within decent range, but my blood platelets were a little off. Nothing too concerning though, so on we went to the two "Fun Bags" of liquids, steroids, "feel good" meds, and appetite accelerators. The infusion lasted two hours and I napped for the last hour of it. When I awoke, I felt like a new person!

Radka had consulted with Dr. Gollard during my nap time. He decided to put me back on Levofloxacin, a high-powered antibiotic to fight the recurring infection in my head and chest that was causing the yellow mucous discharge, wheezing and coughing again. Dr. Gollard also thought I should have a chest x-ray to determine if the walking pneumonia that I carried for two months this past summer had returned for an encore performance. Radka told me to see Wilfredo at the front desk to pick up Dr. Gollard's order for it, so off I went.

The waiting room was packed with existing and new patients. It's both frightening and sad to see how many folks like me are going through their own similar fight with the Big C. Wilfredo told me that the doctor's written order wasn't quite ready yet and that I should have a seat. I got on my phone to check Facebook and out of the corner of my eye noticed a family of three sitting adjacent to me.

There was an older gentlemen in his early 70's, his wife and their 40-plus year old daughter. While she was filling out the pages and pages of necessary paperwork required of all patients, I realized that it was her mother who was ill. She had long, unkempt brown hair, with gray roots, and a worn weathered face. She sat stoically with little emotion and her thin arms crossing her chest. Every now and again, her daughter would ask her to sign on the dotted line of one of the many forms. She'd sigh each time. Her husband was trying to make jovial small talk, but she really wasn't interested in entertaining it or interacting much with him.

I felt bad for all of them. I could tell that they were very concerned and scared. Believe me, I certainly know what those emotions are like having been in the exact same situation twice now. You're just waiting and wondering what's in store for you, how sick you are going to get, whether you'll like the doctor, nurses and staff, if you'll be treated like a person or a number, and most importantly, will the treatment you receive work or fail? And, of course, you can't stop thinking about the very real possibility that death is knocking at your door. Yeah, it sucks...more than most of you reading this will ever know.

I decided that I needed to say "something" to this family. I wasn't sure yet what that would or should be, but I wanted to provide them with some sort of encouragement. So, I turned, smiled and said, "I think you'll like it here. The staff is great, and the treatment areas are bright, airy, and open."

The daughter looked up from filling out all of the forms and the father grinned at me.

The mother shot more of a glare at me and said, "Really? What is there to like about all of this? We have cancer."

Damn. I had opened Pandora's Box. What did I get myself into? I should have minded my own business.

I'm usually pretty good on my feet in uncomfortable situations and when I'm being confronted, so out of my mouth came, "Yes, sadly we do, but I don't think you'll find a better place than here to get the help you need to fight the fight. They really do care about you as a person. And, they've made an unpleasant and untenable situation the best it could possibly be for me. I can't imagine getting my treatments anywhere else."

She cracked a half-smile. I had made progress.

Her husband and daughter lit up. He turned to me and said, "My wife just had surgery two weeks ago to remove a cancerous tumor at the base of her brain, but now needs to get chemotherapy. It all happened so suddenly. We're all in a state of shock and are just trying to get through this."

I nodded. "Yes, it's very hard to understand why bad things happen to good people. I'm dealing with my second cancer battle and often ask myself, Why me? I want to believe that my Higher Power is testing my strength in some way to make me a better person. I know that he is watching over me during this difficult time and that he has much bigger plans for me. I'm just not sure what they are yet or why I have to go through this battle again to realize them. But, I do trust him and have faith that he, along with my angels and the amazing staff here, are moving me along the right path to get there."

They all stared at me with a tilted head and quizzical look. I think they may have had an

"Ah Ha" moment. Perhaps I broke through to them? I smiled and then Wilfredo called for me. I went to the desk and picked up my chest x-ray order. While I was standing there, I reached for one of Dr. Gollard's cards and decided to write the name of my book on it, "From Feeding Tube to Final Table: A Cancer Survivor's Story," along with my name and Amazon.com. I went back over to the family and stood in front of the mother/wife.

I explained that I had kept a blog on CaringBridge.org during my first bout with cancer and that it therapeutically helped me with my own physical and emotional healing process. And, because of the positive feedback I received from so many of my followers, I turned my blog into a book that has provided much hope and inspiration for others going through their own cancer fight.

I handed the woman Dr. Gollard's card with the information I had written on it and said, "I really think my book will help you. It's only $9.99 on Amazon.com. If you order it today, you'll have it in a few days. I know it will make a positive difference for you."

She saw my name on the card, looked up and with a small tear in her eye said, "Thank you, Jim. I think I needed to meet you today."

I reached out, grabbed her hand, leaned over and whispered, "You can do this. I know you can." I smiled, wished them all the best, and left Dr. Gollard's office feeling energized, uplifted, and that perhaps, in that moment, I had just made a real impact on someone else's life. It felt really good!

JAN 7 2018

Positive Expectations

It's amazing how well I'm still feeling after receiving the hydration treatment on Friday morning! That "Fun Bag" really is a miracle worker.

I got a decent night's sleep for a change and I'm ready for a great day! While the majority of the USA is immersed in sub-freezing, frigid weather and digging themselves out of snowbanks, we're having mild winter weather here in Vegas with a beautiful forecast of sunny and 65 for today.

On this past Thursday, while feeling really sick, I somehow managed to place in the top 5% of a field of 144 players in Day 1A of the Venetian's $250 No Limit Hold'em $150K Guarantee poker tournament. In turn, the eight of us who made it through 11 1/2 hours of play, now move on to Day 2 today to compete for the big money against the Day 1B (Friday) and Day 1C (Saturday) qualifiers.

So, out of a total of 810 entrants, I'll be competing with 40 others for the 1st place prize of $23,850. I have a decent chip stack and am currently in 25th place out of the 41 remaining players. Good news is that I'm already guaranteed to win at least $1,000 for my $250 entry, but I obviously want and plan to win it all. This one is mine!

I know I've mentioned this before, but I'm so glad that I have poker in my life to keep me occupied during my days. It keeps my mind focused on something other than "Cancer" and all the "What ifs?" that come along with it. It's quite easy to go there when you're dealing with a serious, life threatening disease, so anything you can do to keep yourself active and involved in an activity or passion you love is a much healthier alternative.

I want to share January 6th's passage from *Jesus Calling*, a book of inspirational daily devotions that I read each morning before getting out of bed. This particular devotion gives me great hope that my prayers for soon becoming operable and ultimately getting the cancerous tumors in my right lung out of my body will be answered.

"I am able to do far beyond all that you ask or imagine. Come to Me with positive expectations, knowing that there is no limit to what I can accomplish. Ask My Spirit to control your mind, so that you can think great thoughts of Me. Do not be discouraged by the fact that many of your prayers are yet unanswered. Time is a trainer, teaching you to wait upon Me, to trust Me in the dark. The more extreme your circumstances, the more likely you are to see My Power and Glory at work in the situation. Instead of letting difficulties draw you into worrying, try to view them as setting the scene for My glorious intervention. Keep your eyes and your mind wide open to all that I am doing in your life."

Ephesians 3:20-21; Romans 8:6; Isaiah 40:30-31(NKJV); Revelation 5:13

JAN 8 2018

Winning Days

Just wanted to provide a quick update on how I fared yesterday in Day 2 of the Venetian's $150K Guarantee poker tournament. I started the day in 25th place of 41 remaining players from a total field of 810 entrants. After five hours of play, I found myself at the Final Table of ten and finished in 8th place after my AdKd lost to AhKh on a board that ran out runner runner hearts. It was a sick way to go out, but I was happy to pocket $4,050 for my overall effort and $250 investment.

I should also mention that a couple of months ago my friend, Liina, gave me a small polished stone with the word "Believe" inscribed on it. I decided to use it as my card protector yesterday and am confident that its good karma and energy helped me do my very best.

Ironically, my poker success continued today in the Venetian's $150 NLH $9K Guarantee tourney. After 8 1/2 hours of play, I placed 3rd of 73 players. Our final seven decided to chop the prize pool as we were all relatively close in chip count. However, since the chip leader had at least double the chips of each of us, we agreed to give him more money. He took home $1740, while we each got $1100 (almost the equivalent of third place money.) So, with back-to-back cashes, it has been a great two days of poker to kick-off 2018!

I'll play again tomorrow and then will take a break for a week as I have chemotherapy on Wednesday, and then Chris comes to visit on Thursday for five days. I'm so excited to see him! It's very hard being so far away from each other, but we're doing our best to make our long-distance relationship work. Hopefully, I'll be feeling well while Chris is here, so we can maximize our time together. I'm sure we'll check out some new restaurants, go to the movies and binge watch some Netflix or HBO series. No matter what we do, we'll just be happy being with each other.

JAN 10 2018

Thinking Ahead

Well, it's almost too good to be true! Last evening, I made my third consecutive Final Table in three days at the Venetian in the $150 NLH $9K Guarantee poker tourney placing 3rd of 91 players for $1400. It feels awesome to be playing and running so well. I hope this transfers over to my cancer fight!

So today is chemo Wednesday. I met with Dr. Gollard first thing this morning for a check-in. He ordered me some more Xanax to help me sleep and Zophran to lessen nausea. Dr. Gollard also reported that my chest x-ray was clean for walking pneumonia. The antibiotic he put me on last week for the coughing and wheezing has been working, so fortunately I've been feeling much better.

I should be here about 7 hours. Janet asked Radka if she could take care of me today to get practice with my specific chemo regimen. I like Janet, so I told Radka I was fine with it. I'm getting my steroid drip now and then the Benadryl infusion before all the lovely cancer meds are pumped into my body. The Benadryl always makes me fall asleep, so I'm going to try to finish this journal entry before I nod off.

I've been starting to think a lot about lung surgery lately and am hoping that I'll have that opportunity, if the chemo has shrunk the tumors in my right lung. In our meeting today, Dr. Gollard put an order in for my PET scan, which will happen shortly after next week's chemo treatment and will determine exactly where I stand. I told Dr. Gollard that I had been researching lung cancer centers online and that I'm now leaning toward wanting to go to MD Anderson in Houston, especially if it looks like the surgery option may be more complicated than usual. I also asked him if he had any recommendations for local Vegas lung surgeons and he gave me two doctors' names, who I will begin to investigate. If, God forbid, surgery is not an option for me, MD Anderson also has a number of active clinical trials for inoperable Stage 3B lung cancer patients. Hopefully, I would qualify for one of them.

Yesterday's *Jesus Calling* reading gave me some comfort with regard to this issue:

"I AM WITH YOU AND FOR YOU. When you decide on a course of action that is in line with My will, nothing in heaven or on earth can stop you. You may encounter many obstacles as you move toward your goal, but don't be discouraged--never give up! With My help, you can overcome any obstacle. Do not expect an easy path as you journey hand in hand with Me, but do remember that I, your very-present Helper, an omnipotent.

Much, much stress results from your wanting to make things happen before their times have come. One of the main ways I assert My sovereignty is in the timing of events. If you want to stay close to Me and do things My way, ask Me to show you the path forward moment by moment. Instead of dashing headlong toward your goal, let Me set the pace. Slow down and enjoy the journey in My Presence."

Romans 8:31; Psalm 46:1-3 (NKJV); Luke 1:37

JAN 12 2018

Chris is Here

I have some good news to share! After I wrote my last journal entry during my chemo treatment this past Wednesday, Dr. Gollard came by to tell me that my chest x-ray showed that the large tumor in my right lung has definitely shrunk from when we started treatments back in October. We don't exactly know by how much or if it has become disconnected from my arteries and other organs, but the mass is now smaller. The PET scan I'll be having later this month, after my final chemo next week, will give a more accurate picture and tell the true story. So, needless to say, I'm feeling really optimistic that surgery will become an option for me!

Right now, I'm sitting in my usual recliner chair at Dr. Gollard's this morning receiving my Friday hydration treatment. It will ensure that I have a good weekend of feeling well and having some renewed energy, which is great because Chris arrived yesterday afternoon.

I'm really glad Chris is here! It's hard being so far apart, but we're managing the best we can. We only get to see each other once a month and given my current situation he unfortunately has to do all the traveling right now. Zing, Zang and I get an immediate "pick me up" when "Daddy Chris" is here with us. We plan on cooking some healthy dinners together (Chris is working out with a trainer now and is on a special diet plan), seeing a number of movies like *The Post*, *The Shape of Water*, *Molly's Game*, *Call Me By My Name*, and *The Commuter*, and binge watching some Netflix series, along with taking a day trip to Mt. Charleston. The weather forecast is sunny and mid-60's for the next week, which is warmer than normal for this time of year here in Vegas. It's absolutely beautiful....and NO SNOW, ever!

Although I've been running really well at poker over the past week, it will be nice to have a break until Tuesday when Chris leaves. It's important to take time off and rejuvenate, so I'm welcoming the temporary hiatus. Louise is taking a break from poker, too, enjoying her time off with her beau at her California home for a long weekend.

I'm excited that my last chemo treatment is this coming Wednesday and that the PET scan will soon follow. I want to keep moving forward, find an awesome lung surgeon, schedule the surgery, and get these cancerous tumors and nodes out of my body. That's all! #PetzingStrong

JAN 14 2018

A Busy Weekend

Having Chris here for almost five days is a real treat, especially since I'm alone so much. We've really taken advantage of our time together this weekend and have kept so busy that I can barely move off the couch today. So I'm writing this journal entry, lying on the couch, watching the Jacksonville vs. Pittsburgh AFC Divisional playoff game while Chris is doing employee reviews on his computer.

Already this weekend, we've seen four movies: *The Post*, *The Shape of Water*, *The Commuter* and *Wind River* (on OnDemand.) I'm not going to provide reviews here, but do highly recommend *The Post* and *The Shape of Water*. Both movies were nominated for multiple Golden Globe awards and are likely to be Oscar contenders in a number of categories, so definitely put them on your viewing list. We also really enjoyed *The Commuter* for the pulse-pounding thriller it is starring the always good, Liam Neeson. *Wind River* was also very good, but quite depressing. Don't watch it if you're feeling sad or might be bothered by a story centered on the search for a rapist and murderer of an 18-year old young woman.

Last night, after seeing *The Commuter*, Chris and I went to the Las Vegas Knights vs. Edmonton Oilers hockey game at the T-Mobile Arena. I hadn't been at T-Mobile yet, so I was eager to experience the new venue. I also love hockey and have been wanting to see a Knights game, so we killed two birds with one stone. The energy was electric, and we had a very fun evening, even though the Knights lost the game in overtime, 3-2.

By the time we got home around 10:15pm, I was exhausted. We hadn't eaten anything since breakfast, so we were hungry. Chris made a taco salad for himself and a grilled turkey and muenster cheese sandwich for me. It hit the spot and I passed out on the couch watching an old Saturday Night Live rerun from March 2015.

I have been really tired lately, especially during the past two weeks. I think all of the poison from the seven chemo treatments I've had over the past 2 1/2 months have saturated my body to the point where my energy level is at a bare minimum. Even the simplest tasks, like walking up three flights of stairs, changing the cat box, vacuuming my condo, and folding a load of laundry makes me short of breath and wears me out. It's very frustrating because that's not me! I know it's temporary, but it's still quite bothersome.

Since Chris just went down to the gym to work out, I think I'm going to take a nap. We're having great weather here in Vegas, 65 and sunny, so Chris is going to grill us some chicken and shrimp for dinner tonight down by the pool. Did I say how nice it is to have him here!? I'll really miss him when he leaves on Tuesday morning.

JAN 15 2018

Waves of Uncertainty

My Dad commented this morning on yesterday's journal entry and was really excited to let me know that today's *Jesus Calling* passage, in our book of daily devotions, was quite relevant to me and my battle with lung cancer. When I read it myself, I felt the same and want to share it with you:

"My face is shining upon you, beaming out Peace that transcends understanding. You are surrounded by a sea of problems, but you are face to face with Me, your Peace. As long as you focus on Me, you are safe. If you gaze too long at the myriad problems around you, you will sink under the weight of your burdens. When you start to sink, simply call out, "Help me, Jesus!" and I will lift you up.

The closer you live to Me, the safer you are. Circumstances around you are undulating, and there are treacherous-looking waves in the distance. Fix your eyes on Me, the One who never changes. By the time those waves reach you, they will have shrunk to proportions of My design. I am always beside you, helping you face today's waves. The future is a phantom, seeking to spook you. Laugh at the future! Stay close to Me."

Philippians 4:7; Matthew 14:30; Hebrews 12:2

I definitely feel like I'm "surrounded by a sea of problems," but I've been able to find my way... taking one day at a time and staying focused on the goal of shrinking my tumors. I not only believe that my Higher Power is watching over me keeping me safe, but also know that my angels on earth and in heaven have been next to me each step of the way keeping me buoyant, supported and secure.

There definitely are "treacherous-looking waves in the distance" full of many uncertainties, but I am at Peace and ready to face them, whatever form they take. By the time these waves reach me, which will be soon, I'm confident that I'll be able to ride them out and manage through whatever complexities they may bring.

Honestly, I'm not able to "Laugh at the future," but I am capable of not letting it "spook" me. I'm more than ready to take on the next step, no matter what that may be. My future is a bit tentative and undefined. It's the hand I've been dealt. I'm going to play it the best way I can, fully believing in myself that I can and will win! Losing just isn't an option.

#PetzingStrong

JAN 17 2018

Last Day of Chemo, Healing in Motion!

FINALLY, after three long months of intensive chemotherapy, today is my last treatment! I've been eagerly awaiting this day and brought a dozen donuts in for the nurses so we can celebrate! It's the end of my first phase in battling Stage 3B lung cancer, and now I'm so ready to move on.

The preliminary indication from a recent chest x-ray is that the one large tumor in my upper right lung has shrunk. My PET scan is being scheduled at this very moment. It will unveil the real situation and answer the questions: How much have both tumors shrunk and are they small enough to be operable? Are the tumors disconnected from other vital organs and arteries so that surgery is now a viable option? Have the cancerous lymph nodes in the middle of my chest been eradicated? Of course, I'm hoping and praying for YES, YES and YES!

On my drive to Dr. Gollard's office today, I was listening to Steve Harvey's morning radio show on FM 105.7. It's a classic oldies station that I really enjoy. I also get kick out of the hosts' daily banter. I have to admit that I'm not a huge Steve Harvey fan, but I do admire his spirituality and motivation to be the best he can be. This man is like Ryan Seacrest. He does everything from hosting a radio show and multiple television shows, like Family Feud, to having his own talk show, and being the *Master of Ceremonies* for the *Miss Universe Pageant*.

Today, Steve got serious about how we look at our lives. He proclaimed that each day we wake up is a gift from God. We may not be fully happy with where we are in our life today or with how it's going (or not), but the fact that we each have the ability to impact our daily existence in a positive way is our individual responsibility and another gift that we shouldn't ever take for granted.

Steve mentioned that God is always watching over us and is by our side when we deal with difficult challenges. Something he said that really resonated with me is that God has given us the opportunity to live and be vital in 2018. We're all alive because God wants us to be. I believe, as Steve does, that God only gives us what he knows we can handle. If every day was easy, we wouldn't really appreciate life in a truly meaningful way. It's those tough times and difficult moments that we often need to suffer and work through, that make us better, stronger people, and allow us to prove to ourselves that we can overcome even the most difficult of obstacles.

We must remember that what has happened in the past really shouldn't matter, because we can't affect it. We can't go back and change history, so why dwell on it? I've had Cancer twice now. It is what it is! I could feel sorry for myself and wallow in self-pity, but why? It's not going to make me any better. In fact, a negative attitude will only deter my physical and mental well-being and healing. I need positive energy to fight the fight and win the battle! I know I can't do it by myself, which is why it's so important to remain optimistic, let others in to help you, and have complete trust in them, including your Higher Power.

In "Your Healing Journey," a pamphlet that my Pastor Sal from Douglas UCC sent me, there is an article titled, "God Is Healing You Now," a Unity Classic by Rev. Mary Kupferle. I'd like to share a few passages with you:

"If you are facing a healing challenge of any kind, you can be sure God's healing power will see you through. Indeed, it is happening at this instant. God is healing you now! Whether you are in your home, hospital, office, bus, plane or car, God's great love is there, healing you now. Whether you have a lot of spiritual understanding or a little, whether you are old or young in physical years, whether you have a great deal of faith or little, you can grasp these few words: God is healing me now. This can bring you into a realization that will lead you into total healing, total rebirth, and total change of life experience for good.

The change may come instantly. If you are going through medical tests or are under the care of a physician, you can silently know: God is healing me now. God can and does work through anyone or anything in an infinite variety of ways and means to help, bless, and heal us. You need not question, reason, or seek out the ways. God will open them up to you, at the right time and appropriate moment, for God is already at work within every detail of your life, bringing about healing in every aspect."

I'd like to close with a couple of "Healing Prayers From Silent Unity" that are very meaningful to me:

"Perfect life is flowing through my entire body right now, doing its mighty work--cleansing, energizing, and strengthening every cell. The wisdom of God is present and working through every medical professional as they support my healing journey."

"The doctors and staff who care for me are divinely guided in their thoughts, words, and actions. The all-powerful presence of divine love expresses through each of them. I am safe and secure."

Yes, I am!

JAN 18 2018

Simple Gestures Make A Difference

Yesterday was a long, but good, chemo day. I got started at 9am and wasn't finished until 4:15pm, when Radka applied the Neulasta Onpro patch on my lower left stomach. You've seen this advertised on tv. It's specifically designed for advanced stage lung cancer patients receiving chemo and is always applied during the last chemo before an "off" week. It's purpose is to stimulate the body's bone marrow to produce extra white blood cells to help thwart possible infections. Common side effects are bone pain and body aches, but I've been so fortunate not to have any of these during my entire chemo cycle. Overall, I have to say that my three months of chemotherapy have been easy breezy, especially compared to what I experienced with the 35 daily radiation and 7 weekly chemo treatments I endured during my neck cancer battle.

When Elizabeth came to visit me during Christmas, she brought me the red "Superman" cape I wore at my final neck cancer chemo treatment and made me promise that I'd wear it yesterday at my last lung cancer chemo treatment. So, I did! I got some smiles from the other patients who were dripping with me and a couple of "Congratulations," so it felt good. Jackie took a few pictures, which I posted on Facebook, and it has been fun to read everyone's "Superhero" comments. I really don't feel at all like a superhero, but more like a regular guy who is just trying to do what's needed to have the opportunity to extend my life.

If you go online and read the life expectancy statistics for Stage 3B non-small cell cancer victims, they aren't good. Basically, they indicate a 15% best case scenario of still being alive five years from my October diagnosis.

After conversations with Dr. Gollard and Dr. Tavares, they reminded me that it's very unusual for folks under 65 to have lung cancer. Additionally, since I've never smoked and am otherwise healthy in body, mind and spirit, that we can consider doubling the 15% to 30%. Of course, there are no guarantees, but I'll take that! As a poker player, I'm good with a 30% chance of hitting the card I need to make my hand, so I'm optimistic and hopeful that I'll beat these difficult odds.

While receiving my chemo treatment yesterday, a group of six nursing students arrived. I was asked by their supervisor if I'd be open to chatting with one of them as part of their clinical training for the day. Of course, I happily obliged. Trevor was assigned to me and we had an awesome conversation for about a half hour.

I learned that Trevor was currently working as a security officer at a local casino, riding a bike all day in and around the parking garage. He told me how unfulfilling it is for him and that he really wants to make a difference every day. His wife doesn't understand why he would want a job where he has to "clean up pee, poop and dirty butts" and "see people dying every day." Trevor told her that he doesn't even think about those things as they are just inherent parts of the job. But, what really motivates him is the chance to help others who are in need every day and make a positive impact on their lives in some way, shape or form. He wants to get up in the morning excited to go work and come home at night feeling fulfilled, and I'm confident that's going to happen for him.

Our conversation flowed easily. Trevor wanted to know my whole "story" and I shared it with him. Of course, he was surprised to learn that I was in Cancer Battle #2 at such a young age, and that I've never smoked. He was curious about how I was handling the intensive chemo treatments and the expected side effects. I told him that we're all in a bit of disbelief with how well I've gotten through them, and that we're all hopeful that they have worked to shrink my right lung tumors and eradicate the cancerous lymph nodes in the middle of my chest so that I can be operable.

We then talked about my first neck cancer battle and how difficult and painful that process was for me. Trevor was so interested and engaged, that I decided to give him a signed copy of my book, "From Feeding Tube to Final Table: A Cancer Survivor's Story." He got tears in his eyes. I was touched that my simple gift meant so much to someone I had only met 30 minutes earlier.

Radka came by to check on my IV drip and saw the book, which I had also given her a copy of a couple of months ago. She said to Trevor, "You are really going to get a lot out of Jim's book. I loved it!"

My Benadryl drip was kicking in and I was starting to get drowsy, so Trevor and I wrapped things up. He thanked me again for the chat and book. I feel like my simple gestures made a big impact on Trevor and I know he is going to become an outstanding nurse, giving back to others in spades. When we finished, Trevor ran over to his supervisor to tell her about our conversation and show her the book. They were smiling, almost giddy. It was special. It really made my day!

At about 4:15pm, Jackie and I left to meet Ardys and Louise at The Cheesecake Factory to celebrate my last day of chemo with an early dinner. All of "my girls" have been there to fully support me, from when I was in the hospital getting my biopsies through the three months of chemo treatments. I feel so fortunate to have such good friends in my life, who I know are there for me and I can count on when I need them. It provides me with so much comfort.

I received some really good news this morning! My PET scan has been scheduled for Wednesday, January 24 at 8am. It will tell the true story of where things stand. I'm praying hard for shrunken and disconnected tumors, and no floating cancerous lymph nodes. My guess is that the results won't be available until Friday, January 26 at the earliest, and more likely on Monday, January 28. Waiting is the hardest part.

Once my doctors have the information they need, Phase 2 will commence. Hopefully, that will begin with a discussion of the type of surgery they recommend and how complicated or standard they believe it will be. I'm sure there will be differences of opinion, so I plan to interview and consult with multiple lung surgeons, likely visiting local and out of state hospital and cancer center locations, to determine who/where I think will be best for me and my needs. My goal is to be on an operating table by mid-February to get this horrific cancer out of my body!

I've got this! #PetzingStrong

JAN 21 2018

Fortunate to Be Cared About

At my hydration treatment on Friday, I got my "Fun Bags" so I'm having a really good weekend so far. On Friday night, I played the 7pm $200 NLH Rebuy tourney at the Venetian and won over $4K after placing 2nd of 69 players and coming back from a short stack. My buddy, Andre, took 1st place, so I was happy for him. We didn't finish until 4:15am on Saturday morning and I wasn't in bed until 5:30am, but the steroids I received earlier in the day gave me much needed energy and kept me going without a problem.

Thankfully, I slept until 11:30am on Saturday and then took a quick shower before heading over to The Wynn to play the $225 NLH Rebuy tourney. That didn't go so well, so I took a shot at the $200 NLH SuperStack Turbo at the Venetian last night but was equally unsuccessful. So, I've decided to take a "day off" from poker today and get some much-needed rest before heading over to Jackie's home for dinner at 5pm. She's making fried okra, mac 'n cheese and cornbread!

I posted a passage on Facebook yesterday that has received a lot of likes. It means a lot to me and seems to be resonating with others, too. Here it is:

"If you find someone who makes you smile, who checks up on you often to see if you're okay, who watches out for you and wants the very best for you, don't let them go. Keep them close and don't take them for granted. People like them are hard to find."

The comment I added with the Facebook post was, "I'm so fortunate to have many people in my life like this!"

I truly am. Let's start with my family.

My Dad & Cheryl, who live in Florida, had planned to come visit me back in December, but Cheryl came down with shingles and couldn't make the trip. We re-scheduled their visit for this coming week, but now my Dad is having severe stomach pain. When we spoke on the phone yesterday, he was very upset and cried because he is so sad and disappointed that they again cannot come see me. I reassured them that it's totally okay and I completely understand. In fact, I think it would be great if they can be with me after my anticipated lung surgery and during my recovery period, which could last up to four weeks or more. I'm not good being in bed or on the couch doing nothing, so having them here to "entertain" and take care of me would be awesome.

Mom still lives in Connecticut where I grew up. She's in a beautiful assisted living center where she gets excellent care from the staff and her daily aides. Unfortunately, given her condition, Mom can't travel. Similarly, she was unable to travel to see me the last time I had cancer, so I know how bad she is feeling about that. Additionally, Mom is a "worrier", so it adds to her frustration. Although she can't physically be with me, she calls a couple of times to week to check in and make sure I'm doing okay. I know I'm loved.

Ed and Sharon are wonderful. They came to Vegas to see me for a long weekend in December. We had a great time! I know how worried and concerned they are about my cancer battle, but they continue to be positive and inspirational. Ed is really good at calling once a week or so. It's always nice to catch up and know that he is thinking of me.

And then there's Chris, my boyfriend of 3+ years. Although we only see each other once a month or so for four- or five-day visits, we text and talk almost every day and are very emotionally connected. He knows me so well and has the gift of picking me up when I'm feeling down. Chris is a "giver" and it's so nice to be pampered by him when we're together. I miss him a lot and wish that there wasn't so much physical distance between us.

So not only do I feel fortunate to have a family that really cares about me, I also have an amazing support network of friends who keep in touch with me daily, weekly, or every now and again. Within that group, are some really "special" friends (my angels) that I know are always there for me! It's friends like these, who would do anything for you, that are really hard to find. Knowing they're in my life and that I'm not alone in my fight, is so reassuring and such a relief. I especially love when they can make me laugh, because I don't find myself doing much of that lately. I hope I'm as good of a friend to them, as they are to me!

And, finally, thanks to all of you who keep me in your prayers and are regular readers of my blog here on CaringBridge.org. You are important friends, too! I so appreciate the comments you make on my journal entries. They make me smile, while motivating me to keep fighting the fight!

#PetzingStrong

JAN 24 2018

PET Scan in the Books

I had been very much looking forward to today! It has been three months since I started four cycles of chemotherapy (two "on" weeks and one "off" week in each cycle) for a total of eight chemo treatments, which I completed last Wednesday.

For "graduating" from chemo, I got to have my PET scan this morning. Its purpose is to determine if the two large tumors in my right lung have shrunk enough to be operable and to see if the cancerous lymph nodes in the middle of my chest have been eradicated.

I arrived at Steinberg Associates at 7:45am and was there for 2 1/2 hours. For those of you who have never had a PET scan, here's how it works:

First, I checked in at the main desk with my license and insurance card, and then signed a paper confirming that the name, address, phone, and insurance info they have in their system is correct. Then, I sat for 15 minutes in the main waiting room before my name was called by the Accounts Payable specialist. She collected my co-pay of $950, which I paid via credit card, and gave me a receipt which I'll file with my taxes as a non-reimbursable medical expense. Back to the main waiting room I went, where HGTV's "Love It or Leave

It" was on the big screen tv. I really didn't like the couple on the show and was thinking that they'd be divorced before they decided on keeping their renovated home or buying a another one. The husband was unreasonable and full of himself, making it painful to watch.

Another 20 minutes passed until I was called by an aide and escorted to a "special" men's restroom with lockers in it. I was instructed to take off my vest, jeans and sneakers and to put on two hospital gowns, one forward and one backwards. Clearly, I looked like a fashion model ready to hit the runway with my bright red, long sleeve Fila shirt, blue socks, and speckled green, orange, blue and brown gowns hanging off of me. After exiting the bathroom, I took a seat in another waiting room and five minutes later was taken to a "quiet room", where I sat in a leather recliner and was haunted again by the same "Love It or Leave It" show.

Mitzi came in to place an IV, which took three tries. I suggested that she do it through the port in my chest, but she explained that there was no one there trained to do it and that they'd have to find a vein in my arm to use. I informed Mitzi that I got the port because the veins in my arm had become crusted and hardened, and that I thought she'd have a problem. Well, she did. First attempt in left arm didn't work. Second attempt in right arm, similarly, was a bust. She apologized for having to prick me multiple times. I gave her an annoyed grin and mumbled, "I told you so." I then suggested that she try the top of my right hand. BINGO, that worked!

Mitzi left the room indicating that she'd be back shortly with the radioactive material to inject into my IV. Five minutes later, in she walked with a sealed box containing a large syringe. She pulled it out and shot the serum into my IV. Mitzi then said that I'd have to relax for 45 minutes while the radioactive material worked its way through my body and attempt to drink a mixture of barium and water. I was given the option of a vanilla or mochaccino flavor, and chose mochaccino. Then, I whined about how horrible sucking down that crap is and that I was already feeling nauseous.

She said, “Well, do your best.”

I think I rolled my eyes behind her back.

Ten minutes later, the aide came in with a large size cup of vanilla barium, not mochaccino as I had ordered. I took a taste of it and decided that it was okay, much to the relief of the aide who was worried she may have to mix another drink. So, I napped on and off, while drinking about 2/3’s of the barium cocktail.

The aide came in about 35 minutes later and woke me saying it was time for the PET scan. First, we stopped at the bathroom again so I could “clear my bladder” and then we walked into a low-lit room with the large PET scan machine. Think of the apparatus as a 5 ft in diameter acrylic donut with a covered tunnel coming out of it and a narrow 3 ft wide flat padded table to lie on. Mitzi was back and placed a pillow under my legs and under each shoulder, as I raised my arms over my head and put my hands together to hold a plastic ring. Mitzi indicated that the table would move back and forth through the tunnel for about 20 minutes.

I said, “I knew the drill and it wasn’t my first rodeo.”

The scan itself was easy breezy. I fell asleep for most of it, and before I knew it the scan was over. Mitzi escorted me back to the “special” bathroom with the locker holding my clothes and said that I could just leave when I got dressed. And so, I did at about 10:15am.

I was starving because I hadn’t eaten anything all morning, so went to the Tuscany for some breakfast. From there, I went to the Wynn to play a poker tourney at noon and 5pm, but was not successful. I got home about 10:45pm, fed Zing & Zang, turned on Don Lemon (CNN), made a grilled turkey & cheese sandwich and heated up some loaded potato with bacon soup.

It’s 12:25am on Thursday now and time to go to bed. I’m feeling good about the day and am optimistic that the past three months of chemo treatments have worked! I'll know for sure on Monday, when I get the PET scan results from Dr. Gollard in our 9am meeting. I'm praying hard that Phase 2 will be a surgery to remove 2/3's or all of my right lung. I know that sounds odd. Who wants any kind of surgery, let alone one where your whole lung might be removed? Well, I do. I can live on one lung and want the cancer out my body NOW!

I'm so hopeful that I'll have this opportunity and be operated on by the end of February.

JAN 25 2018

I'm Being Transformed

I'm in a bit of shock this morning. I just received some very sad and disturbing news that a poker friend of mine, Eric B., who lived in Texas, passed away suddenly during a CT scan procedure. He went into cardiac arrest and was without a pulse for 33 minutes. Apparently, Eric had fallen a couple of weeks earlier, which is why he went in for the scan. This is the second time in six months that I have lost a good friend to a heart attack during or after a standard hospital procedure. I have to say it's putting me on edge a bit when I think about my upcoming lung surgery.

It's so hard to make sense of why bad things happen to good people. Eric, in his mid-50's, was a passionate poker player and an awesome guy who regularly checked on me to see how I was doing with my treatments. He kept me in his daily prayers, and we had plans to meet up at Choctaw Casino Resort in Durant, OK when I got better. I'm just stunned.

Yesterday morning, I made a Facebook post when I was at Steinberg Associates getting my PET scan. Since then I've received over 230 responses, including 80 comments of prayers, hope and inspiration. You have no idea how good it makes me feel to know that I continue to have such amazing support from such wonderful people. It keeps me positive and really makes a difference in my attitude.

After doing a large load of laundry and cleaning up a bit around my condo, I decided to take some quiet time to reflect on a number of things: Eric's death, my Dad's unknown stomach illness (he's in a hospital in Florida and getting an endoscopy today), my upcoming PET scan results and next steps. Is surgery an option? What does the future hold? What will life look life for me now? You know, and other general life stuff. It's so easy to go on overwhelm, but I'm an expert at compartmentalizing and am able to manage through it fairly well. I also get great comfort from my daily readings in *Jesus Calling*.

Today's passage is a meaningful one for me:

"Let My Love enfold you in the radiance of My Glory. Sit still in the Light of My Presence and receive My Peace. These quiet moments with Me transcend time, accomplishing far more than you can imagine. Bring Me the sacrifice of your time and watch to see how abundantly I bless you and your loved ones.

Through the intimacy of our relationship, you are being transformed from the inside out. As you keep your focus on Me, I form you into the one I desire you to be. Your part is to yield to My creative work in you, neither resisting it nor trying to speed it up. Enjoy the tempo of a God-breathed life by letting Me set the pace. Hold My hand in childlike trust, and the way before you will open up step by step."

Hebrews 13:15; 2 Corinthians 3:18; Psalm 73:23-24

I truly believe that my Higher Power has bigger plans for me and that I'm on a continual journey of transformation. After battling and winning my first fight with neck cancer, I saw many positive changes in myself: more personal strength, more appreciation for true friends, more patience, more empathy, less rigidity, more appreciation for the simple things in life, less tolerance for those feeling sorry for themselves, and the continued importance for living life fully every day you have it. Every minute we have on this great Earth is a gift.

I do trust that my Higher Power again is looking out for me in this second battle with the Big C. Clearly, there's more I'm supposed to learn, along with more growth I'm destined to experience. It's hard, but there must be a greater purpose for me that is to come out of all of this. I'm excited to see where this path is taking me and how I can help others along the way. #PetzingStrong

JAN 27 2018

Moved to Tears by an Unexpected Letter

I went in for Happy Hydration yesterday, received my "Fun Bag" and have been wired ever since. In fact, after busting the Wynn poker tourney in the afternoon, I had so much energy that I was able to play the 7pm $200 NLH Rebuy tourney at the Venetian. At 3:30am, I was eliminated in 9th place of 72 players for $500. I was disappointed that I didn't do better but was happy with my second consecutive cash on back-to-back nights.

I'm just finishing breakfast now at Marilyn's Cafe in the Tuscany Suites Hotel Casino across the street from where I live. It's 1:45pm. Yes, I got a later start than usual today because I slept in until 9:30am, lied around in bed until 11:30am checking emails and Facebook and called Chris.

I was excited to tell him about an unexpected letter I received yesterday. It was from Ryan B, a guy I met 5 years ago on a Mediterranean gay cruise. We really don't know each other very well but have re-connected via Facebook and intermittent texting over the past few years. Ryan B. is a casual poker player and was here in Vegas both last Summer and a few weeks ago, but we weren't able to coordinate our schedules to get together in person. He was eager to meet with me because he wanted to let me know how much my book, "From Feeding Tube to Final Table: A Cancer Survivor's Story", had impacted him and changed his life. And, of course, I wanted to hear what he had to say!

Well, that happened yesterday when Ryan's 4 1/2 page single-spaced, typed letter arrived. I read it in bed at 4am this morning, when I got home from poker, and it brought tears to my eyes. I know I've been positively impacting many people with my cancer story and my book, but I guess I didn't realize how significant of a difference I've made for some, like Ryan B.

So, I'd like to share with you some selected passages from Ryan's letter. It has touched me at my core and filled my heart with happiness. I hope it will do the same for you.

January 19, 2018

"Jim,

When I met you in the pool on the Celebrity Millennium on first day of the cruise in May 2013, although I knew nothing about you initially--you had a spark that made you different, special, and I felt that immediately. I didn't know why exactly, but your zeal and special unique spirit struck me. You were the first person I really spoke with on that trip, aside from the great friends I traveled there with, and loved talking with you in the pool. I know we didn't get the chance to connect much throughout the trip from there, but it was a special interaction for me. You might wonder how that is relevant--hopefully, with any ability for me to be even remotely articulate--I'll get to how you've made an impact.

"We connected on Facebook, and I followed my friends' lives, and I posted, myself too. Despite not knowing you much, yet knowing a bit about your drive, your professional accomplishments, and by reading your character by my gut, I've always looked up to you. I know that might sound weird... but I mean that as a high compliment. When I learned of your first Big C diagnosis (via Facebook, and thank you for sharing the most raw, tough times so candidly, as I would learn more through your book), I was also learning of my sister's (my very best friend) diagnosis with cancer."

"In 2013 (right after the cruise), I left everything I knew in Arizona. I had no network awaiting me in Houston, which would become my new home for an undecided period of time. I ventured away from comfort, family and friends, toward an amazing albeit very challenging and often lonely job. After about three personally very difficult years there, I had grown in some ways and regressed in others. With my Mom's condition worsening (Parkinson's), and now my best friend (my sister) receiving a cancer diagnosis, I knew I needed to be closer to them. I left Houston and went home. There was no hesitation or doubt. My sister is a very private person, asks for nothing, and I knew I needed to be with her. I tell you this because, as I read your book, it resonated so much with me that although I personally cannot even begin to know what it's like to deal with cancer (and my heart breaks that now you are facing it again on a different front), I do empathize so much with all that you went through and are going through. I admire your decision to share it so candidly, even on the days that I'm sure you just wanted to curl up in a ball and sleep. I know 'quit' is not in your vocabulary (another thing I admire about you.) I'm sure, truth be told, there were moments when even the 'q' word might have seemed appealing. You didn't."

---Side note from me: Ryan is right. I'm not a quitter, but the pain I was experiencing in my first cancer battle was so intense and overwhelming, that I did consider it. But, thankfully, my motivation and drive to not let the Big C win and get the best of me took over and helped me persevere!

> "Fortunately, my sister is now on the right side of things, and it has been a blessing to be close in proximity. We've always been close in spirit. As I read your book, and learned of the characters in your story, your beautiful angels in your life, I was touched by the honesty of the dynamics of your relationships. I respected your candid disclosure of the realities and difficulties of sex life (or lack thereof), which of course makes 100% sense. I was full of joy and awe to learn of your relationship with Chris and have so much respect for getting a new relationship off the ground, especially amidst what can only be described as one of the toughest possible scenarios. I admire your relationship with Elizabeth, and the humor that you both injected into raw and difficult times. Love and laughter do wonders. Let modern medicine help heal the body and let love help heal the mind and soul. It is evident that everyone around you -- so many in the Douglas community, those that patronized Zing, and, of course, your angels -- care deeply for you, as you do them. This is such an inspiriting reality, and it's such a blessing that makes my heart sing.
>
> "I'm going to get personal here and delve a bit deeper to explain the impact you've had on me without even knowing it, by sharing your difficult, brave, and admirable journey. When I moved back to Arizona from Houston with no job, a mildly scary set of circumstances, I had just ended a relationship. It hurt -- we've all been there, and I'll leave it at that. Everything was scary, unknown, and my emotions were raw. Jobs, social interactions, reconnecting with home, and

even getting out became tough. On that level, in addition to knowing chronic illness from my family's experience, I could partially relate on some level to many of the chapters in your book. I didn't have consistent insurance, and after always having stable jobs all my life, I was in a position of flux longer than I ever I thought I would be. I let friendships wane because I wasn't 'up for stuff.' During this process, the silver lining and my purpose for coming home was that I was able to be there for my sister and Mom as much as possible. This was/is a gift!

"Over the past few years, a piece or two of me died. Mostly emotionally. I let it. I began to say, "I missed opportunities". I shut off a part of my heart and began to feel that settling for my current path wasn't quitting--it was just being realistic and pragmatic. This is all different for me, as historically, people have always seen and described me as very 'driven'. It's sometimes funny how people see us, versus how we see ourselves.

"I purchased your book within days of its release. Because my sister's situation was better, but still a little raw, your book of experience, honesty, pain, wisdom, friendships, devotion, community, and spirituality sat on my nightstand for months. I looked at it daily. It sat until I was ready to read it. A couple of weeks ago, right after I returned from my recent Vegas trip, I knew I would read it very soon. I wanted to do so when I could be very focused, as I knew it would strike many chords. About 10 days ago I picked it up, put it in my day bag, and carried you with me, but didn't read it.

"I recently felt the need for a cleansing given all the twists and turns in my life during the last few years. Being in a spot I didn't guess I'd be in at 35 years old, I supposed I'd even further minimize clutter, personally, professionally, spiritually, etc. I've kind of always been a minimalist that way. Experiences matter to me more than things. Part of this cleansing meant that for whatever reasons, I decided to go through my phone and clear out some 'noise.' I deleted a number of contacts from my phone, not to be spiteful or anything like that, but simply as a way of keeping priorities in check – reorganizing -- to keep the people who are true friends, family, loved ones, etc., close and to relieve myself of contacts who were only that--contacts. This cleansing or re-organization served two functions, a bit of an odd duality which unbeknownst to me would come full circle immediately after reading your book. I believe that reading about your strength, your relationships, your pain and your joy, harmonized very well with a bit of a 'reset' button I was about to push (or was maybe already in the process of pushing) and that was much needed. Simply put, you gave me the gift of perspective.

"So, it was on Friday, January 12, that I boarded the roughly five hour flight from Phoenix to Baltimore for what had historically been a poignant and significant weekend event for me, which I had attended three of the last four years. And, each year something major has happened in my life while I've been in attendance.

"As soon as I took my seat on the plane, I opened your book. I read it cover to cover from the beginning of the flight to almost the end of it--nearly to the minute, experiencing quite a range of emotions, some of which I had forgotten what they felt like. And, that was YOUR gift to ME. You touched my heart with your journey and gave me a reminder of how simultaneously rotten and beautiful life can be.

"During the course of this big event weekend, something extraordinarily unexpected was about to happen, unbeknownst to me. I had already felt like this reset, renewal, or whatever we want to call it was in motion. I was humbled by your journey and by your strength. I re-lived some of my experience with my sister, and even my mother. I shed many tears on the plane, reading your words. I have been uplifted by my time with my family. I have been frustrated with my own health but am starting to get those pieces in place. What happened to me that weekend, I do not think was coincidence. I would categorize myself easily as a skeptic. I want proof of things. I don't jump on bandwagons. I question authority. I challenge what many readily accept. I have never believed in fate or 'everything happens for a reason' or 'it was meant to be.' I started to write this letter to you, even before most of the events of this past weekend...so many of these elements of my message of gratitude to you were already formulated before this moment.

"As my friend Richard and I were walking together leaving this social event, I had literally just finished a conversation with him about how I have accepted, for some time now, the reality that some things I'd wanted in life -- really referring to love, meeting my match -- were just not in the cards for me. Suddenly, a man walked by me. I felt electricity. I sensed something here that I've never even particularly believed in. I was not only very attracted to him, but I had this very odd, and even startling (in a good way) feeling that I've never experienced. I really can't even put it into words. Despite my reluctance to 'go for things' in the past...I noticed him pause. We both did a double, then a triple take. I walked over to him and introduced myself. He did the same. I felt like we were the only two people on Earth, amidst a room full of hundreds of men. I never believed in love-at-first-sight. In fact, I'd probably be the first to tell you how ridiculous that concept is. I changed in that moment. I believe, without a shadow of a doubt, that he will be the man I will marry. We spent an amazing weekend together.

"Al and I regularly talk on the phone for hours, have already delved deeply into each other's souls, and have a very bright outlook on what life can look like moving forward. I almost gave up on that happening for me. I was resigned. And in the blink of an eye, things changed.

"I've wanted to catch you in Vegas for a long time, and I know meeting up can be a series of sliding doors, especially with two poker players whose schedules can be a bit unpredictable. Even prior to reading your book (which only reinforced my gut about your qualities), I always wanted the opportunity to chat with you and just say thanks for making a mark on me, even if you didn't know you did!

"In this letter, I humbly write to thank you for being one of MY angels, who has helped me renew my perspective and nourish my soul. I thank you for the gift that you've given me, in an unexpected way. I thank you for your story, which helped soften my heart, feel moments of all ranges of emotions, and appreciate the honesty and truth each of our voices can have to lift each other up, even when we feel we are falling. Jim, thank you for your strength.

Humbly and sincerely,

Your friend,

Ryan B."

Wow....I am a bit overwhelmed having just shared this with all of you. I want to thank Ryan B. from the bottom of my heart for taking the time to write me this amazing letter! I'm so glad that my book made such a huge impact on him. It's why I decided to write it...to provide hope, inspiration and motivation for others that may be struggling with or affected by cancer or may be facing tough difficulties or challenges in their lives that may seem insurmountable.

JAN 30 2018

The Results Are In

I rarely get nervous about anything, but I was certainly anxious yesterday morning when I woke up at 7:15am because I knew I'd be getting my PET scan results from Dr. Gollard in a few hours. To pass the time, I threw myself into paying bills and miscellaneous administrative stuff. At 9:30am, I jumped into the shower, quickly got dressed and ran out the door.

On my drive over to the Nevada Cancer Specialists' building, I was actually a bit nauseous. It was a combination of both excitement and fear about what Dr. Gollard was going to say. I had asked Jackie to join me for the meeting because I didn't want to hear the news alone. I also thought it was important to get a second point of view on the information.

Jackie and I met in front of the building and went up to the office together. I told her that I was a bit nervous and she reassured me that everything would be just fine. We sat in the waiting room chit-chatting until they called for me. Jackie and I had agreed that she would tape the meeting on her phone, so we could go back and listen again if we needed to.

Kevin, a nursing aide, took us back to an examination room where he took my blood pressure and checked my air capacity. All was good. Dr. Gollard came in shortly thereafter and greeted us both. I introduced him to Jackie, and we got started.

He asked me how I was feeling and if there had been any changes in anything over the past week or so? I told him that I was doing well, relatively speaking, but that I had developed re-occurring night sweats over the past five days. He wasn't sure what that was all about and recorded it in his notes to revisit at another time.

We then got into the PET scan results.

Overall, Dr. Gollard was very pleased with my progress. The chemotherapy plan I've been on for the past 12 weeks has been working. He indicated that the large tumor in my upper right lung has shrunk by about 1/3, and that the smaller tumor in my lower lung is almost non-existent. He also said that many of the cancerous lymph nodes in the middle of my chest were much smaller or gone. Unfortunately, however, the large tumor has not shrunk enough to be operable and more of the cancerous lymph nodes in my chest need to be eradicated before surgery can be an option.

Since the chemo IS working and I'm managing it quite well, Dr. Gollard has decided that we should continue with the chemotherapy plan for another six treatments.

I was definitely disappointed that the chemo hadn't shrunk my tumor enough for surgery, but did understand the need for the tumors and nodes to be as small as possible to increase my chances for a successful outcome when I do have it. So, I'll be back at chemo again tomorrow for #9 of 15 treatments. I was hoping for immediate gratification, but it looks like I need to be patient and wait for delayed gratification.

During the appointment, Dr. Gollard determined that it was time to add some other specialists to our group. So, a radiation oncologist and thoracic surgeon will join our team that currently consists of Dr. Gollard (chemo), Dr. Tavares (pulmonary) and Dr. Tahir (general.) I'm also being scheduled for a

Pulmonary Function Test (PFT) that will evaluate my ability to potentially live with only one lung. Although not specifically said by Dr. Gollard, Jackie and I got the sense that if surgery does happen it likely will be the removal of my entire right lung. I'm okay with that as my understanding is that many people are able to lead fairly normal lives with only one lung.

IF the chemo continues to work and I pass the PFT, Dr. Gollard recommends that surgery happen next. He mentioned that it will be extensive, complex and intricate. I told him that I wanted to have surgery at the best place possible with a surgeon that specializes in addressing my specific situation. Dr. Gollard asked me where I had looked and I told him that I had researched MDAnderson in Houston, Mayo Clinic and Cancer Treatment Centers of America in Phoenix, and UCLA in Los Angeles. The only one he really responded favorably to was Mayo Clinic, so I will pursue his opinions further when and if surgery becomes viable. If surgery is not an option in a few months, it looks like I'll start receiving a combination of chemo and radiation therapy.

Of course, life expectancy is always on my mind. If you go on the internet, you'll learn that only 5-15% of Stage 3B cancer victims who receive treatment live for five years beyond their diagnosis date. However, there are those that have beat the odds. I plan to be one of them!

On that note, Dr. Gollard actually mentioned (for the first time) that he is cautiously optimistic there is still a possibility we can cure this, versus just treat it. He confidently stated that he has treated many folks with the chemo/radiation combo that have gone on to live much longer lives than expected.

I'm not getting too excited right now about possibly being cured of lung cancer because I just don't want to suffer through the massive disappointment later, especially if it doesn't become reality. However, it is good to know that there's an outside chance. I'll take that and work with it...one day at a time!

#PetzingStrong

JAN 31 2018

Trying to Be Strong

I woke up in a funk this morning. If I'm being completely honest, it's because I'm feeling sorry for myself today. I really don't want to be here at chemo, but I know it's necessary to continue the shrinkage of the large tumor in my right lung.

After going through eight chemo sessions during the past three months, I now need to endure six more treatments over the next nine weeks. FUN! I'm just not looking forward to feeling "blah" for another three months. It's kind of depressing, but I know it's what I need to be doing. By shrinking the tumor and cancerous nodes further, I have a better chance for a positive outcome. So, I'm just going to grin and bear it and work hard at maintaining a positive attitude.

On an uplifting note, my reading today from *Jesus Calling* has given me some added motivation:

"I am your Strength and Shield. I plan out each day and have it ready for you, long before you arise from bed. I also provide the strength you need each step of the way. Instead of assessing your energy level and wondering about what's on the road ahead, concentrate on staying in touch with Me.

My Power flows freely into you through our open communication. Refuse to waste energy worrying, and you will have strength to spare.

Whenever you start to feel afraid, remember that I am your Shield. But unlike inanimate armor, I am always alert and active. My Presence watches over you continually, protecting you from both known and unknown dangers. Entrust yourself to My watch care, which is the best security system available. I am with you and will watch over you wherever you go."

Psalm 28:7; Matthew 6:34; Psalm 56:3-4; Genesis 28:15

I don't think it's a coincidence that this was my January 31 passage. I've tried so hard to be strong and will continue to do so, but I really needed this extra kick in the butt today!

#PetzingStrong

FEB 2 2018

Struggling Emotionally This Week

I'm back at Dr. Gollard's for Hydration Friday. I'm looking forward to getting my "Fun Bag" of goodies to get me through the weekend.

It has been a tough week for me emotionally.

Additionally, it hasn't been a good week at the poker tables and I miss Chris. It's hard to be alone so much, especially when going through something like this. My friends have been great, but sometimes you just want that special someone to be there when you're feeling down and out and need a pick me up.

And, finally, I still haven't sold my damn restaurant/martini lounge in Douglas, MI after 28 months of being on the market. Sadly, this tiny town of 1200 residents and its neighbor, Saugatuck, with 800 folks are not especially good for commercial businesses because they comprise a very seasonal resort area that's totally dependent on a good weather Summer. Winters are brutal and there are very few full time locals who have significant disposable income to spend on eating out at nicer restaurants.

Basically, Douglas is a second home retirement community that hasn't evolved and desperately needs more full time residents. It's stuck in the past and not poised for a prosperous future. I've recently lowered the price of my restaurant/martini lounge (and the two beautiful condos above it) to a "fire sale" level just to get rid of it. Hopefully, someone will buy it soon and remove this big black cloud that continues to suffocate me.

Given my negative attitude this week, I've been looking and hoping for some spiritual support and healing. Ironically, the *Jesus Calling* passages for yesterday and today have given me some renewed energy and inspiration.

This was yesterday's passage:

"Follow me one step at a time. That is all I require of you. In fact, that is the only way to move through this space/time world. You see huge mountains looming, and you start wondering how you're going to scale those heights. Meanwhile, because you're not looking where you're going, you stumble on the easy path where I am leading you now. As I help you get back on your feet, you tell Me how worried you are about the cliffs up ahead. But you don't know what will happen today, much less tomorrow. Our path may take an abrupt turn, leading you away from those mountains. There may be an easier way up the mountains than is visible from this distance. If I do lead you up the cliffs, I will equip you thoroughly for that strenuous climb. I will even give My angels charge over you, to preserve you in all your ways.

Keep your mind on the present journey, enjoying My Presence. Walk by faith, not by sight, trusting Me to open up the way before you."

Psalm 18:29; Psalm 91:11-12 (AMP); 2 Corinthians 5:7 (NKIV)

And this is today's passage:

"I am renewing your mind. When your thoughts flow freely, they tend to move toward problems. Your focus gets snagged on a given problem, circling round and round it in attempts to gain mastery. Your energy is drained away from other matters through this negative focus. Worst of all, you lose sight of Me.

A renewed mind is Presence-focused. Train your mind to seek Me in every moment, every situation. Sometimes you can find ME in your surroundings: a lilting birdsong, a loved one's smile, golden sunlight. At other times, you must draw inward to find Me. I am always present in your spirit. Seek My Face, speak to Me, and I will light up your mind."

Romans 12:2; Psalm 105:4

These two passages are so fitting to my situation this week. I will take them to heart and work hard to change my attitude. I will send up my issues and let him guide me to where I need to go.

FEB 4 2018

A Challenging Week Ahead

After receiving my hydration treatment on Friday, I decided to play Day 1B of the $250 NLH $50K Guarantee poker tourney at South Point casino, which is very close to Dr. Gollard's office. I had a good run, placed 2nd in my group, and started Day 2 yesterday in 3rd of the remaining 44 players from a total field of 296 entrants. Of course, I had hoped to win the $12K 1st place prize, but I had an up and down day and only finished in 13th for a $909 payday. It felt good to cash, but I was disappointed that I didn't fare better. On to the next one....

I have a busy week ahead full of doctors' appointments and treatments. Tomorrow morning, I meet Dr. Dean, my new radiation oncologist, who has been added to my treatment team. Although radiation is not yet part of my program, it may be needed down the road if surgery doesn't become an option or if radiation is required post-surgery.

On Wednesday, I'll be back at Dr. Gollard's for chemo treatment #10 of 14, and then again on Friday for hydration.

Then, on Thursday, I'm having my Pulmonary Function Test (PFT). This is a breathing test that I believe will determine how well I can function living with one lung, if my right lung is removed. I'm really not sure what to expect, but I don't think it will be "fun." In fact, it'll probably require a lot of "huffing and puffing." I purposely scheduled it on Thursday, after Wednesday chemo, because it's the day of the week that I feel my best and strongest. It's important that I pass this test for surgery to remain an option, so I'm a little nervous about it.

Today's *Jesus Calling* devotion is very appropriate for my situation. It reads:

"Bring Me your weakness and receive My peace. Accept yourself and your circumstances just as they are, remembering that I am sovereign over everything. Do not wear yourself out with analyzing and planning. Instead, let thankfulness and trust be your guides through this day; they will keep you close to Me. As you live in the radiance of My Presence, My Peace shines upon you. You will cease to notice how weak or strong you feel, because you will be focusing on Me. The best way to get through this day is step by step with Me. Continue this intimate journey, trusting that the path you are following is headed for heaven."

Psalm 29:11; Numbers 6:24-26; Psalm 13:5

Yes, I will continue to take one day at a time, believing that I am doing all of the right things to get to where I need to be. I will work hard at staying in the moment and not looking too far ahead, which is necessary, but quite difficult to do. And finally, while I can, I will live each day to its fullest maximizing every minute with not a moment to waste.

#PetzingStrong

FEB 6 2018

Radiation in the Picture

Yesterday I met with Dr. Dean, the radiation oncologist that has been assigned to my case. He was absolutely amazing! I was so impressed that he had taken the time to prepare for our appointment by re-creating my entire cancer history dating back to July 2014. Dr. Dean spent over an hour with me, answering all of my questions and providing valuable insight into my situation. I didn't exactly like what I heard, but I was certainly glad to be hearing it from him. Radiation will definitely become a part of my program, along with chemo, as a replacement for surgery if I don't qualify for it. Or, it will be used for post-surgery treatment.

Based on my last PET scan, after I finished my first four cycles of 8 chemo treatments, Dr. Dean is very concerned about the location of the large tumor in my right lung and the numerous cancerous lymph nodes that still exist in the middle of my chest. From his vast experience, he believes that I have a 50/50 chance of a thoracic surgeon being willing to perform a pneumonectomy, the surgical removal of a lung, on me. Apparently, there is a lot of complexity and risk involved. A lot will depend on how well I perform in Thursday's PFT (Pulmonary Function Test) breathing test and if the next five chemo treatments make a significant difference in eradicating the cancerous nodes and reducing the large tumor even further. He even mentioned that I might be referred to UCLA by the thoracic surgeon.

Interestingly, while I was meeting with Dr. Dean, I got a call from Health Plan of Nevada's scheduling office and I have a consultation appointment set up with a thoracic surgeon on Monday, February 26 at 8:45am. I'm already anxious about what he is going to say.

Dr. Dean indicated that the decision of whether surgery is an option or not will be totally up to the thoracic surgeon.

I asked Dr. Dean, "If you were me and, in my situation,, would you choose surgery if it was available to you or would you go the route of a radiation/chemo combo treatment?"

He paused and said, "I would certainly consider the surgery. But I'd need to be very sure that I have full confidence in the surgeon and that he is not 'wishy washy' at all on its potential success."

Dr. Dean and I then got into the discussion of the alternative to surgery. Basically, I would start a new six to seven-week program with daily radiation for 33 days, a less intensive chemo with hydration once a week, and a full hydration every Friday.

ARGH!!!!

It's exhausting to think about having to go to radiation everyday (Mon thru Fri) for 6 1/2 weeks. He assured me that this radiation would be much less intense than the radiation I received when I had neck cancer, which made me very sick and was almost unmanageable. I'm still coming to grips with the fact that I have a chronic disease that will require treatment in some form for the rest of my life. The "good news," if any, is that Dr. Dean's office is only a seven minute drive for my home, so getting to and from should be easy.

After my meeting with Dr. Dean, I was quite bummed out. I went to Albertson's and spent $141. I decided that I needed to get my mind occupied quickly, so I played Day 1A of the $400 NLH $100K Guarantee poker tourney at the Venetian, which started at noon. At 11pm, I was one of 24 out of 206 players remaining who qualified for Day 2 on Wednesday. I have a decent chip stack of 76K/25bb going into Day 2, so hopefully I'll make the $$$$!

Given that my normal chemo day is Wednesday, I called Dr. Gollard's early this morning and they were able to squeeze me in today. So, I'm at chemo right now writing this journal entry. I filled in Radka on yesterday's meeting with Dr. Dean and she tried to keep me positive. I just love her. She's so caring and wonderful. Radka told me that Dr. Gollard and Dr. Dean have been good friends for many years, so I feel like I'm in the best hands possible for moving forward.

Now my goal is to snap out of my funk, work at staying positive, take one day at a time, and live fully in the moment. I can and I will!

#PetzingStrong

FEB 7 2018

Spiritual Support from an Old Friend

Chemo lasted a surprising 6hr and 45mins on Tuesday. All went smoothly, but there was a lot of liquids and meds to drip through. I took two naps for a total of 3 hours. Louise came by to keep me company for about 1 1/2 hours, so the time really flew.

I left Dr. Gollard's office around 5pm and drove to the Venetian. Since I was starving, I got a ham & cheese stromboli in the food court and it hit the spot. At 7pm, I entered the $200 NLH Progressive Bounty tourney and cashed in 8th place of 126 players for a net win of $422. I busted out horribly with AK vs 99 post flop with a board of A97. Just very unlucky.

During the tournament, I received a text message from an old friend who has been following my journey on CaringBridge.org, just like all of you. He's going to be in town in the near future and wants to get together to catch up. I'm really excited to see him. We had an amazing text conversation that I'd like to share here, as there is so much to learn spiritually from it.

Here's how it went:

> Friend: "Try to kick some of that C's ass before I get there!"

Me: “I’m working on it.”

Friend: “I know you are my man. And He is with you every step. Just like with all of us.”

Me: “Yes, I believe that.”

Friend: “The challenge is always toughest with those He loves most!”

Me: “Wish He didn’t make it so difficult.”

Friend: “Yes, you do. Do you think your love and faith in Him would be as strong had you not been put to the test?”

Me: “Probably not. Just tired of being tested.”

Friend: “And don’t you think your confidence in your personal salvation is at an ALL TIME HIGH?"

Me: “I do. I have to be sure it is.”

Friend: “They say the mark of a completely lost relationship is indifference.”

Me: “I agree with that. I’ve been in some of those.”

Friend: “That’s why I make great friends with my Uber drivers They want 5-Stars and so they love me!»

Me: “LOL”

Friend: “You hang in there, even though it’s no fun to endure. But the power of the relationships you have is so neat to watch. I really love all these people in your life that I just don’t know. And I’m proud to be a part of the #PetzingStrong community.”

Me: “I’m glad you’re there with me.”

> Friend: "Same. You're giving us all a gift you can't understand. By the way, I'm trying to be there for you even though it has been a long time. And, responding to your journal entries on CaringBridge is my way to message you support and energy. I'm here for you anytime you want to pick up the phone."

This text dialogue with my old friend meant a lot and I'm looking forward to seeing him soon!

FEB 9 2018

YAY...Breathing Tests Completed

It's Hydration Friday. So, while I get all of my "Fun Bag" goodies, I thought I'd write today's journal entry.

I've been on a nice poker run for the past week or so. On Wednesday, I cashed in 15th place of 524 entrants in the Venetian's $400 NLH $100K Guarantee tourney. It was a $2K+ payday so that felt good, but I was really disappointed that I didn't fare better and win the $37K 1st place prize! I'll be playing later today in Day 1B of the $800 NLH 8-Max $250K Guarantee, so hopefully this one will be mine!

Yesterday morning I had my Pulmonary Function Test (PFT) at San Martin Hospital. Basically, it's an hour of breathing tests where you are required to inhale and exhale in different ways through a tube that's stuck in your mouth, while nose clamps are attached to prevent any kind of air passage through the nostrils.

I had this same test back in October when I was first diagnosed with lung cancer, so I knew what to expect going into it. It was a very unpleasant hour full of coughing, hacking, eye-watering and feeling like I was going to throw up. Fortunately, Mari, the tech assigned to me, was incredible! She walked me through each of the tests before I had to do them and then tried to keep me motivated when I wasn't.

The purpose of the tests is to determine my overall lung capacity and whether I might be able to function well on only one lung, if my right lung is removed during surgery. The sense I got is that I did better on some of the tests and worse on others, but decent overall. Dr. Gollard will receive the results today and I'm set to meet with him next Friday before hydration to review the findings. Of course, my fingers are crossed hoping that I did well enough to keep surgery as a possible option in the mix of future treatment plans.

I believe my Higher Power will help guide the ultimate decision of the path I'm supposed to take. He will work through me and all my doctors (my earthly angels) to ensure we do the right thing. I am putting my faith in Him and am confident that all will work out for the best.

This keeps me grounded and living in the moment without too much worry. I can't change the past and I really have no control over what the future holds for me, but what I can do is make the most of today! And, that is my daily goal.

FEB 12 2018

Needing to Sleep

I didn't fare well in Day 1B of the $800 NLH 8-Max tourney on Friday, but after busting out I entered the 7pm $200 NLH Rebuy tourney. 11 hours later (at 6am), I found myself in 3rd place of 114 players for a net win of $4424! It definitely was worth playing all night. Luckily, I was able to do so because the steroids from my hydration treatment had kicked in and kept me energized.

February has been a good poker month for me so far. I've played in 14 tourneys, cashed in 4 and bubbled 1 (just missed the $$$ by one spot). The average cash rate is 10% and I'm at 29%, so I'm definitely feeling good about that.

I also had a nice weekend seeing and hanging with April and James from Vancouver. They came into town to celebrate James' 50th birthday and treated me to breakfast on Saturday. It was so fun catching up. I really enjoy them. Then, on Sunday, I went to Ardys' home for brunch. Her husband, Jimmy, made a fabulous meal and I got to see Rachael, Ardys' youngest daughter, who was here from Sydney, Australia for a fashion convention. We had a very laid back and enjoyable time. It was exactly what I needed.

Sunday afternoon I attempted to play the $200 NLH Rebuy poker tourney at the Venetian. I wish I hadn't. I was so tired and out of it. The Friday "fun bags" had started to wear off and all I wanted to do was put my head on the poker table and take a nap. I couldn't fathom playing for a total of 10 hours, so when I got low in chips, I just busted myself out and went home.

I got in bed at 2:30pm and napped until 6pm. For dinner, I warmed up some of Jackie's asparagus soup and reheated leftover lasagna, enjoying them both while I watched the Winter Olympics. By 10pm, I was falling asleep on the couch, so I put myself back in bed and slept until 7pm this morning. Even after 12 1/2 hours of sleep yesterday, I still woke up tired and not feeling well. I stayed in bed another 45 minutes watching *Good Morning America* until the cats drove me crazy and I had to get up to feed them. After showering, I went to CVS to pick up some meds, got a haircut, and treated myself to a manicure/pedicure. By 2pm, I was back in bed for another nap. All my body wants to do is sleep.

I can tell this is going to be a tough week for me, as I usually feel the worst during my off week from chemo and I'm already so tired. I'll receive a hydration treatment on Friday, but that seems like it's a month away. Hopefully, all of the sleep I'm getting will provide me with a little pick me up. We'll see.

I went back and re-read the February 3 *Jesus Calling* devotion because I remember it having a positive impact on me. It states the following:

"I am with you and for you. You face nothing alone...nothing! When you feel anxious, know that you are focusing on the visible world and leaving Me out of the picture. The remedy is simple: Fix your eyes not on what is seen, but on what is unseen. Verbalize your trust in Me, the Living One who sees you always. I will get you safely through this day and all your days. But you can find Me only in the present. Each day is a precious gift from My Father. How ridiculous to grasp for future gifts when today's is set before you! Receive today's gift gratefully, unwrapping it tenderly and delving into its depths. As you savor this gift, you find Me."

Romans 8:31; 2 Corinthians 4:18; Genesis 16:13-14 (AMP)

I have faith that He is with me, guiding me day by day. I am doing my best to stay in the present and truly appreciate all that the gift of each day has to offer, even when I'm not having a good one.

#PetzingStrong

FEB 16 2018

Loneliness is Hard

It's Happy Hydration Friday! I'm in my leather recliner right now receiving my "Fun Bags" of goodies: electrolytes, steroids, Pepsid, and anti-nausea. It's the perfect cocktail to start off the weekend. I really needed this today, as I've been overly tired this past week, especially on Monday when I slept and slept and slept.

On Tuesday, I had to get out of my condo, so I played Day 1B of the $400 NLH SuperStack poker tourney at the Venetian. At 11pm that night, I found myself with a stack of 443K chips and in 2nd place moving into Day 2 of the tournament. So, from a total field of 399 players, I returned on Wednesday to compete with the remaining 46 players for the 1st place prize of $27K.

It was a roller coaster ride of a day for me. I lost half my stack within the first two hours but fought hard and battled back to make the Final Table of ten players. By 9pm, I had outlasted seven of the players and was now in the Final 3. Unfortunately, I didn't advance further. However, on a very positive note, I won $13,232 for my effort finishing in 3rd place. It was my biggest cash of the year so far! I've been really happy with my play this month and have cashed in 5 of 15 February tournaments, which is well above the average cash rate of 10%. I'm hoping my hot streak continues.

I know this all sounds fabulous, but if I'm really being honest, I have to tell you that I've been feeling really lonely lately. Yes, even social folks like me get lonely. I struggle with why I feel this way because I have an amazing group of loving and supportive friends who I know will do anything for me if I ask them. And, I have an awesome boyfriend, Chris, who I know loves me. But, unfortunately, he's in Michigan. I know my Mom, Dad, stepmom, brother and sis-in-law are praying for me every day, but I'm still lonely.

I've been in treatment now for 4 1/2 months and have another month of chemo to go. It's hard being sick alone. It makes me sad to think about other cancer patients like me who don't have a hobby, like poker, that can help keep their mind focused on something else other than their illness. And, I worry about those that don't have good friends, a spouse, a special someone or a social network like I have. They must feel really lonely.

What's most difficult for me is coming home every night to an empty home. Zing & Zang are always there to greet me, but it's not like having someone physically there that you can talk to about your day, how you're feeling, and what your concerns and worries are that keep you up at night.

This is my second time fighting cancer "alone," meaning by myself without a partner who lives with me. It's just hard and there is nothing I can do about it. Fortunately, I've had practice and am used to it, but it's still a lonely existence. I'm not being critical of Chris here. I know he cares about me very much and is awesome about checking in on me, but it's just not the same as having him here. Unfortunately, his other life responsibilities (job and four kids) keep this from becoming a reality for us.

Anyway, I continue to try to stay positive and upbeat, but some days it's a chore and exhausting. There are so many of us fighting this awful battle "alone"... without a significant other right there with us by our side every day. So, we have become independent warriors. We have learned to face our obstacles and fears on our own and persevere through both the good and bad days.

We are strong! We can and will do this! I believe in me.

#PetzingStrong

FEB 20 2018

Relying on Him

I've taken a few days off from making a journal entry. Most of my time has been spent at the poker table where I've cashed in two of the six tourneys I've played over the past three days. I'm really happy with how I've performed this month and feel like I'm playing at my best right now.

I know that my last journal entry about "Loneliness" was concerning to many of you. It was emotionally raw and real. I'm feeling a little better now, but I know I'll continue to struggle with it. It's important that I embrace and work with it, and not let it bring me down.

I'm thankful for Sarah Young's *Jesus Calling* book of daily devotions. I read it each morning before I start my day. It provides me with words of hope, encouragement, comfort, guidance and reassurance.

Two recent readings from Sunday (February 18) and yesterday (February 19) made a significant impact on me, especially given how I've been feeling lately. I'd like to share them with you:

"You are feeling weighed down by a plethora of problems, both big and small. They seem to require more and more of your attention, but you must not give in to those demands. When the difficulties in your life feel as if they're closing in on you, break free by spending quality time with Me. You need to remember who I am in all My Power and Glory. Then, humbly bring Me your prayers and petitions. Your problems will pale when you view them in the Light of My Presence. You can learn to be joyful in Me, your Savior, even in the midst of adverse circumstances. Rely on Me, your Strength."

Exodus 3:14; Habakkauk 3:17-19

"I am with you. These four words are like a safety net, protecting you from falling into despair. Because you are human, you will always have ups and downs in your life experience. But the promise of My Presence limits how far down you can go. Sometimes you may feel as if you are in a free fall, when people or things you had counted on let you down. Yet as soon as you remember that I am with you, your perspective changes radically. Instead of bemoaning your circumstances, you can look to Me for help. You recall that not only I am with you, I am holding you by your right hand. I guide you with My counsel, and afterward I will take you into Glory. This is exactly the perspective you need: the reassurance of My Presence, and the glorious hope of heaven."

Zephaniah 3:17; Psalm 73:23-26

When I'm feeling down and out about my situation and turn to these words for hope and encouragement, I gain renewed strength knowing that I'm not alone in my fight. I also know that all of you are consistently sending me positive, energizing thoughts and prayers. I do feel them! They mean so much to me, so please keep them coming.

#PetzingStrong

FEB 21 2018

Pulmonary Test Results Are In

I met with Dr. Gollard this morning, before the start of my chemo infusion, for an overall review of how things are going and to get the results from my recent Pulmonary Function Test(PFT) that I had on February 8.

The good news is that surgery is still in the realm of consideration. The bad news is that there are some potential issues that have been exposed by the breathing test. First, it appears that I may have a mild case of emphysema or COPD, which Dr. Gollard believes might be coming from exposure to secondhand smoke over the years. Second, during the PFT, I did not respond at all to bronchial dilation medications. And third, apparently the oxygen/carbon dioxide gas exchange through my alveoli, the tiny air sacs of the lungs which allow for rapid gaseous exchange, is quite weak. Together these issues could become a bigger problem if my right lung is removed.

Since Dr. Gollard is not the expert in this area, he asked me to set up an appointment with Dr. Tavares, my pulmonologist, to go over the PFT results and get his opinion. I'll be meeting with him on March 1. I was impressed with Dr. Tavares the first time we met, so I'm sure he'll have some great insight to provide on this situation.

Ultimately, the decision of whether my next step should be having surgery or a radiation/chemo treatment combo, will be dependent on the PET scan results I get in mid-March and the collective opinion of my excellent group of doctors: Dr. Gollard (chemo), Dr. Dean (radiation), Dr. Tavares (pulmonary) and Dr. Mavroidis (thoracic surgeon), who I will be meeting for the first time next Monday, February 26.

It's a bit frustrating that there are no clear answers right now, but it's part of the process. Fortunately, I learned this from my neck cancer experience, so I know what to expect. Basically, we're dealing with a complex puzzle that has many pieces that need to come together to complete the picture. It takes time, so patience is a virtue and I have a lot of it! Poker certainly has helped me hone that ability.

As I write this journal entry, I'm comfortable in my chemo chair getting my 7-hour drip. Louise is dropping by in a minute to say "hi" on the way to her accountant, and Ardys will be here at 1:30pm to spend the afternoon with me. I have such great friends!

Yesterday I played in Day 1B of the $1600 No Limit Hold'em $1MM Guarantee poker tourney at the Venetian and after 12 hours of grueling competition, I found myself with 71400 chips and 60bb going into Day 2 tomorrow. I've been playing really well lately and hope that my run continues.

Finally, Chris comes tonight for a 5-day visit. I'll pick him up at the airport around midnight and can't wait to see him. We're going to see Diana Ross in concert at the Wynn on Friday night and likely will see a number of movies over the weekend. We'll definitely maximize our short time together.

FEB 23 2018

Don't Be Trapped by Self-Pity

Chris arrived yesterday morning after having his Dallas to Vegas connecting flight cancelled on Wednesday evening. Luckily, he hadn't left Grand Rapids yet, so he was able to go home, get a few hours of sleep, and fly out at 5:45am on Thursday through Chicago to avoid the freezing rain and bad weather in Dallas. I'm so glad he's here. He always boosts me up, especially when I'm feeling down.

Today I'm in a bit of a chemo fog.... slow moving, forgetful, not on top of things and generally out of it. This happens sometimes. I'm not in any pain. I just don't feel like myself.

Thankfully, it's Happy Hydration Friday! So, I'm in my usual chair at Dr. Gollard's receiving my "Fun Bag" drip of electrolytes, Pepcid, anti-nausea meds, magnesium, vitamins and steroids. I'll leave here feeling a lot better and ready to take on the weekend with much more energy. Tonight, Chris and I are going to see Diana Ross at the Wynn, so we're quite excited about that.

Over the past week or so I've been in a bit of a funk... feeling sorry for myself. I try hard to stay positive and not go there, but sometimes it's difficult and

I just can't help it. Today's daily devotion in *Jesus Calling* is so timely and clearly meant for me.

"Be on guard against the pit of self-pity. When you are weary or unwell, this demonic trap is the greatest danger you face. Don't even go near the edge of the pit. Its edges crumble easily, and before you know it, you are on the way down. It is ever so harder to get out of the pit than to keep a safe distance from it. That is why I tell you to be on guard.

There are several ways to protect yourself from self-pity. When you are occupied with praising and thanking Me, it is impossible to feel sorry for yourself. Also, the closer you live to Me, the more distance there is between you and the pit. Live in the Light of My Presence by fixing your eyes on Me. Then you will be able to run with endurance the race that is set before you, without stumbling or falling."

Psalm 89:15-16; Hebrews 12:1-2 (NASB)

I really needed to read this today. It's an important reminder for me, and all of us, that self-pity can be quite destructive. It serves no constructive purpose and only feeds our soul with unwanted negativity. We are better than this and must not fall into the trap. If we do, we'll continue to spiral downward and find ourselves in a worse place that will be so much harder to get out of.

I know that if I reach out to Him, he will continue to be there for me during my times of need. Don't be afraid to ask for His help. Stay close to Him.

FEB 26 2018

In the Black Hole

It has been great having Chris here since Thursday morning. Given my low energy level, we've been fairly low key but did manage to see the amazing Diana Ross in concert at the Encore on Friday night and a couple of movies over the weekend.

We thoroughly enjoyed our 90 minutes with Diana as she took us through 18 of her greatest hits and made four fabulous costume changes. The crowed loved her, too. She's so down to earth and still sounds and looks incredible. We definitely left on a high!

On Saturday, we saw the movie, Game Night with Jason Bateman and Rachael McAdams. It had very good reviews on Rotten Tomatoes, but I absolutely hated it! Chris was slightly entertained. It was so bad that I fell asleep during it out of boredom and pure silliness. I definitely would not recommend it. Chris would not pay full price to see it at the theater but would consider renting it. Honestly, don't waste your time on it.

Yesterday, we saw *Black Panther,* and both really liked it! At 2 hours+ in length, there was never a dull moment. The story, cinematography, music, costumes, and acting were excellent. The African setting really made it unique and different. Overall, it was very easy on the eyes and full of good energy. It's perfect for all ages and many positive messages flow from it. We give it two thumbs up!

On a more serious note, I met this morning with Dr. Mavroidis, the thoracic surgeon, referred to me by Dr. Gollard. I've been anxiously waiting for this appointment to see if lung surgery is a viable option for me.

Chris and I left my place at 8:15am and stopped at Dunkin' Donuts on the way, so Chris could get his morning coffee fix. He didn't like their Hazelnut blend. When we arrived at Dr. Mavroidis' office at 8:45am, I checked in with the receptionist and gave her the six pages of paperwork I had filled out at home, along with CD copies of various CT scans and chest x-rays that were requested. We waited 45 minutes before my name was called. I was hopeful that Dr. Mavroidis had been reviewing all of my information in preparation for meeting with us.

At about 9:45am, we met Dr. Mavroidis. Initially, he seemed a bit frenetic, disheveled, and not very well grounded in my case. He had reviewed my scans, but I still had to re-create my cancer and treatment history for him. Once we were all on the same page, I felt better.

What I liked about Dr. Mavroidis was his straightforward, "lay it out there," New Yorker style of communicating. I appreciated his "no holds barred" honesty. It was actually quite refreshing, although I wasn't happy with or expecting some of the things I heard.

The bottom line is that all of the cancerous and pre-cancerous lymph nodes that have been floating throughout the middle of my chest have to be eradicated in order for surgery to even be an option. This is the biggest concern right now versus the size of the large tumor in my right lung that we're trying to reduce with the chemo. Apparently, there is too much risk of the cancer spreading if I'm opened up and these contaminated nodes still exist. So, I have to hope and pray that after completing chemo #14 in mid-March, when I have my CT and PET scans, that I am clear and no longer considered "hot." This is the real deal breaker right now. Interestingly, Dr.

Mavroidis thought that my PFT results from the recent breathing tests I had looked good and he had no concerns there.

So, basically, I'm in that unfortunate situation again of being in a "black hole." No plans can officially be put in place because we don't have the full complement of information we need right now to make good, informed decisions. There's no reason to get a second or third opinion yet or further weigh one possible treatment option versus another (e.g. radiation/chemo combo vs. surgery followed by radiation) because there isn't enough data to work with until I get the next round of CT and PET scans. It's frustratingly a "wait and see" game. I want to move forward in making a plan but can't. So, I feel like I'm flailing around with no clear direction.

Dr. Mavroidis was very clear today that the only possible chance I have to be cured of lung cancer is via surgery. He said that a radiation/chemo treatment combo cannot remedy it. This came as a bit of a surprise, as I got the sense from Dr. Dean that I could be cured by a radiation/chemo treatment combo. Perhaps this was wishful thinking on my part, or I misinterpreted something Dr. Dean said?

I do vividly remember Dr. Dean saying that it's very rare for someone with Stage 3B lung cancer to have a pneumonectomy (full lung removal.) Apparently, twenty years ago, this was common practice. But not today for someone in my situation. Yet, Dr. Gollard and Dr. Mavroidis are both "thumbs up" for rolling the dice and moving forward with surgery, if I qualify for it, because of my age and good general health...and, of course, the chance to be cured.

This is where things get confusing, when one doctor says one thing, and another says something quite different. I faced a similar scenario when dealing with possible neck cancer treatment options and outcomes, so I'm not foreign to this. However, it's still quite frustrating and a bit disturbing. I'll certainly be working toward getting clarity on many things as we progress through the next few weeks.

Chris and I both asked Dr. Mavroidis many questions and he answered them to the best of his ability. As previously mentioned, there are still a lot of unknowns, so it was hard for him to be definitive. When questioned about getting additional opinions on my case, Dr. Mavroidis was very supportive of that concept. I told him that I had researched MD Anderson in Houston and that they were renowned for their lung cancer treatment and clinical trials. He agreed. He also recommended UCLA, as have two of my other doctors and a number of friends. Once I have my next set of CT and PET scan results, I plan on visiting both institutions to talk with their experts and see where they net out.

So, it's business as usual for the next few weeks. I'm back at chemo (#12) on Wednesday and hydration on Friday. Next week, I'll be meeting with Dr. Tavares, my pulmonologist, to get him up to speed and obtain another opinion. He'll also have a lot more input and feedback on my recent PFT breathing test results. Dr. Mavroidis mentioned today that if my lung is removed, I may need to be on oxygen. I want to discuss that with Dr. Tavares and get his thoughts on my ability to have quality of life with only one lung.

There are just so many issues and variables involved with my situation. Sometimes it's so overwhelming that I just want to scream and stop the madness. However, I'm doing my best to not freak out, keep a level head, and remain calm and positive. It's not always easy, but I know it's important.

There is nothing I can change or do about what has happened. It is what it is. I have to trust that my Higher Power and angels will guide and help me move in the right direction with good decision making and continue to support and protect me through the remainder of my chemo treatments and beyond. I know have a long road ahead of me. I can do this!

#PetzingStrong

FEB 28 2018

Don't Worry, Be Happy!?

I arrived 15 minutes early at Dr. Gollard's office today for my chemotherapy drip. His practice used to be part of Nevada Cancer Specialists, but they were recently acquired by a much larger organization, OptumCare Cancer Care. In fact, they finally removed the "Nevada School of Medicine" sign off the office building and changed it accordingly.

When I walked off the elevator this morning, there were orange and white balloons everywhere, along with the entire reception and office staff wearing orange t-shirts and fun, feathery orange headbands. Of course, I inquired about what was going on and Ronnie excitedly said, "It's Optum Day!" I asked why I didn't get the memo and what's in it for me? They laughed and indicated it's an Employee Appreciation Day and that they got bagels. I just love the staff here! They are so helpful, caring, and nice.

When the chemo team was ready for me, Ronnie sent me back to the drip room. I always sit in the same cubicle and recliner at the end of the room. It's "reserved" for me, since I'm a regular.

Today is chemo #12 of 14.

It's hard to believe that I've been coming here for chemo and hydration treatments since October 2017 and still have three weeks to go. By the end of March/early April, I should have my next round of CT and PET scan results, so that decisions on next steps can be made. I'm really anxious to get there and tired of waiting. I've been so patient for so long, but it's becoming more and more difficult. Unfortunately, I have no control over the situation, so I have to continue to go with the flow.

I had a heart to heart with Radka this morning. I told her that I was a little disturbed and confused by my meeting with Dr. Mavroidis on Monday, and have been having trouble processing some of the information Chris and I heard, which appeared to be contradictory to what some of my other doctors have previously told me. I've been in my head a bit a lot lately, and asked Radka if she could schedule an appointment for me with the counselor, Kathy, who is on staff here. She agreed that was a good idea and also wants me to chat with Dr. Gollard about how I'm feeling. It's really hard not having someone by my side on a regular basis to share my innermost concerns, feelings and issues. So, I think it's time to reach out for help.

Louise will be stopping by around 1pm-1:30pm to hang with me this afternoon.

It's always nice to have one of "my girls" visit. It makes the time go by so much faster. I'm so proud of Louise. She just won a WSOP Circuit ring by placing first in a $365 No Limit Hold'em poker tourney at the Rio last week. It's a big achievement in the world of poker, which I have yet to realize. I'm so happy for her!

This week has been a bit of an emotional struggle for me. Ironically, yesterday's daily devotion from "Jesus Calling" was a good reminder of how I need not worry so much because He is watching over and protecting me. I'd like to end my journal entry today by sharing it with you:

"Keep your eyes on Me! Waves of adversity are washing over you, and you feel tempted to give up. As your circumstances consume more and more of your attention, you are losing sight of Me. Yet I am with you always, holding you by your right hand. I am fully aware of your situation, and I will not allow you to be tempted beyond what you are able to bear.

Your gravest danger is worrying about tomorrow. If you try to carry tomorrow's burdens today, you will stagger under the load and eventually fall flat. You must discipline yourself to live within the boundaries of today. It is in the present moment that I will walk close to you, helping you carry your burdens. Keep your focus on My Presence in the present."

Psalm 73:23; 1 Corinthians 10:13

MAR 1 2018

Thank You, Earl!

I awoke at 5:15am with a really bad case of indigestion and haven't been able to get back to sleep. Plus, the steroids from yesterday's chemo have me wired. Even though I didn't go to bed until 1am and only got 4+ hours of sleep, I'm still wide awake so I'll use the extra time this morning to write a journal entry.

Chemo went well. I was only there for six hours and slept for 2 1/2 hours of it. When Louise arrived at 1pm, I was sleeping like a baby and didn't wake up until 1:50pm. Louise was worried that I might be awakened by the gentleman's phone that kept ringing in the room next to me, but I was out like a light. She laughed when I sat up and saw the long vertical sleep streak on the left side of my face caused by my sleeping hard on the pillow.

There was black coffee and chocolate covered Oreos waiting for me! Perfect.

An interesting event happened while we were chatting. The gentlemen from the next room emerged and stopped by to say "hello." His name was Earl. We learned that he is 74 and has Stage 4 metastatic cancer that has spread throughout his entire body. He also is a patient of Dr. Gollard's and comes three times every week for hydration. Earl has had a number of surgeries, including removal of part of his lung, and was given 4 to 8 months to live a year and half or so ago. You would never know how sick Earl is. He looks great, has amazing energy, walks with a pep in his step, and exudes a very positive attitude! Earl was a breath of fresh air.

We talked a little about my situation and how I was feeling frustrated after my Monday meeting with Dr. Mavroidis, the thoracic surgeon. Earl asked if I had heard of the Fiekes family of surgeons. Apparently, Randall did his lung surgery and he was very impressed by him. Louise did a Google search to check him out and up came Randall's wife, Quinn, who is also a thoracic surgeon and was listed as a top surgeon by US News and World Report. We took down the information so I could share it with Dr. Gollard in our next meeting.

Earl was my divine intervention yesterday. He was meant to chat with us and provide me with some much-needed hope, inspiration, and new direction regarding my choice of a thoracic surgeon. Ironically, after he headed on his way, Radka, my chemo nurse, came by. I had asked her earlier in the day if I could possibly see Dr. Gollard and/or Kathy, the counselor, to discuss some of the concerns that were weighing heavily on me. It was my lucky day. Radka was able to squeeze me into Dr. Gollard's schedule at that very moment.

Sometimes it amazes me how things just come together when you least expect it. Radka detached me from my chemo drip and Louise and I headed to Room #5. I was glad she was there because I wanted her to hear what Dr. Gollard had to say, too. I think it's important that those friends closest to me (Chris, Louise, Ardys and Jackie) hear what I hear, so we're all on the same page and can together discuss and evaluate the information were given. It's also a good dose of reality for them because they're all trying so hard to be supportive and keep me positive, but sometimes the news isn't good and I don't want them to think I'm over-dramatizing it.

When Dr. Gollard arrived, I gave him the top line notes and outlined my concerns and issues from my Monday meeting with Dr. Mavroidis. I asked for clarity on Dr. Mavroidis' statement that "ONLY surgery could possibly cure me," while Dr. Dean, my radiation oncologist, had told me that "a combination of daily radiation for 33 days combined with weekly chemo for seven weeks and a follow-up regimen could possibly do the same." Dr. Gollard was a bit surprised by Dr. Mavroidis position and indicated that he did not agree. However, he did concur with Dr. Mavroidis point of view that if the cancerous lymph nodes in my chest area are not eradicated, that surgery will not be an option for me.

I told Dr. Gollard that if surgery does become an option, I would like someone other than Dr. Mavroidis to do it. Chris and I had not gotten a "warm fuzzy feeling" or the confidence level necessary from him to be the one to open me up and remove my entire right lung during an extreme surgery. I mentioned the conversation Louise and I had just had with Earl and asked Dr. Gollard about the Fiekes'. Apparently, Randall has retired, but his wife, Quinn, is still active. He reacted favorably and is setting up a referral for me to meet with her. We also discussed my getting a second and third opinion from UCLA and MDAnderson in Houston and Dr. Gollard is supportive of that, too.

Lastly, I put Dr. Gollard on the spot and asked him to tell me his thoughts on my cure rate potential. Because I'm responding well to the chemo program and continue to have a positive attitude (most of the time), he put me at 50/50. This is a much better statistic than Chris and I received from Dr. Mavroidis, even after going through surgical removal of my right lung. So, I'm feeling a little better about possible outcomes than I did earlier this week.

Dr. Gollard ended our session indicating that we will finish the two remaining chemo treatments and then do a series of CT and PET scans to see where we stand. Additionally, I'm meeting this morning with Dr. Tavares, my pulmonologist, to bring him up to date and review the results of my PFT breathing tests. It will be interesting to obtain another opinion and hear what he has to add to the conversation.

After leaving Dr. Gollard's office, Louise and I went to the Peppermill Restaurant and Lounge, a Vegas institution, to have a late lunch/early dinner as I'm always starving after chemo. We then went over to the Wynn to play the $300 NLH Sattie event, which was a qualifier for the $1600 NLH Main Event that starts today. Out of 108 players, 20 would win their $1600 seat. Unfortunately, I finished in 39th, but Louise made the top 20 and won her seat. She's on fire lately, which is great to see!

So, all in all, it was a good day yesterday! I'm back on track with my attitude and will continue with business as usual.

#PetzingStrong

MAR 2 2018

Better than Expected PFT Results!

It's Happy Hydration Friday! I'm getting my 90 minute "Fun Bags" drip, which should help keep me energized and feeling well over the weekend until about Sunday evening when I'll start to fade a bit. Hydration has been such a "life saver" for me. I rarely feel nauseous, achy, or really sick because of the magic it provides! It picks me up when I'm feeling down and keeps me going.

Yesterday morning I had an awesome appointment with Dr. Tavares. He spent a full hour with me providing his observations and insights into my situation. We started with the results of the Pulmonary Function Test (PFT) I had a few weeks ago. I was a little nervous about what I might hear based on some of Dr. Gollard's previous feedback on the results, but Dr. Tavares reassured me that I passed with "flying colors."

The key measure he looked at was the FEV1. It's an indicator of the strength my current lung capacity/breathing power and whether I'd have enough left to function well if my right lung were to be removed. The minimum acceptable score is a 2.0 and I got a 3.96! This means that he supports me being a surgery candidate if the chemotherapy treatments eliminate the floating cancerous nodes in the middle of my chest and continue to reduce the size of the large tumor in my right lung. He felt very confident that I should do well with only one lung and definitely prefers the surgery option over the alternative of a radiation/chemo combo. He also agreed with Dr. Gollard that either approach could potentially cure me.

What was most encouraging to me is that Dr. Tavares has no selfish reason to "push" for either the surgery or radiation/chemo option as my next step. His objectivity was much needed and appreciated. He felt good about Dr. Quinn Fiekes, the new thoracic surgeon I'm going to meet with in the next week or so, and also was a big proponent of me getting a second, third and maybe even a fourth opinion from MDAnderson in Houston, UCLA and the Mayo Clinic in Phoenix (in that order.). He was very familiar with MDAnderson's expertise in lung cancer treatment and their clinical studies with Stage 3B lung cancer patients like me and gave them a big "thumbs up."

I left Dr. Tavares' office feeling so much better. Surgery is still on the table as a viable option right now. I just need to get through two more chemo treatments. My last one will be on March 21. Then my CT and PET scans will likely be scheduled for the following week, so we should know where I stand by early April. I will continue to be patient, go with the flow, and do my best to stay positive and hopeful.

There is a *Jesus Calling* daily devotion from February 3 that I keep referring back to because it gives me strength when I'm feeling "up against the wall."

"I am with you and for you. You face nothing alone--nothing! When you feel anxious, know that you are focusing on the visible world and leaving Me out of the picture. The remedy is simple: Fix your eyes not on what is seen, but on what is unseen. Verbalize your trust in Me, the Living One who sees you always. I will get you safely through this day and all your days. But you can find Me only in the present. Each day is a precious gift from My Father. How ridiculous to grasp for future gifts when today's is set before you! Receive today's gift gratefully, unwrapping it tenderly and delving into its depths. As you savor this gift, you find Me."

Romans 8:31; 2 Corinthians 4:18; Genesis 16:13-14 (AMP)

MAR 6 2018

I Know I'm Not Alone

I've taken a few days off from posting a journal entry because I needed a bit of a break. Plus, I really haven't had much to say, which I know may come as a big surprise to many of you!

This week I don't have a chemo treatment, so I added a hydration session today. I'm really glad I did that because I'm really dragging and there's no way I could wait until Friday for it. I've been experiencing a dry cough for the past few days, along with the onset of dizzy spells. Radka told me that "there's something going around in the valley" and that three other patients here getting treatment today also have the cough. It looks like the dizzy spells are a common side effect from chemo, so Radka did a blood test this morning. My red blood cell count is down a bit, which explains that situation. Hopefully, the hydration treatment will help address both of these issues.

My friend from Canada, also named Louise (nickname Bling), is here visiting and staying with me. We had a good conversation over coffee this morning about my battle with the Big C and how I'm holding up. She, along with Ardys, both said that they don't think they'd be handling it as calmly as I am and that they'd be freaking out. I completely understand how that could be. Being told you have cancer is quite a shock and then emotionally dealing with that information is quite difficult.

I know this may sound odd, but because this is my second time around, I've actually been quite calm and even keeled. I've learned to embrace my "sick" status and go with the flow. Clearly, there's nothing I can do to go back and change it, so why look back at the past? There's no reason to feel sorry for myself and dwell on the "bad beats" I've received because that will only bring me down. I need to stay as positive as possible and continue to believe that I can beat this bastard! Realistically, the odds are not in my favor, but I've conquered them before in life and in poker, and there's no reason to believe that I can't do it again, right!?

Sometimes I do feel alone in my battle because I spend so much time by myself. I try not to get too much in my head during those lonely times and think I've done a good job managing my emotions. Of course, my anti-depressant meds have made a huge difference with this, too! They truly have been a life savior, keeping me balanced and hopeful.

I also know that the power of prayer has had a hugely positive impact on me. My angels in heaven and on this good earth are continually watching over me, as is my Higher Power. They are doing their best to protect, guide and support me. Today's daily devotion from Sara Young's, Jesus Calling, is so relevant here:

"Continue on this path with Me, enjoying My Presence even in adversity. I am always before you, as well as alongside you. See Me beckoning to you: Come! Follow Me. The One who goes ahead of you, opening up the way, is the same One who stays close and never lets go of your hand. I am not subject to limitations of time or space. I am everywhere at every time, ceaselessly working on your behalf. That's why your best efforts are trusting Me and living close to Me."

Hebrews 7:25; Psalm 37: 3-4

MAR 10 2018

Don't Wait to Make Your Dreams Happen

Live your dreams now! Please don't wait. I know this sounds cliché, but you just don't know if you're going to be around tomorrow. You could have a heart attack, die in a fatal accident, be shot, get run over by a bus, taxi or speeding car, fall and hit your head on the sidewalk or succumb to cancer. If you happen to be lucky enough to live, your life may be changed forever. Don't take it for granted. Live it fully every day and make those dreams become your realities as soon as you can.

I have always been a dreamer with big goals. When I was a kid, I thought the coolest thing ever would be to own a bakery. My Mom would take my brother and me to Rita's Bakery on Sunday's to get these huge, yummy chocolate chip cookies. I can still see, smell and taste them. They will forever be embedded in my mind. So, I taught myself to bake and often made cakes and brownies from mixes. It was a start. I knew I had to practice being perfect.

As I got older, I realized that a bakery might not be a very profitable business venture, so I set my sights on being strong academically and learning as much I could from being involved in a myriad of extracurricular activities. I was a sponge and floated through high school without trying very hard. I was bored most of the time and told my Mom I wanted to skip my Junior year and go right on to college. Unfortunately, that wasn't an option, so I had to endure my Senior year.

My guidance counselor saw my potential and pushed me to be the best I could be. I played varsity basketball, was President of my church youth group, rang handbells in a choir, performed in school plays and talent shows, and volunteered in the community. I graduated high school as Valedictorian, won some scholarships, and went on to Cornell University where I majored in Business Management & Marketing with a minor in Communications and Spanish. Now my dream was to graduate with academic distinction, get recruited by a major company, land a great job, and make a lot of money!

Right out of college, I earned $20,500 (1982) working for General Foods in consumer promotion, when most of my peers were getting offers at $10-12K. I was on my way. Now I started to dream even bigger and was hopeful to have my own business one day. I knew I had a long way to go. I'd have to gain a lot of experience and earn my credentials to be viable. There was no stopping me. I was up for the challenge!

I fast tracked through General Foods and Nestle. At the age of 28 (1988), only seven years out of college, I found myself as a Sr. Vice President of Marketing Services at Citicorp POS Information Services in Stamford, CT making $100K/year and part of a "think tank" for developing a national consumer purchase behavior database. I couldn't believe I had landed this amazing opportunity. It was crazy. I was the youngest Sr. VP in our division and headed up a department of ten folks, each of which I individually hired. It was an amazing job and I was on Cloud 9. I had to pinch myself. I had so much responsibility at such a young age and didn't even have a Master's degree. Unfortunately, after 2 1/2 years, our division had made many mistakes and we failed big time. We were given very lucrative severance packages and I needed to find something else. I wasn't going to let this setback stop my dreams!

I decided to round myself out and, in 1991, took a strategic planning Sr VP job at a large New York City promotion marketing agency. Having been a client for so many years, I would bring a lot of value to the agency side. My dream was still to have my own business one day and this would be an awesome steppingstone for doing so. Ultimately, I was sent out to Chicago to start a regional office.

Ahhhhhh... now I'd be running my "own" business with their money. What a great way to learn with no real skin in the game. And it was!

Fast forward to 1994 and I now had realized my dream of having my own business at the age of 34! It was called The Synergy Group, Inc and we were an integrated marketing communications agency in Chicago serving clients like Kraft, Helene Curtis, IBM and others. Five years later, I merged my company with another agency, became the Chief Marketing Officer of the joint operation, commuted to Connecticut from Chicago every week, and hated every minute of it! I felt a bit derailed. It was time to move on after two years of pure hell. My new dream was now to travel internationally for business and see the world!

I broke loose and started another company, Exceleration Training & Consulting. We trained marketers in marketing strategy and integrated communications. Kraft Foods was my largest account and we trained all of their domestic marketers. Kraft's Sr. VP of domestic marketing became the head of international marketing and wanted our training program implemented WORLDWIDE!

OMG...My new dream was going to become a reality, too!

For over 15+ years, I and my team traveled the world conducting training and consulting for not only Kraft, but also IBM, Heineken, and other major corporations. It was an awesome and lucrative gig, but not without its sacrifices.

Every day I was under pressure to be "on" and "perform" in a foreign country where I had to learn their culture, work on bonding with the class participants, and make sure I was getting the job done effectively so I'd be invited back and/or referred on to another international company for more work. And there were many countries I went to that weren't Pro-American, like Russia, Romania, Ukraine and China to name a few. Many of the European countries, especially the UK, France and Germany, weren't especially fond of an American teaching them how to be better marketers either, but they came around. For those 15+ years, I was physically in the United States only 50% of the time. I was always traveling, BUT I was seeing and experiencing the world! In fact, I've now been to over 90 countries. This dream became a reality, too, but I had to work very hard at it.

As I turned 50, I had burned out from the travel and constant pressures of the job. I had made enough money to retire but had too much energy to not be doing something challenging. I couldn't picture myself sitting around doing nothing. So, I closed down Exceleration Training & Consulting in 2010, and bought a restaurant/martini lounge out of foreclosure in a seasonal resort area of southwest Michigan called Saugatuck/Douglas. Think of it as the Provincetown of the Midwest, with a vibrant art community, gorgeous beaches, and a significant gay population.

This became my new dream...and ultimately the biggest challenge of my life! I would take this sad, cold building that had been sitting unoccupied for over six years and make it into something incredible! It would be my "baby." I'd nourish, care for it and make it grow into something substantial and meaningful. Well....it didn't quite work out that way. Let's just say I was overzealous and quite naive. I had never worked in the restaurant business and honestly had no idea what I was getting into, BUT I learned a lot! The name of my restaurant was Zing Eat Drink and we were a steak and seafood house, with 4 stars on Trip Advisor and 3 1/2 stars on Yelp.

Everything you hear about how difficult restaurant ownership is is absolutely true! It's even worse in a seasonal resort area where you really only have three months to make it work because the off-season weather is so brutal, and tourism is way down. I could write another book detailing all of the craziness that happened to me during these five years. It was ridiculous. BUT, the one thing I do know is that I made a difference for the community and for the 50+ employees I had each Summer. Most of these folks were living paycheck to paycheck and barely making ends meet. I kept them employed and they had a "home" with a family of people who cared about them. We were a good team. I just couldn't make it a profitable venture no matter how hard I tried.

So after battling neck cancer from August 2014 to April 2015 and surviving a commercial plane crash in March 2015, I decided it was time to pursue my next dream while I still could! I would move to Vegas and work at becoming a professional poker player. I had been playing tournament poker part-time for seven years, traveling to Vegas about six times a year to get my fix and was doing quite well at it. Like anything, I knew that if I devoted myself 150% to working on my game, I could be really good and maybe even make some decent money doing it.

So, I officially retired, packed myself up and moved with Zing & Zang here to Vegas in January 2016. Unfortunately, dreams do come with sacrifices. It was a very hard decision leaving Chris in Michigan, but pursuing this dream was something I needed to do while I still could. And, as you've seen, Chris and I have been able to manage through it fairly well.

The minute I got to Vegas, I threw myself into the poker world. I had an amazing first year playing full time. In 2016, I grossed over $238K and was ranked 2nd in the world in number of major tournament cashes out of over 500K players. In 2017, I was ranked 31st in tournament cashes and grossed over $135K. I've already started off this year strongly and am currently ranked 20th in tournament cashes. However, what I'm most proud of is that after only playing full time for 2+ years, my overall GPI Index rank is 700th (out of 500K) in the world. And, I'm currently in 93rd place for 2018 Player of the Year. How crazy is that?! YES, Dreams Do Come True! But you have to work very hard to make them a reality.

Well, I'm sad to say that with dreams come nightmares. And, as you know, I've been living my second cancer nightmare since October of last year. Life has a way of balancing things out, doesn't it? As amazing and blessed as my life has been, it doesn't come without significant threats to it. So now my new dream is to conquer THIS cancer nightmare! I am not going to let fucking Stage 3B Lung Cancer take me down before it's really my time to go. I have so much more to do and give to others. I truly believe that my Higher Power is continuing to test me. He has a purpose for me when I come out clean from this, but I'm just not quite sure what it is yet. I will continue to fight and win. That's all there is to it because I have more dreams to make a reality.

Just like me, you can make your dreams become a reality too, whatever they may be! You'll have to make them your priority though and work very hard to achieve them. They won't come easy, however they are absolutely attainable IF YOU REALLY WANT THEM and you implement a well thought out action plan. Unfortunately, you just can't "wish" for your dreams to come true. YOU have to make them happen! Time is fleeting, so don't wait. The time is NOW, while you're here, healthy and can!

#PetzingStrong

MAR 10 2018

Finally Got Out of Town!

I have been absolutely stir-crazy since last October when I started my series of chemo treatments. Given that I have doctors' appointments and/or infusions at least twice a week, it has been really tough for me to get out of Vegas.

Prior to being diagnosed, I had been traveling a lot to play poker and now I'm really missing doing that. I was lamenting about this to Ardys the other day and she said, "Well, let's do a road trip and get out of town. I'm game!"

So this morning we hopped on a Jet Blue flight (only $97 RT) from Vegas to Long Beach, CA (instead of driving 4 hours each way) and took an Uber to The Bicycle Hotel & Casino, where the LA WSOP Circuit event is being held.

It felt so good to pack my stuff and get Zing & Zang settled before leaving. They looked at me strangely when I pulled out my duffle bag and started to fill their dry food canister. I'm sure they were wondering, "What's up here? Where's dad going?"

Lynnore will look in on the boys until I return on Tuesday afternoon in time for chemo on Wednesday. They love when Aunt Lynnore comes to visit because she always brings treats or toys.

Ardys and I got to The Bike around 10:30am, but our room wasn't ready, so we had coffee at the Starbucks in the hotel. Finally, at 11:20am, we got into our room, unpacked and got ready for the $230 NLH noon satellite, which was a qualifier for tomorrow's $1675 NLH Main Event. Unfortunately, neither of us made it through, so we'll buy straight in tomorrow. The combined field of today's players plus tomorrow's will be huge, so there should be quite a significant prize pool approaching $1MM! Hopefully, we'll both do well and advance to Day 2 on Monday.

I was really tired after I busted the satellite, so I went upstairs and took a two-hour nap. I think all of the poison in my body, from the 12 chemo treatments I've had so far, is starting to take its toll on me. It's really odd. I can be wide awake one minute and then twenty minutes later feel like I need to get in bed and sleep.

When I awoke from my nap at 4pm, I had renewed energy, so I decided to play the $1100 NLH Survivor tourney, where the top 10% of the field each wins $10K. As has been standard for the past few days, I had crappy cards for most of the tourney and was constantly folding. Then, when I did have a decent hand and raised or called with it, I'd completely miss the flop. Sadly, after four hours of play, my better starting hand of AK lost to AQ all-in pre flop when a QJ4 hit the flop and no K or T came out for me on the turn or river. Great, another suck out! I finished in 35th of 67 players.

Tomorrow's another day and we're both due for a good run, so here's hoping for a successful outing! I think we're going to start the morning off with breakfast in our individual beds, so that should be fun and a great way to kick off the day.

MAR 14 2018

Fun Weekend Away

Ardys and I had such a fun weekend in LA at The Bicycle Casino Hotel. I don't think I'll ever do the 4+ hour drive again because flying was such a breeze. Although we weren't "winners" at the poker tables, we still managed to enjoy ourselves. Both of us caught up on much needed sleep and were glad to just have the chance to get out of Vegas for a while. We even treated ourselves to "breakfast in bed" (separate beds) on Sunday morning. We were perfect roommates!

I've been so freaking tired lately. Even with a solid nine or ten hours of sleep, I find myself needing to nap for 2 to 2 1/2 hours each day. My body just goes into "check out" mode and I can barely function. It's very frustrating, because I often I feel pretty good right up to the time when my body decides to short circuit. I've learned to deal with it as it's part of the process.

Ardys gave me some interesting feedback yesterday and said that my body is exuding a metallic, medicinal smell. No one has mentioned it previously, so I'm going to bring it up with Dr. Gollard in my appointment with him today. Ardys thought that maybe a chlorophyll pill would help with the issue. I guess since it has become a part of me, I don't smell it. But clearly I need to take care of the situation.

As I write this journal entry, I'm in my "Lazy Boy" chair getting chemo infusion #13 of 14. Next week will hopefully be my last one. I'm praying that these last six sessions will have further shrunk the large tumor in my right lung and eradicated the cancerous lymph nodes running up and down the middle of my chest. The PET scan I'll have in late March will give us a clear picture and determine next steps. I'm still hoping for surgery to remove my lung and am looking forward to meeting a new thoracic surgeon in the next week or so. Hopefully, I'll like her way better than the last one I met with.

My bestie, Jackie, will be coming by this afternoon to keep me company after my Benadryl nap. We haven't had a chance to spend good quality time together in a while, so I'm looking forward to catching up with her. She has been so busy with work and family stuff that she hasn't had a minute to breathe. Depending on how I'm feeling late this afternoon, we may have an early dinner with her husband, Mike.

Lastly, on a really positive note, it looks like I FINALLY sold my restaurant/ martini lounge that has been on the market for the past 2 1/2 years in Douglas, MI. It has been a big, black cloud hanging over my head that I just needed to have disappear. The commercial real estate market is so bad in the tiny, seasonal resort towns of Saugatuck/Douglas, that I had to go the route of an online auction to get rid of it. I got just enough to cover my mortgage nut, so hopefully I'll be free and clear from it by mid-April. It has been a never-ending stress point and I pray that I'm done with it for good. AMEN!

MAR 16 2018

I'm Officially Anemic

It's Happy Hydration Friday...again! I'm back in my chair getting my "Fun Bag" drip, but today I found out that I'm officially anemic. I have what's called Iron Deficiency Anemia, a condition in which the body does not have enough healthy red blood cells. Without iron, blood cannot carry oxygen effectively to tissues and organs in the body, which, for me, has resulted in ongoing tiredness, fatigue from performing simple household tasks, concentration problems, shortness of breath, and light-headedness/dizziness when I stand up after sitting for a while or get out of bed.

I started taking an iron pill about a month ago and it helped a bit, but not enough. A special iron test was done on this past Wednesday's blood draw and the anemia showed up. It's a 2 out of 5, so not too bad, but it does need to be addressed. So hopefully today, I'll also get the first of two iron infusions with a drug called, Injectafer. It costs $800 a bag, so Dr. Gollard's office is negotiating with the insurance company right now as I write this journal entry.

Injectafer is an intravenous (IV) form of iron that is used to treat iron deficiency anemia in adult patients who have had unsatisfactory response to oral iron. That's me! Injectafer delivers a high dose of iron in a short period of time, only 15 minutes, and in as few as two infusions 7 days apart. The side effects don't look bad at all, so I'm game to get this going. I think it will help me feel a lot better and give me the energy I've been missing.

I was also successful this week in getting an appointment set up with a new thoracic surgeon, Dr Quinn Fickes, who has come highly recommended to me. It's not until April 11, but that should work out just fine because I should have my updated scan results by then. So the pieces of the puzzle are starting to come together.

I'm continuing my work on staying positive, optimistic, and hopeful for being able to qualify for surgery. I pray every day that the chemo treatments are doing their job at killing off the cancerous nodes in my chest and reducing the tumor in my right lung to a manageable and operable size. We'll know where I stand shortly. Please keep your prayers and good thoughts coming on this! I need every one of them.

I remain #PetzingStrong!

MAR 18 2018

Be Kind...Always!

After my hydration treatment and iron infusion on Friday morning, I went to CVS to pick up a prescription and ran into Albertson's to get a few groceries. While I was checking out, I witnessed a very sad situation.

The lady in front of me had purchased a dozen or so items, almost all on sale. Her bill came to $10.20. She was shocked at how "high" her bill was and asked the cashier to re-check it, which she gladly did.

It was correct.

The lady opened her wallet and only had a $10 bill. She told the cashier that she'd need to forego something and chose a $1 can of dog food, instead of one of her other food items. I was kind of stunned by what was happening, but it really bothered me that she chose the dog food.

I couldn't help myself. "I'll buy the dog food!" I said and handed over a dollar bill to the cashier. The lady turned to me, smiled and said, "Thank you so much!" with a little tear in her eye.

I nodded and told her it was my pleasure.

Now I'm mad at myself for not buying all her groceries for only $10! It would have been such an easy thing to do. I felt good about helping out this woman but wish I had done more. So many people are less fortunate than ourselves and are likely fighting a battle we know nothing about. That's why it's so important to be kind...always! I think deep down we all want to do what we can to help others in need. Please look for those opportunities and pay it forward.

After going home and unpacking my groceries, I played a noon poker tournament at the Venetian and busted out quickly in three back to back ridiculous hands. Frustrated, I went home and took a nap. When I woke up at 5:30pm, I was wired. The "Fun Bag" steroids from hydration had kicked in and I was ready to rock and roll.

There was a 7pm $300 NLH Rebuy tourney at the Venetian, so I decided to go play it. Do you believe in karma? I do. After playing all night from 7pm to 4:30am Saturday morning, the final ten of us decided to do a chip chop. I finished in 4th of 89 players and won $3388! All I could think about was the lady I gave $1 to at Albertson's earlier in the day. In some odd way, I think my winning was an extension of her "thank you" for my simple gesture of caring.

Since last evening, I haven't felt well. I had chills all night and was nauseous this morning. I didn't get out of bed until 11am and barely moved off the couch all day. The NCAA "March Madness" basketball games were so entertaining to watch and kept my mind off how bad I was feeling. It's 9pm now and thankfully I'm doing much better tonight. Hopefully, I'll have a good day tomorrow!

MAR 21 2018

Hopefully My Final Chemo

It has been three days since I've posted a journal entry. There are two reasons for this:

1) I have felt absolutely horrible. 2) I really haven't had anything to say.

It's quite clear that all of the poison is finally wreaking havoc on me. Since Sunday, I've barely moved off of the couch or out of my bed, except to drag myself to breakfast with friends on two occasions and to try to play in a poker tournament on Monday, which was a bad idea. I've had absolutely zero energy and no desire to do anything. I have never been soooooo tired day after day, even with getting 9 to 11 hours of sleep a night and at least a 2-hour nap during the day. It's so frustrating, because it's so not me.

With this ongoing lethargy, I've been a bit depressed and haven't felt like writing either. I'm feeling stuck, bored and deflated. It's like I'm stuck in a plane's holding pattern as it circles around the airport where it's supposed to land. I keep waiting for air traffic control to give the thumbs up so we can begin our approach for landing. Honestly, I'm really tired of waiting and wondering if all of these chemo treatments have done their job to eradicate the cancerous lymph nodes running up and down the middle of my chest and to reduce the large tumor in my right lung enough to qualify for surgery.

I've been in this "black hole" before when I had neck cancer, so I know the feeling but it's still not easy to handle.

The good news is that today is hopefully my FINAL chemo (#14 of 14). Radka is on a well-deserved vacation in the Dominican Republic, so Marianne is taking care of me. She's awesome, too! The chemo treatment, which includes an energizing set of steroids, should give me a "pick me up" for the next couple of days. I'm very hopeful for that, especially because my Dad & Cheryl are coming from Florida tomorrow for a 5-day visit and I really don't want to be sleeping and feeling "blah" the whole time they're here.

Fingers crossed! I'm excited to see them and it will be nice to have family in town.

On another positive note, Christine, Dr. Gollard's insurance admin, was able to convince the insurance company today that I must have a PET scan next week to see where I'm at so we can quickly move forward on the decision-making regarding my next steps. Generally, there needs to be three months between scans in order for insurance to cover them but, given my "special circumstance," they are making an exception. Hopefully, I'll be able to have the PET scan next week and have the results available for my April 11 consult with Dr. Quinn Fickes.

I'm about to get my Benadryl injection, so nap time will be coming on shortly. Ardys is coming by around 1:30-2pm to hang with me this afternoon. It's always nice to have a friend to chat with for the last couple hours of chemo. It makes the time pass so much faster.

Now that I've written this journal entry, I'm feeling much better emotionally. I think I just needed to vent and get things off my chest. Staying positive is so difficult sometimes, but I know how important it is to keep that mindset and will continue working hard to do so!

Staying #PetzingStrong!

MAR 23 2018

Happy Dad & Cheryl are Here!

Finally, after four days of feeling crappy, I felt really good yesterday! The timing couldn't have been better as Dad & Cheryl flew in from Florida for a much anticipated five-day visit. Their third attempt over the past few months was the charm, as both of them conquered their ailments and were able to make the trip this time! It's so great having them here and catching up. I have really missed seeing family.

Tonight, we're going to see WOW! at the Rio. It's a new Vegas-type variety show with singing, dancing, acrobatics and unusual acts, so we're looking forward to it. Then, tomorrow night, we'll be mesmerized by the magic of Mat Franco, the winner of America's Got Talent. Chris and I have seen his show and it's really good. I think Dad and Cheryl will enjoy it, too!

Thankfully, I'm in my chair now at Dr. Gollard's getting my hydration and iron infusions. I only have half of the energy I had yesterday, so these are much needed to help me get through the weekend. Today's iron infusion is the follow-up to the one I received last Friday. I'm told that the cumulative effect of both iron infusions won't kick-in for two or three weeks, at which point I should start feeling MUCH better. Apparently, it takes a while for the body to absorb, assimilate, and distribute the iron. Naively, I was expecting to feel "brand new" next week, so I'm a bit disappointed and will just have to wait.

Similarly, I continue to wait for my PET scan to be scheduled. Although I have received insurance authorization for it, the company doing it still hasn't called me to get it set up. Christine has really been pushing them hard. My fingers are crossed that they'll call soon, and I can have it done next week. I just want to keep things moving forward as I'm tired of being in limbo. Waiting is tough.

I earmarked a passage from Sarah Young's *Jesus Calling* that is helping me today. It's from

February 2 and states:

"I am renewing your mind. When your thoughts flow freely, they tend to move toward problems. Your focus gets snagged on a given problem, circling round and round it in attempts to gain mastery. Your energy is drained away from other matters through this negative focus. Worst of all, you lose sight of Me.

A renewed mind is Presence-focused. Train your mind to seek Me in every moment, every situation. Sometimes you can find Me in your surroundings: a lilting birdsong, a loved one's smile, golden sunlight. At other times, you must draw inward to find Me. I am always present in your spirit. Seek my face, speak to Me, and I will light up your mind."

Romans 12:2; Psalm 105:4

MAR 27 2018

Scared for My Life

I took Dad and Cheryl to the airport early this morning at 6am. We had such a nice visit! Although I was extremely tired during their stay, we did manage to do a lot. We saw two very entertaining shows (WOW! at The Rio and Mat Franco), had dinner out a few nights and enjoyed breakfast with my besties (Jackie, Ardys, Louise and Lynnore.) I'm really glad that Dad & Cheryl got to see where I live, meet my friends, and experience a bit of Vegas. It was a treat having them here with me.

I had a very disturbing and scary situation occur yesterday. After hanging with Dad and Cheryl in their room after breakfast, I decided to go pick up two prescriptions at my CVS a mile down the road. I parked close to the entrance, made my way to the pharmacy and got my cancer meds. On my way out, I was walking down the main aisle to the exit when an adorable, little black toddler came "running" at me, giggling all the way. I'm guessing he was close to 2 years old. I had a big smile on my face as he quickly waddled toward me. He was so darn cute!

It looked like the toddler might actually run into me, so I side stepped and he went on by. At that very moment, the toddler's big, muscular father came around the corner and was glaring at me.

He said, “Hey! You!” -- pointing at me-- “Did you just trip my son?”

I quickly retorted, “What? Of course not.”

He indignantly said, “Oh yes you did! I saw you trip him.”

I exclaimed, “Why would I trip your adorable son? I would never do something like that.”

Now he was in my face and screamed, “You’re a racist and a liar! You tripped my son.”

I was trying to maintain my composure and again reiterated, “I absolutely did not trip your son.”

Apparently, when I side stepped his son, he lost his balance and fell behind me as he passed by. He wasn’t crying or anything. I was really confused and was starting to get concerned because his dad was seething mad.

At this point, we were making a scene in the store as I moved toward the exit. Shoppers and workers were all watching us.

The father didn’t believe anything I said. He then yelled, “We’re taking this outside.”

I watched him go out the door and cross over to the parking lot where he leaned over and picked up a large stone the size of his palm.

He came running back into the store toward me and said, “I’m going to pound your head in with this.”

Now I was really scared. The store manager told the father to get out. I screamed, “Call the police!”

The father reluctantly left the store saying, “I’ll be waiting for you out here.”

Meanwhile, the mother of the toddler picked up her son, chuckled a bit and headed toward the pharmacy.

One of the cashiers got the police on the phone and reported the incident. They indicated that they would send a car right over. Thirty minutes later, I was still inside the CVS waiting for the cops, while he was still outside waiting for me. The cops never came.

Finally, one of the CVS cashiers -- an older, mature black woman -- said to me, "I know you didn't trip that little boy. I'll go talk to him and try to calm him down."

She went outside and chatted with the father for about ten minutes. I was anxious, not feeling well and concerned for my safety. Where the hell were the cops?

The cashier came back in the store and told me that she assuaged the father and that they were leaving. Thank God for her! I saw the family get in their car and drive off. I was relieved, but shaken and waited another five minutes before going out to my car. The cops still never came.

Honestly, I felt like I was in a bad episode of *The Twilight Zone*. It all just didn't make any sense. This guy was so full of anger and hatred, and just wanted to pick a fight with someone. I really think he intended to hurt me. It was the first time in my life that I feared for my safety and well-being.

I ran out to my car and drove home. This was not an experience I ever want to have again.

MAR 30 2018

Meaningful Devotions

After numerous tries and with much help from Kristina at Dr. Gollard's office, I was finally able to get my PET scan approved by insurance and scheduled for April 9. The timing is perfect as I have my appointment with the new thoracic surgeon on April 11 and a meeting with Dr. Gollard on April 12. My hope is that we'll have a plan coming together by the end of that week. I continue to pray that the chemo program I've been on for the past six months has worked by sufficiently shrinking the tumor in right lung and eradicating the cancerous lymph nodes in the middle of my chest. This will enable me to have lung surgery and I'm mentally prepared for it. If the chemo didn't 'work', I'll be looking at 35 days of daily radiation and seven more weeks of weekly chemo, which isn't sitting well with me right now. Been there. Done that. And don't want to do it again!

I received a sweet text yesterday from Elizabeth. She, too, reads Sarah Young's book of daily devotions and wanted to be sure that I saw the March 29 reading because it's so relevant to what I'm going through:

"Stop trying to work things out before their times have come. Accept the limitations of living one day at a time. When something comes to your attention, ask Me whether or not it's part of today's agenda. If it isn't, release it into My care and go on about today's duties. When you follow this practice, there will be a beautiful simplicity about your life: a time for everything, and everything in its time.

A life lived close to Me is not complicated or cluttered. When your focus is on My Presence, many things that once troubled you lose their power over you. Though the world around you is messy and confusing, remember that I have overcome the world. I have told you these things, so that in Me you may have Peace."

Ecclesiastes 3:1; John 16:33

I have worked so hard at trying to live in the present and not jumping ahead to plan for tomorrow. It's easier said than done, but does make life simpler when you can embrace what it offers in the given moment and not worry about the future.

Today's daily devotion from *Jesus Calling* is also meaningful to me:

"I am taking care of you. Trust Me at all times. Trust Me in all circumstances. Trust me with all your heart. When you are weary and everything seems to be going wrong, you can still utter these four words: "I trust you, Jesus." By doing so, you release matters into My control, and you fall back into the security of My everlasting arms.

Before you arise from your bed in the morning, I have already arranged the events of your day. Every day provides many opportunities for you to learn My ways and grow closer to Me. Signs of My Presence brighten even the dullest day when you have eyes that really see. Search for Me as for hidden treasure. I will be found by you."

Proverbs 3:5; Deuteronomy 33:27; Jeremiah 29: 13-14

I am putting my trust in him and believe that he will help make me well!

#PetzingStrong

APR 2 2018

Time for an Attitude Adjustment

I have to admit that I've been feeling really sorry for myself the past couple of weeks. Last week, I clearly hit bottom and on Friday, during hydration, I had a heart to heart with Radka and Marianne. Actually, it was more like a venting session for me. I have been so frustrated with how lethargic, tired, achy, unmotivated and depressed I've been. They listened intently as I told them that there's no way I can continue feeling like this every day.

It has been six months since I've felt "normal" and I don't like my "new normal" at all. Both of them reassured me that the physical way I'm feeling is totally expected, especially now that I've had fourteen 6 1/2 hour chemo drip sessions over the past six months. The 90+ hours of "poison" that has invaded my body has definitely taken a toll on it in a big way.

Radka and Marianne both reassured me that I'd start feeling better this week, since the chemo ended almost three weeks ago and the two iron infusions I had should start taking effect. I've also added iron and magnesium pills twice a day to my pill regimen, which should help with how I feel. So.... the good news is that yesterday I actually had enough energy to play in a poker tourney for 11 hours at the Venetian, where I cashed in 7th place of 79 players and won $1585 for a $400 entry! It was very exciting, as I felt almost human again.

I woke up early this morning to do a few things before heading to hydration. We decided last week that I would start doing hydration three days a week (vs. two), since I've been feeling so badly. I'm in the chair now as I write this journal entry and am pleased to say that I think Radka and Marianne were right! I feel 150% better than I did on Friday and Saturday. I got my energy back. This is a good sign!!

I really fell into a dark place last week that I didn't like. I always try so hard to stay positive and optimistic that all will work out for me, but sometimes the chemo cave I fall into just takes over. It messes with my mind, and negatively affects my attitude and demeanor. It's an ugly feeling, so that's when I reach out to my Higher Power and ask for his help, support and guidance. I know he wants what is best for me.

Coming into this week, I had already decided that I need a major attitude adjustment. So, I thought about all the things I have to be thankful for and it put into perspective how lucky I really am, even though I'm in the fight for my life with this horrific disease, called CANCER. This isn't a comprehensive list, but it does cover many of the things that keep me going:

* A small, but loving family who truly cares about me

* My boyfriend, Chris, who does what he can to be there for me, when he can

* A wonderful group of close friends (and good acquaintances), who are there to support and help me, as needed, and treat me like I'm part of their family

* A spectacular set of doctors and nurses, who are doing their absolute best to make sure I defeat the beast

* My angels on this great earth and those looking down at me from heaven, who are watching over and protecting me every day

* Poker, which has helped occupy my mind and time and given me a purpose to wake up each day and get out of my apartment versus staying in bed or on the couch and becoming a hermit

* Insurance coverage that is paying for most of my exorbitant and costly bills

* Waking up each day and being able to live my life fully, with some slight adjustments

* Being retired and not having to work or be concerned about earning an income while being in treatment

* My two amazing cats, Zing & Zang, who know that I'm sick and never leave my side when I'm home with them

* All of you, who regularly read my journal entries and provide me with hope and inspiration through your encouraging comments

Honestly, I have so much to be grateful for. I feel very blessed and need to remind myself of that, especially when I'm feeling down and out. It's so important to take a step back and inventory all the wonderful things we have going for us in our lives, even when it seems like "life" isn't going our way. Perhaps you'd like to try making your own list!?

#PetzingStrong

APR 4 2018

Feeling Human Again!

You've heard the expression many times, "I feel like a million dollars!". Well, I'm excited to say that "I feel like $750K!" After bottoming out last week and almost losing hope that I'd ever feel "normal" again, I started my upswing this past Sunday morning after not feeling so great on Saturday night. I was very surprised to wake up to renewed energy and motivation because Sundays historically have been my worst days of feeling badly.

Radka and Marianne were right! Apparently, the two iron infusions I received three and four weeks ago have started to take effect. This was confirmed today when my blood draw revealed that my iron levels are increasing, but aren't quite yet where they need to be for me to receive a supplemental iron treatment. All I can tell you is that I'm starting to feel human and like ME again. It feels sooooooo good!

As a result of feeling better and not being so tired, my poker play has improved, too. I cashed in 7th of 79 players for $1585 in the Venetian $300 NLH Rebuy poker tourney on Sunday. Then, on Monday, I qualified for Day 2 of theVenetian $340 NLH $100K Guarantee tourney, which I play in today after finishing my hydration treatment. 83 of 590 players remain and the top

63 will make the money. I'm starting with a solid chip stack, so am feeling positive about the outcome. 1st place is $35K!!

And, finally, last evening I won a $1650 entry into the Heartland Poker Tour (HPT) Main Event this coming weekend by placing in the top 10 of 38 players in a $375 NLH satellite qualifier. This will be a televised event, so hopefully I'll do well enough to get some TV time.

I met with Dr. Gollard this morning for a general update meeting before starting my hydration drip. We discussed my journey over the past six months and are both hoping that the 14 chemo treatments I've endured (90+ hours of drips, not including hydration) have shrunk the tumor in my right lung enough and eradicated the cancerous lymph nodes in the middle of my chest so that surgery becomes an option versus the alternative treatment plan of 35 days of daily radiation combined with seven more weeks of weekly chemo.

We'll know a lot more after I get my PET scan this coming Monday, April 9 and review the results with Dr. Fikes, the thoracic surgeon, on April 11 and Dr. Gollard on April 12. I'm hoping and praying that I qualify for surgery and can have my right lung removed. It is my best chance for having more years to live my life to its fullest.

Please keep your positive thoughts and good energy coming. It really helps! #PetzingStrong

APR 6 2018

Coincidence or Not?

It's amazing how well I've been feeling this week compared to last week. I'm so grateful that the iron infusions of a few weeks ago have been absorbed into my system and are getting me out of my anemic state. Additionally, the three "Fun Bag" hydration infusions I've received this week (at #3 as I'm writing this) have also made a huge difference. We've decided to do the same next week and then drop down to only two the following week, so my body doesn't become too dependent on them.

Today, I'd like to share something unusual that happened yesterday. Let's begin with a little background information. When I was sick with neck cancer from July 2014 to February 2015, I was living in tiny Douglas, MI (pop. 1200.) My treatment plan was 35 consecutive weekdays of radiation, plus 7 weekly chemo infusions. I was so sick that I really couldn't do much of anything and I was on a feeding tube for three months.

Everything went into that tube...my meds, painkillers (liquid morphine), fluids, and food (think high-powered Ensure.) My throat was a festival of pain and I could barely swallow, talk, or breathe. It was just horrible.

During that time, I lived alone and needed help getting to and from my radiation/chemo treatments. The Cancer Center was a 40-minute drive each way every day. My amazing friend and angel, Elizabeth, was always there for me, anytime I needed her. She took me to and sat with me during every one of my seven chemo treatments. We laughed. We cried. And, we tried to make the best of my situation. Elizabeth is like the sister I never had. We would do anything for each other.

After I recovered from neck cancer, I moved to Vegas in January 2016. A year and a half or so later, Elizabeth moved to Scottsdale, AZ, where she now resides. We keep in touch via texting, monthly/bi-monthly phone calls and Facebook. And, as mentioned previously, we spent this past Christmas together here in Vegas and had a great time!

Elizabeth texted me about 10 days ago and wanted to chat, but I was tied up in a poker tourney. Time got away from me and with not feeling well, I just didn't want to call her and be a "Debbie Downer." So yesterday, feeling great, I decided to give Elizabeth a call. She immediately answered her phone and told me she was at the dentist upside down in the chair waiting for her numbing drugs to take effect. She was there to get a couple of temporary crowns and some other work done.

Elizabeth hates going to the dentist, as many do, and had put her visit off for quite a long time. She finally acquiesced and got herself there. We had an awesome chat catching each other up on what has been going on in our lives during the past couple of months. After about 15 minutes, her dentist came back into the room and was ready to get started. We said our "goodbyes" and ended the call.

Five minutes later, I received a text from Elizabeth. She said, "You're not going to believe this, but I just told my dentist about you and he told me that his dad is a lung cancer survivor! First, he suffered with renal and brain cancer and then it moved to his lung. Now he's 58, fully cured, living on one lung and leading a healthy active lifestyle!"

Elizabeth is sure that this situation was not a coincidence, but rather a message to both of us from our Higher Power to continue to be hopeful and optimistic that everything will work out for me, too. It really is strange when you look at all the pieces. What are the odds?

Coincidence or not, I'm really encouraged by this event. I think it's important to keep oneself open to receiving these types of messages, however they may be delivered. Often, they have meaning beyond our normal state of understanding and are hard to explain when they happen, but that's okay. I'm totally on board because I'm a believer and feel inspired!

What do you think?

APR 9 2018

PET Scan Done, Results on Wednesday

I had a really good weekend of feeling well for a change! The combination of the iron infusion taking effect and the every other day hydration treatments is definitely keeping my energy up. It was a profitable poker weekend too, as I cashed in 12th of 413 players for $3370 in the $600 NLH SuperStack $200K Guarantee tourney at the Venetian last night. Louise placed 11th, so it was a good run for her, too.

Today, I had my PET scan. I've been "patiently" waiting three weeks to get this done. The results will determine the next steps for me in my battle against Stage 3B lung cancer. If the scan shows that the cancerous lymph nodes in the middle of my chest are gone and the tumor in my right lung has shrunk enough to be operable, then I will be eligible to have my right lung removed. If one of these two conditions does not exist, then I will have to endure 35 consecutive weekdays of daily radiation in conjunction with seven more weeks of weekly chemo.

Honestly, my heart is set on the surgery. It's the best option for me to extend my life. I will be devastated if, after six months and 90+ hours of chemo dripping, I'm told later this week that I'm inoperable. When I had neck cancer back in July 2014-March 2015, I had to do the exact same radiation/ chemo treatment plan mentioned above and it wasn't fun. The thought of having to do it again is painful and I really don't want to go there.

On Wednesday, I meet with Dr. Fickes, a thoracic surgeon. She will review my PET scan results from today, compared with the previous two, to determine if surgery is the right approach and doable. If for some reason she says "No", I will likely travel to MD Anderson in Houston and/or UCLA in Los Angeles to get a second opinion, which I may do anyway depending on how confident I am overall with our conversation. I'm hopeful that I'll like her because I wasn't at all impressed with the first thoracic surgeon assigned to me. The "good news" here is that my friend, Marika, is a nurse and knows and likes Dr. Fickes. She has a great reputation and has favorably been written about in US News & World Report.

On Thursday, Dr. Gollard and I will regroup for him to tell me his thoughts on the new PET scan results. At this point, he would like me to go the surgery route too if I'm eligible. We're all holding our breath. I'm trying not to obsess about it, but it's hard.

For those of you not familiar with the PET scan, it's a pretty simple test. The purpose of it is to locate any tumors or cancerous cells that may be active or dormant in my body from my head to mid-thigh area. The procedure started with a line pick being inserted into a vein so a radioactive serum could be injected into my blood stream.

Unfortunately, given all the chemo I've had previously via veins in both of my arms and hands, they have pretty much dried up. And, for this procedure, they are not able to access the port in my chest. It took the technician five tries to find a good vein, so there was a lot of pricking before we found success. Then I was given a 16-ounce vanilla flavored barium drink that I sucked down with a straw. It tasted awful and must be consumed prior to the scan because the sugar in it helps attract the cancer cells. These bad cells then light up during the scan.

After 45 minutes of letting the barium and radioactive serum settle into my system, I was asked to change into a hospital gown and was taken into the scanning room. There was a very large,

5 1/2 ft in diameter, doughnut-shaped apparatus with a long, narrow straight board, covered in sheets and extending from the hole. I got onto the board and laid on my back with my head propped up and a pillow under my knees. The technician told me that I'd need to be still for 20 minutes, while the board traveled back and forth through the "doughnut" hole/tube. I've had this test three or four times before, so I've gotten over the claustrophobic aspect of it, but it definitely is tight in there. Overall, it was easy breezy and no big deal.

So that's it! Everything is out of my control now. The results will be the results. All I can do is pray for the outcome I hope for and put my trust in my Higher Power for the right next steps. I'll be sure to provide an update here on Wednesday or Thursday. Please keep your prayers, virtual hugs and love coming. It means a lot to me and really makes a difference!

APR 12 2018

Bad Day of News, Back to Square One

It's 3:37am and I can't sleep. My mind is on overdrive from a really bad day of news yesterday. I feel like I was kicked in the gut. The good news I had hoped and prayed for didn't come. In fact, what I did learn was so not expected. I'm still shocked, frustrated, disappointed and confused. Here's what transpired:

I woke up early yesterday so I could pull together the final documents for the closing on my restaurant/martini lounge in Douglas, MI. It has been on the market for 30 months with minimal activity due to the very seasonal nature of this Lake Michigan coastal area, the depressed commercial market there, the lack of regular weekly tourism (weekends only), and the other seven restaurants that have been for sale longer than mine in the Saugatuck-Douglas community.

I closed Zing on October 31, 2015 because I couldn't come to terms with spending another $60K in yearly overhead costs: taxes, license fees, utilities, storage and building/ground maintenance, etc. to keep things afloat waiting for a buyer. So, I auctioned off the property, which also included two beautiful apartments above the restaurant and a martini lounge. It went for a steal at $379K and was just enough for me to pay off my mortgage nut. The closing will be finalized today or tomorrow, so I will be glad to have this albatross off my back and the gray cloud gone that has been hovering over me for way too long.

At 9:15am, I drove back to Steinberg Associates where I had my PET scan done on Monday. I needed to pick up the CD of the scan and the corresponding written report, so Dr. Fiekes could review it at our 11:15am appointment. I only had to wait ten minutes to get it, as they had prepared the CD the day before and it was ready for me. The report was stapled to the paper cover of the CD. When I got back in my car, I read the report. I couldn't believe what it said. It was like reading a foreign language, but it was clear that the news wasn't good. I took a few deep breaths and kept on reading. The news got worse. I wanted to cry but couldn't. I was numb.

I think what I posted on Facebook yesterday does a good job at summarizing the situation. Here's what I wrote:

"Well, it wasn't a good news day for me. The PET scan results showed that the tumor in my right lung grew by 25% over the past three months and the cancerous nodes on my bronchial tubes in the middle of my chest still exist. Additionally, I have what appears to be a new cancerous spot in my lower right lung, which is of concern.

The thoracic surgeon, Dr. Fiekes, said that I'm currently not a candidate for surgery and recommended that I have another bronchoscopy to biopsy the cancerous nodes to see if they have morphed into a different cell type. Additionally, she suggested a needle biopsy of the new spot in my lung to see what exactly we're dealing with there. Dr. Gollard agrees and these two procedures are being set up.

So, basically, I'm back to square one after six long months of chemo treatments. I'm frustrated, confused and very disappointed. This was the last thing I expected to hear today. I feel like I can't catch a break. Just another bad beat. I will try to remain positive, but it's really hard right now. CANCER SUCKS!"

My appointment with Dr. Fiekes was scheduled for 11:15am, but we didn't see her until 12:45pm. Louise met me at her office. I've learned from past experience that it's really important to have someone else with you (preferably a calm, supportive, smart, level headed, and non-emotional person) during doctor meetings who can hear and process the information along with you.

While we waited for Dr. Fiekes, Louise held my hand and put her arm around me. I was really struggling to keep my emotions in check because I already knew the bad news Dr. Fiekes was going to share with us given the scan report I had already read and shared with Louise. As we continued to wait, Louise went online and researched clinical trials that are going on for Stage 3B lung cancer folks like me.

Our meeting with Dr. Fiekes was worth the wait. She was generous with her time and explanations, and even showed us the PET scan on her computer. I have a much better understanding now of the complicated nature of my situation. She reinforced how the right lung cannot be taken out now due to the size and intertwining nature of the main tumor and because there is not enough safe margin between the lung and the location of the cancerous nodes residing on the bronchial tubes in the middle of my chest. Opening my body up at this point, could cause those nodes to go elsewhere, which would be an even bigger problem.

After 45 minutes of Louise and I asking a lot of questions, I put Dr. Fiekes on the spot and said, "If you were me and in my situation right now, what would you do?"

She paused, thought for a moment and said, "I would get a bronchoscopy to see if the cancer cell type has changed and to determine if the tumor markers are the same or different, so a new chemo program can be developed AND I would get a needle biopsy of the new spot in the lower right lung to see what's going on there."

I left Dr. Fiekes' office and immediately drove to Dr. Gollard's where I was already scheduled for a hydration treatment. I was supposed to meet with

Dr. Gollard on Thursday to review the PET scan results, but I was so worked up after getting the bad news that I called Radka and asked her if she could convince him to somehow meet with my during my hydration treatment.

I just love Radka! She's the best. When I arrived, they had the one private drip room ready for me. Radka and I chatted about the results and she told me how everyone on the staff, including Dr. Gollard, was also shocked by the news. She explained to me that sometimes the cancer cells build up a resistance to the chemo meds and figure out a way to still maintain and even grow their presence. Cancer is a fucking devious devil...my words, not hers. Radka tried to keep me calm and said that Dr. Gollard would be stopping in to chat with me, which he did.

Dr. Gollard was almost speechless. He clearly was surprised at the report and I could tell the wheels were spinning in his head. I don't think he had enough time to process it all, so he deferred to Dr. Fiekes' recommendation and agreed that the bronchoscopy and the needle biopsy were the appropriate next steps. He indicated that he would have his staff immediately get started on getting both of the procedures set up and that I should meet with him again in a week. After my two hour "Fun Bag" drip, I was told by Princess, the office manager, that she was on it and we should know something soon.

When I got home, I got on my couch and tried to decompress. I had already called Chris, Elizabeth and my Dad & Cheryl from hydration to give them the bad news. Louise had already called Ardys, Jackie, Lynnore and Susannah to fill them in. I just didn't have the emotional strength to have any more conversations about the situation. The calls I had already made were hard enough. However, I still needed to call my Mom, which I did. She struggled with the news, but I think understands the next steps. I haven't spoken with Ed yet, but plan on doing so today.

While decompressing, I checked the Facebook update I posted yesterday. I continue to be so touched by all of the loving, supportive comments I have been receiving. It's truly amazing and makes a huge, positive impact on me!

Louise called to check in on me. I had intended to play a 7pm poker tourney but told her I felt paralyzed and emotionally exhausted. She told me to disconnect from my phone and Facebook and just veg. I took her advice, made some pork burritos, watched CNN, and threw myself into bed at 9pm. I slept until 2:30am but have been up since then. It's now 5:15am. I'm meeting Jackie at 9:30am for breakfast and will play a poker tourney at the Venetian at noon. I need to get back on track and do what I normally do. I can't let this bad news keep me down. So, I will continue to fight the good fight, work on an attitude adjustment, take one day at a time, and beat this FUCKER! Yes, I will!

#PetzingStrong

APR 13 2018

Renewing My Trust in Him

I've had a couple of days now to process Wednesday's bad news. I'm in a much better place emotionally and still feeling pretty good physically. The three hydration treatments I've received both this week and last week have really helped with my overall energy and well-being. Next week, I'm being reduced to only two hydration treatments, so we'll see how that goes.

So next steps at this point are to get the bronchoscopy and needle biopsy scheduled. Kristina and Princess at Dr. Gullard's office are on it and hopefully I'll be having both of these procedures in the next couple of weeks. I really don't want to wait. We've got to get back on track here and keep things moving along!

I want to thank all of you from the bottom of my heart for your kind, caring words of love, support, inspiration, compassion and hope. You have no idea how good it feels to know that I have an army of prayer warriors out there fighting along with me. I don't feel alone in my battle and definitely need all of the help I can get.

As you can imagine, I'm having a hard time understanding why things aren't going my way right now. I've always been a bit of a control freak, so it's very frustrating and difficult to not have control in a critical life or death situation like this one. There's really nothing I can do except follow what my doctors say, research other treatment options and clinical trials, and determine if I need to get a second and/or third opinion, which I likely will do after I get the test results from the upcoming biopsies and a new recommended plan from my current team of doctors. Only time will tell.

Since I'm feeling a bit helpless, I know I need to put my Trust in my Higher Power. Ironically, yesterday's daily devotion in Sarah Young's *Jesus Calling* spoke of this:

"Trusting Me is a moment-by-moment choice. My people have not always understood this truth. After I performed miracles in the wilderness, My chosen children trusted Me intensely--but only temporarily. Soon the grumbling began again, testing My patience to the utmost.

Isn't it often the same way with you? You trust Me when things go well, when you see Me working on your behalf. This type of trust flows readily within you, requiring no exertion of your will. When things go wrong, your trust-flow slows down and solidifies. You are forced to choose between trusting Me intentionally or rebelling: resenting My ways with you. This choice constitutes a fork in the road. Stay on the path of Life with Me, enjoying My Presence. Choose to trust Me in all circumstances."

Exodus 15:22-25; Psalm 31:14

I am renewing My Trust in him. I believe that he will make things right for me. I just need to be patient and follow the path he has put me on. These sentiments are also reinforced by a beautiful email I received today from my friend, Silvio, who is a regular reader of my CaringBridge posts and a talented documentary film producer.

He writes:

"Jim,

I read your latest blog with a heavy heart. I'm deeply sorry it wasn't the news you and all of us were hoping for. It's almost impossible to understand why this is happening to such a wonderful, giving person.

All I can offer is that no matter how bad things are, He is there with you and always will be. He will never abandon you. I know this because He carried me through my darkest hour (dying mother, disintegrating marriage, disillusioned career and loss of my kids).

The 'bizarre' incidents you've recounted to us reveal His presence along your journey. Remain strong in that knowledge. Continue to witness His work and stay connected to Him for guidance and comfort.

Through our struggles, the love between Him and us grows. The more difficult the struggle, the deeper that love becomes. And it is that love which matters more than anything since with it, anything can be endured.

your brother-in-Christ,

Silvio"

I was so moved by Silvio's note. I too believe that He will not abandon me but is poised and ready to help me breakthrough this temporary setback. I know He will guide me to the right place, the right people, the right treatment plan, and the best outcome possible. I will take comfort in that right now. Thank you, Silvio.

#PetzingStrong

APR 18 2018

A Very Full Day

I took a five day hiatus from writing, since basically I've fallen back into "wait & see" mode. It's very frustrating that I ended chemo about a month ago, the large tumor in my right lung grew by 25% over the past three months and I have a new cancerous spot/tumor in my lower right lung.

Finally, I was able to get an appointment with Dr. Osman for a week from today. Ironically, he's the same surgeon that did my original bronchoscopy when I was in the hospital over six months ago. He'll be doing the same procedure again, hopefully a week or so after we meet. Unfortunately, the needle biopsy to see what's going on with the lower lung invasion has not been scheduled yet. Our insurance system is so fu*k*d up. It takes forever to get approval on procedures and then even longer to get them set up. For every week of not moving forward, I feel like I'm losing a month of my life. It's not a good feeling.

Thankfully, I'm at hydration today. My last one was this past Friday (4 days ago) and its effects wore off by Monday morning. So, Monday and Tuesday were "chemo cave" days, where I felt woozie, dizzy, tired and very lethargic. The good news is that I dragged myself out on Monday to play a $150 NLH poker tourney at the Venetian and cashed in 5th out of 107 players for $884, while being a short stack the entire day.

After my hydration today, I will meet with Dr. Gollard to continue our conversation about "WHY" the second three months of chemo didn't work like the first three months. I'm still confused and concerned as to what exactly happened. Now that he has had some more time to process the situation, I'm hopeful he'll have some better answers than the last time we spoke. Once the test results come back from both the bronchoscopy and needle biopsy, it will be interesting to see what my team of doctors recommend as a plan. As I've mentioned previously, I will be taking that plan and getting 2nd and 3rd opinions at MD Andersen in Houston, UCLA Medical, and/or Mayo Clinic in Phoenix. I think it's time to get "the best of the best" on my case!

This morning, I had an appointment with an attorney to go over the total amendment revision I need to have made to my Declaration of Trust (Will), Living Will, and DNR should anything unfortunate happen to me in the near term... or long term, for that matter. The last amendment I had made was by my Chicago attorney in 2014. So now that I've lived in Vegas for 2 1/4 years, it's time to get updated here. I want to be sure that all of my "ducks are in a row" and that there's no question about what I want to have happen with me and my estate should I die.

Tonight, I'm having dinner at my friend Lisa's house. She's a poker buddy that has wanted to do something special for me for a while now and is making one of my favorites: a fabulous meat lasagna with cheesy bread. Louise will also be joining us, and she's bringing a tomato mozzarella salad and a yummy dessert. I'm really looking forward to a fun evening with the girls! It will be nice to hang out and enjoy their company.

Then, late this evening, around 12:15am, I'll be heading to the airport to pick up Chris. He's flying in tonight from Michigan and will be here until Tuesday. I'm so excited to see him. It has been almost six weeks since he was last here. We'll be going to some movies (like A Quiet Place), binge watching some

Netflix series, hitting a Vegas show, investigating some museums (The Mob Museum and The Pinball Museum), hanging by the pool, seeing friends, and making some nice dinners.

It will be a full schedule! Hopefully, I'll have the energy to do it all.

So that's it for now. My "fun bag" is dripping and I'm already starting to feel a little increase in my energy. By 11pm tonight, I'll be wired... just in time for Chris' arrival!

APR 20 2018

Finally Moving Forward Again

I met with Dr. Gollard on Wednesday after my hydration treatment. I had a lot of questions for him, but he jumped right in and immediately addressed the key concern I had before I could even present it to him.

The issue is that I haven't had a chemo treatment in four weeks, but my right lung large tumor grew by 25% and a new one has developed in my lower lung over the past three months. So then, what has been happening in my body during the past four weeks without any treatment while we wait for my biopsy procedures to be scheduled? Dr. Gollard thinks that the tumors are probably growing at an even quicker rate and believes that we need to get started on a radiation/chemo combo treatment plan as soon as possible before we get test results from the bronchoscopy and needle biopsy. I fully agree with this recommendation, although I'm not excited about it.

The good news is that through being a bit pushy and having good relationships with Dr. Gollard's staff, I've finally been able to get most of the appointments scheduled. On Monday morning at 9am, I will be meeting with Dr. Dean, who I was quite impressed with during my first visit. He has squeezed me in because of the urgency of my situation. Right after my appointment, I will drive to another location and get a CT scan for radiation treatment planning purposes. This scan will provide measurements and position locations for all the areas that will be zapped by the radiation. My guess is that there will be three key areas of focus: the large right lung tumor, the new lower right lung tumor and the middle of my chest in the bronchial tube area where the cancerous lymph nodes continue to cling on and multiply. I'm feeling relieved that we are finally moving forward in at least some direction, especially since I've been sitting idle for over a month now. I don't know how long it will take Dr. Dean and his team to put a radiation treatment plan together, but hopefully I'll be starting it the following week.

At 11:45am on Wednesday next week, I will meet with Dr. Osman to review my case and discuss the bronchoscopy procedure. Interestingly, Dr. Gollard isn't convinced I need to do it again because he thinks that the squamous cell type hasn't changed, while Dr. Feikes thinks it's important to have one done to be sure we know exactly what we're dealing with at this point. I will also ask Dr. Dean for his opinion and, of course, will see what Dr. Osman has to say about it. If it's determined that I should move forward with a bronchoscopy, it looks like it would be scheduled within 7-14 days from my appointment with Dr. Osman.

After my meeting with Dr. Osman on Wednesday, I'll be going to hydration and seeing Dr. Gollard again at 1:45pm to review where we stand on everything. I'm back on a three day per week hydration schedule (Monday, Wednesday and Friday) in order to keep my energy levels up, especially if I'll be starting radiation shortly.

Finally, on Monday April 30 at 10am, I am scheduled for a needle biopsy. This will help identify what's going on with the new spot in my lower right lung. It's an outpatient procedure that I don't have all the details on yet. However, I have been told that I'll need to have someone available to drive me home after the biopsy as it looks like I'll be receiving anesthesia.

So, overall, I'm glad that everything is starting to fall into place and that we're moving forward again. I've been feeling quite stuck and very concerned that every week we're not doing something, I'm losing a month of critical time that I can't afford. It's my own head game that I try to stay out of, but it's difficult not to go there.

With no ability to control what is happening around me, I am having to put all of my trust in my Higher Power. I'd like to end today's journal entry with this April 15th daily devotion from Sarah Young's "Jesus Calling" that truly fits how I'm feeling and what I need to do:

"Trust Me, and don't be afraid. Many things feel out of control. Your routines are not running smoothly. You tend to feel more secure when your life is predictable. Let Me lead you to the rock that is higher than you and your circumstances. Take refuge in the shelter of My wings, where you are absolutely secure.

When you are shaken out of your comfortable routines, grip My hand tightly and look for growth opportunities. Instead of bemoaning the loss of your comfort, accept the challenge of something new. I lead you on from glory to glory, making you fit for My kingdom. Say yes to the ways I work in your life. Trust Me, and don't be afraid."

Isaiah 12:2; Psalm 61: 2-4; 2 Corinthians 3:18 (NKJV)

APR 21 2018

Breaking News...Opdivo May Be an Option

I just wanted to provide a quick update here on some encouraging news I received yesterday after I posted my journal entry.

Dr. Gollard came by to see me as I was finishing my hydration treatment. He said that after my appointment with him on Wednesday, he called the pathology lab at the hospital where I had my original bronchoscopy over six month ago. He wants them to check the tissue biopsy of my cancerous lymph nodes to see if it indicates the right type of markers for me to potentially be treated with an immunotherapy drug, called Opdivo. It's very similar to Keytruda, another immunotherapy drug used with certain lung cancer patients. Both brands advertise heavily on tv, so you likely have seen their ads.

You also may have heard the news this past week of the exciting research results from Merck's testing of Keytruda, which apparently has helped extend life expectancy by four to six months for about 70% of those lung cancers patients being treated with it. This is very encouraging! My doctor, however, is keener on Opdivo because it has been out on the market longer and has more research behind it. Plus, he has had greater success with it in his practice. It's most often given to Stage 3 or 4 cancer patients, like me, where chemotherapy was unsuccessful and their tumors did not shrink or perhaps grew.

The beauty of Opdivo is that it specifically targets cancer cells while leaving normal red and white blood cells alone, whereas chemotherapy basically poisons all of the cells in your body. If I qualify, Opdivo will be administered to me via a one-hour infusion every two weeks. This would be amazing since my chemo drips lasted 6 to 6 1/2 hours.

So now we are on a parallel path, pursuing the Opdivo option along with evaluating the radiation/chemotherapy approach. If I qualify as an Opdivo candidate, then my team of doctors and I will need to make the decision of which scenario is better for me. I'm, of course, leaning toward the Opdivo option because if it can get rid of the cancerous lymph nodes in my chest area and shrink the tumors in my right lung, I still could be a short term candidate for surgery. If I go the radiation/chemo route, surgery could still be a longer term option if the same results occur, but I'd likely have to wait six months to a year for tissue healing purposes before a surgeon could safely operate on me.

My fingers are crossed for hearing that Opdivo could be my next step! I'm tired of being disappointed and not catching a break, so hopefully things will be different this time!

I remain #PetzingStrong!

APR 23 2018

A New Plan...Radiation Starts This Week

Chris and I got up early at 6:30am so we could leisurely get ready to leave at 7:30am for my 8am appointment with Dr. Dean. I saw him last on February 5. He had pieced together my entire cancer history from August 2014, when I was officially diagnosed with neck cancer. All I had to do was fill in a few details for him. Now, 2 1/2 months later, we will discuss his thoughts on a combo radiation/chemo program, since the overall chemo treatment I recently completed didn't work as expected.

I forgot how close Dr. Dean's office is to my apartment. It's only ten minutes away, so we got there early and sat in the car going over the specific questions we wanted to be sure to have answered. We walked in at about 7:45am and there were already six or so others in the waiting area, some for their radiation treatments and others, like me, for an appointment. My name was called second, only about ten minutes from when we sat down. Honestly, I was a bit anxious and nervous about what Dr. Dean might say, since nothing has been going especially well lately.

Chris and I only waited five minutes in the examining room before Dr. Dean arrived. He is the epitome of a true professional, from his overall demeanor, manner and style to his expertise, knowledge and clear delivery of information. I feel very fortunate to have him on my team of doctors. Chris was similarly impressed.

Dr. Dean jumped right in summarizing the report from my recent PET scan. He showed a lot of concern around the recent growth of the already large tumor in my right lung and the new area in my lower pleural lobe, which is being needle biopsied a week from today. He is 95% sure that it's also a cancerous tumor. He indicated that if in fact it is, I would now be considered a Stage 4 cancer patient because of the spreading of the cancer outside of the main area where it has been previously located. However, this would not be a "death sentence" Stage 4 designation as the cancer is still isolated in my right lung. If it spreads outside of the right lung, that particular Stage 4 diagnosis will be bad for me.

Dr. Dean explained to us that his goal initially with the radiation will be to focus on killing off the cancerous cells in the large tumor with the hope of shrinking it enough to provide me with more overall relief. Currently, I'm back where I was almost seven months ago with the tumor putting significant pressure on my bronchial tubes causing regular shortness of breath, wheezing, and more coughing. His treatment program will be 12-15 days of daily radiation each morning, likely combined with a milder chemo drip once a week and two days of hydration to keep my energy levels up.

Since it has been almost six weeks now since I've had a chemo treatment, both Dr. Dean and Dr. Gollard are very concerned that the tumors have grown even more during this time and want to get started immediately with this new treatment approach. So, right after my appointment with Dr. Dean, Chris and I drove to Steinberg to get a CT scan. Its purpose is to see the exact size and location of the large tumor, along with the others, and to get specific measurements. This scan will be overlaid to the April 5 PET scan, so Dr. Dean can put the proper radiation plan together. His hope is that I will commence radiation on Wednesday or Thursday morning of this week, so we are not messing around here.

In our meeting with Dr. Dean, we also discussed the recommended next step pursuant to the three weeks of radiation/chemo. He and Dr. Gollard both believe that I should start on a three-month program of Opdivo, the immunotherapy drug that I wrote about in my last journal entry.

If all of my markers check out, I would receive a one-hour infusion of Opdivo every other week for three months...a total of six infusions. Then, I would have another PET scan to see if my body is responding appropriately, the cancerous cells/nodes are being killed off, and the tumor(s) are continuing to shrink. If it works, I likely will remain on Opdivo for two or even three years.

I couldn't help myself and had to ask Dr. Dean what likely would happen to me IF I don't respond well to the Opdivo treatment. Basically, he said that within five to six months after stopping the Opdivo, the cancer would likely metastasize and spread somewhere else in my body. Not good! He also indicated that this is the point where my quality of life would likely take a big hit and I would start failing quickly. Apparently, if it's found that the Opdivo treatment is not working after the three-month trial period, this is when obtaining a 2nd and 3rd opinion makes the most sense and/or getting into a clinical trial for Stage 3B/4 cancer patients. So the bottom line is that I'm really banking on Opdivo!

You may recall from previous journal entries, after my meeting with Dr. Feikes, that the plan was to get another bronchoscopy to confirm the type of cancer cell we're dealing with. Interestingly, after speaking with both Dr. Gollard and Dr. Dean, the needle biopsy on Monday will do that for us. So, they don't see the need for it and I cancelled my appointment on Wednesday with Dr. Osman.

As you can well imagine, I've been experiencing a lot of emotional ups and downs over the past six months, and especially lately. It has been wonderful having Chris here with me for the past five days. He's a great sounding board and I've been able to really open up and share my true feelings and concerns with him about my cancer situation. They aren't easy conversations to have, but are very necessary. He's one of my earthly angels and has been so supportive and understanding. I feel so blessed to have him by my side in my ongoing battle.

So there you have it. This is now the plan as of today. Of course, it could change at any moment, but I'm quite confident that we'll be moving forward with it. I'm trying so hard to remain positive and optimistic. Your kind caring words of hope and inspiration really do help keep me going! I'm doing my best and will continue to be #PetzingStrong.

APR 25 2018

Dr. Dean & Dr. Gollard's Plan

It's official! I will start radiation tomorrow morning with Dr. Dean. He has scheduled me for 12 consecutive weekdays of treatments, but without chemotherapy. This will allow him to administer a shorter, more intensive approach vs a longer, drawn out one if chemo were to be added as well.

During the 2 1/2 weeks of radiation treatments, I will continue to come to hydration three times a week. This will be important for managing any side effects, maintaining fluid balance and keeping my energy levels up. At the conclusion of the radiation treatments, Dr. Gollard will likely be putting me on a three month cycle of the immunotherapy drug, Opdivo, or possibly Keytruda, depending on the results from this coming Monday's needle biopsy of the new tumor in my lower right lung and those from the full evaluation he ordered on the original tissue biopsy taken during my bronchoscopy seven months ago.

After the three months of immunotherapy, I will have another PET scan to see if the tumors are responding and shrinking. A new plan will be put in place from there. So, I'm feeling good that we're moving forward and getting things going again!

I had a good day of poker yesterday finishing in 6th place of 160 players in a $150 NLH Bounty tournament at the Venetian and winning $1038 for a net payday of $888. It felt awesome to play well and make another Final Table. I'll be playing again tonight after I finish with today's hydration treatment.

In closing, I want to share the sentiment of a beautiful card I received yesterday from my friends Ron & Jamie. It reads:

"Wishing you PEACE in your heart as you let your body follow its own gentle path to healing, QUIET in your soul as you let go and let God nurture you as only He can do, and CALMNESS in your spirit as you know the blessings of renewal and reflection this time of recovery offers. Thinking of you and hoping that God, rest, and prayer will restore good health to you!"

#PetzingStrong

APR 26 2018

Hope is Eternal

I got up early this morning to go to the Quest Diagnostics clinic to have a special PT/PTT blood draw done in advance of Monday morning's needle biopsy. I got there at about 7:15am and was walking out the door an hour later, so it wasn't too bad. Then, I drove five minutes to Dr. Dean's office and had my first of twelve intensive radiation treatments, which was easy breezy and only lasted 15 minutes. I'm hoping side effects will be limited, but only time will tell.

Today's daily devotion from Sarah Young's, "Jesus Calling", was meaningful to me:

"Welcome problems as perspective-lifters. My children tend to sleepwalk through their days until they bump into an obstacle that stymies them. If you encounter a problem with no immediate solution, your response to that situation will take you either up or down. You can lash out at the difficulty, resenting it and feeling sorry for yourself. This will take you down into a pit of self-pity. Alternatively, the problem can be a ladder, enabling you to climb up and see your life from My perspective. Viewed from above, the obstacle that frustrated you is only a light and momentary trouble. Once your perspective has been heightened, you can look away from the problem altogether. Turn toward Me and see the Light of My Presence shining upon you."

2 Corinthians 4:16-18; Psalm 89:15

I received a bookmark at my hydration treatment yesterday that also helped build me up. On it were the following words:

"What Cancer CANNOT Do:

Cancer is so limited....It cannot cripple love. It cannot shatter hope. It cannot corrode faith.

It cannot eat away peace. It cannot destroy confidence. It cannot kill friendship. It cannot shut out memories. It cannot silence courage. It cannot reduce eternal life. It cannot quench the Spirit."

Author Unknown

I am choosing hope. I believe I will win! I hate losing.

#PetzingStrong

APR 27 2018

It's NOT "My" Cancer!

I woke up early again this morning and went on Facebook to catch up. My good friend, Nancy B., who lives in Florida, saw that I was awake and online, so she texted me to see if I was up for a chat. It was so good to hear from her and to catch up. She has had a tough few months recovering from her father's death. They were very close. Nancy was my first real "poker" friend, who I met almost 10 years ago waiting for an elevator at the Beau Rivage hotel in Biloxi, MS. We were both there playing in a tournament series called "The Millionaire Maker." Unfortunately, neither of us left with $1MM! It will be great to see Nancy in person when she comes out here to Vegas this summer to play in the World Series of Poker.

After a quick breakfast of pear juice, oatmeal with banana, and a bagel, I drove over to Dr. Dean's radiation center for my daily 8:50am treatment. I was in and out and then on my way to Dr. Gollard's chemo clinic for hydration and an iron infusion, as I'm still anemic with a below standard iron level. I'm here now and will drip for about three hours.

My plan for this afternoon/evening is to play in the $340 NLH Bounty tournament at the Venetian. There is a guaranteed $50K prize pool, so I intend to get a big share of it! If I do well today and have chips remaining late this evening, I'll move on to Day 2 this Sunday.

I was treated to a nice surprise last night when I got home from playing poker. In the mail was a package from Elizabeth and a handwritten card that read:

> "Jim,
>
> I am putting my eggs in the Opdivo basket! I am sending this incredible lotion for use on your skin after radiation. Here's the story behind it. I went to a Farmer's Market on Sunday and this wonderful gay man, Nick, had an amazing aromatherapy display. I was immediately drawn to the name, "Heaven to Earth", and then specifically to this particular scent. He had developed this lotion for a dear friend who has lymphoma and is going through radiation, too! No coincidence there! His friend said it was the only lotion that helped with the chaffing caused by the radiation. I hope you like it, honey. Let me know how it works and I'll keep it coming! Stay #PetzingStrong. Love you, babe!
>
> xoxox, Elizabeth"

What a thoughtful gift with perfect timing! Hopefully, my skin won't get too burned or dried out by the radiation treatments, but if it does I'm ready for it with my new super duper lotion.

This past week, I also received a Facebook Messenger note from a Mexican friend of mine, David. He is also very spiritual and studies alternative medicine. David has been following my journey and provided some very interesting insight in his message to me:

"I read you and I get kind of frustrated. My view is that chemotherapy doesn't work. On the contrary, it makes people sicker. I've been working with

Ayahuasca for the last six years and it has amazing power. I'm sorry if my views might upset you, but different points of view are good. I hope all good will come to you on your decisions how to combat the cancer.

Here is a secret: We have trillions of cells and they understand us. So, please, DO NOT MAKE ANY SICKNESS YOURS! Don't say MY this or MY that, as your internal intelligence understands the message. If you affirm it, you will get it. So, cheat your cells and tell them you're doing well and feeling healthy and alive. They will understand the message.

I'm sending you a big hug full of LOVE. I'm sorry if this bothers you, but I needed to get it off my chest. LOVE ya!"

I definitely could see David's point about not using the word, MY, when talking about my situation. It makes a lot of sense to me. So, this is what I wrote back to him:

"I really like this! You're right. I will stop using MY. The Cancer is NOT mine! I love this perspective. Interestingly, chemo worked for me when I had neck cancer and for the first three months this time around. But then the cells got smart and resisted. I've had good luck in the past with radiation, so hopefully it will help a bit. I'm feeling optimistic about the immunotherapy drug approach following radiation, too. We'll see how it goes. I started my CBD pills today and maybe they'll make a difference. I'll definitely read about Ayahuasca. Thanks for all of your prayers, hugs, and suggestions. Really appreciate it!"

So, I'm going to work very hard at not using the word, MY, from here on out! I'm kicking it out of my vocabulary and into the gutter....right where cancer belongs.

MAY 1 2018

Needle Biopsy Cancelled!

Wow, it's hard to believe that we're already in May! Time sure does fly. That's why we need to live in the present and fully enjoy each day we are blessed to experience.

Today's daily devotion from Sarah Young's "Jesus Calling" captures this concept well:

"You are on the path of My choosing. There is no randomness about your life. Here and Now comprise the coordinates of your daily life. Most people let their moments slip through their fingers, half-lived. They avoid the present by worrying about the future or longing for a better time and place. They forget that they are creatures who are subject to the limitations of time and space. They forget their Creator, who walks with them only in the present.

Every moment is alive with My glorious Presence, to those whose hearts are intimately connected with Mine. As you give yourself more and more to a life of constant communion with Me, you will find that you simply have no time for worry. Thus, you are freed to let My Spirit direct your steps, enabling you to walk alone the path of Peace."

Luke 12:25-26; Luke 1:79

So yesterday I got some great news for a change. I went to Steinberg Diagnostic for the needle biopsy of the hot spot in my lower right lung that showed up in my early April PET scan. After getting prepped, being put on the operating table and having another CT scan, the radiologist told me that the scan showed that the lesion they were going to biopsy had shrunk by 50% since early April, so it's likely NOT a cancerous tumor but rather the remains of some kind of infection! In turn, they cancelled the biopsy. So now I'm just dealing with the large tumor, undergoing daily radiation for the next two to three weeks before getting put on one of the new immunotherapy drugs. I feel so blessed that I don't need to deal with another tumor right now!

This morning was radiation treatment #4 of 12. Afterwards, I met with Dr. Dean. He was very surprised and happy that the hot spot was not cancer. Given this new information, he told me that he's considering expanding the number of radiation treatments for the large right lung tumor to 15 or 17 in total. Since I'm getting a double dosage each time, this is equivalent to six to seven weeks of radiation (30-34 treatments.) Dr. Dean definitely seemed more optimistic, but also more confused, about my case. He indicated that he and Dr. Gollard had been in dialogue about me and my situation and that they still had more to discuss regarding next steps.

Dr. Dean's optimism has given me some new hope, so we'll just have to wait and see how things play out.

I'm in my hydration chair at Dr. Gollard's office finishing up this journal entry. My eyes are starting to shut while I am typing this entry, so clearly I need to take a nap. I'll get a good two hours in before we finish. Then I'm heading over to my new attorney's office just down the street to sign my Declaration of Trust, Living Will, DNR and other important papers. I think it's important to get my "house in order", just in case anything unexpected might happen. It will be nice to have this work completed as it will give me additional piece of mind.

Depending on how I feel later this afternoon, I might play a 7pm poker tourney at the Venetian or just go home, hang out with Zing & Zang, make a nice dinner and watch some TV. I'll be back at hydration again tomorrow morning after my radiation treatment.

I continue to be #PetzingStrong!

MAY 2 2018

Don't Be Trapped By Your Problems

I'm back in my hydration chair today getting my "Fun Bag" at Dr. Gollard's. My weekday mornings are very busy as I have radiation every day at 8:50am followed by hydration on Monday, Wednesday and Friday at 9:30am. Today I had radiation treatment #5 and, so far, I'm not having any severe side effects.

I have done a good job at letting go of the feeling that I need to be in control of solving my own problems. That's not to say that I don't take an active role in helping overcome them, but I have acquiesced to knowing that more often than not, I can't do it alone....and that's okay. I reach out to others when I need to and/or "send up" my insurmountable problems when I really need help.

Sadly, I think many of us believe that we need to deal with our problems on our own and not involve others because it may show "weakness" or the inability to step up to the plate. Or, we don't feel it's right to burden others with them. In a way, this is a bit selfish. Most of our families and good friends WANT TO HELP and always have our best interests at hand. Let them!

And, if necessary, don't be afraid to take the additional step of reaching out and embracing your Higher Power....and angels. You may not know them, but they are always there for you.

MAY 7 2018

Same Old, Same Old

I've kind of been in a funk for the past week or so. I can't really explain it other than to say that I feel like my life is "on hold", which in essence it is. I'm also in a rut. Basically, I play poker every day, if I'm up to it. I go back and forth from my apartment to the Venetian or Wynn. When I get home, I lie down on my wraparound red faux leather couch or spread out on my bed to watch CNN and some of my other favorite shows: American Idol, The Voice, Rise, For The People, Dateline and 20/20, to name a few. I'm also a closeted Bachelor/Bachelorette fan (Do not judge me!)

In reality, I'm just not used to not having the freedom to do what I really want, when I want. For the past 7+ months, I've been in treatment for Stage 3B lung cancer and it has required me to spend two to five days a week at doctors' appointments, chemo/radiation and hydration. This has severely limited my ability to travel and do the things on my "bucket list." I feel stuck and not in control of my destiny. This is quite frustrating and I'm still working on embracing it. I know my higher power is trying to show me the way and I do believe he is looking out for me.

Hopefully, the current radiation treatments I'm receiving and the planned immunotherapy program I'll be starting in a couple of weeks, will both do their respective jobs and extend my life. On that note, I picked up my revised Living Will and other important documents from my attorney last week. I want to be sure that my wishes are known in case things don't go as "planned."

I haven't talked about this, but each day I take some combination of nine different medications and vitamins, including:

* Venaflexine (for medical depression)
* Xanax (to help me sleep and be calm)
* Zofran (as needed, for nausea)
* Docusate (for constipation)
* Iron (for anemia)
* Magnesium (for energy)
* Turmeric (known to fight cancer cells)
* CBD (50mg daily, known for killing off cancer)

I've been taking a Z-Pack for the past five days, too, to knock out the infection and wheezing I've been battling. So, I'm a pill popper. And, the counter top of my bathroom sink looks like a pharmacy.

I finally broke a ten tournament streak of not cashing yesterday when I placed 56th of 612 players for $651 in the Venetian $340 NLH SuperStack event. It felt really good to get back on the board.

I'm writing this entry as I sit in my hydration chair. My eyes keep closing and I'm regularly nodding off, so I'm going to take a nap now. Please keep the following passage in mind as you live life fully every day this week and in the future:

"We can't always see where the road leads, but God promises there's something better up ahead. We just have to trust him."

I believe this to be true.

#PetzingStrong

MAY 11 2018

Exploring the Options

It has been a tough week physically and emotionally for me. I've been feeling really down and out.

Today was my final radiation treatment (#12) and for the past three days I've been very fatigued from them, which has required a daily two-hour nap. Dr. Dean has expressed concern about my situation as the "puzzle pieces" just haven't been fitting together for him. He also continues to use the word "complicated" when talking about my case. My cough has gotten worse and my wheezing is really bad. He decided to do an "emergency" CT scan this past Wednesday to see what impact the radiation has had to date and if there was anything odd going on. What he saw was that my airway had opened up a little wider, but nothing unusual. Now that I've finished the radiation treatments, it will stay in my system for a month or so, hopefully doing its job of shrinking the large right lung tumor. I'm scheduled to meet with Dr. Dean four weeks from today to review where we are.

Dr. Dean and Dr. Gollard have been talking regularly. They decided that it was best to stop the radiation and start on the immunotherapy treatment with Opdivo. I've been doing my own research on Opdivo and have found that it only "works" for about 20% of folks who take it. Unfortunately, I have a non-existent PD-L1 count, which puts me in a group that generally does not respond favorably to Opdivo. I already feel a bit defeated by this statistic, but you never know. I'm worried that if this doesn't work for me, I have a very few options remaining. It's kind of like I have "all of my eggs in the Opdivo basket" right now, but the basket has some holes in it.

Since I've been feeling so anxious, I've dug into researching non-traditional, alternative medicine approaches and clinical trials. What I tend to get most excited about are the "treatments" and "medications" that get mentioned the most and have numerous people providing amazing testimonials about their efficacy. However, many of these potential treatments have no validating research to support their findings.

As you've seen, I've added turmeric and CBD capsules to my regimen, but what I'm learning is that a regular, strong dosage of THC oil is what I really need to help kill cancer cells. The issue with taking it is that I'd be on a constant high and likely require 10-14 hours of sleep a day. I'd need to ingest the oil by putting it under my tongue or adding drops of it to tea or coffee. Apparently, it tastes awful and its consistency is a big turn off. I spoke with Dr. Gollard about taking it. He said he didn't think the THC would interfere or cause a negative reaction with the Opdivo, but that there's no research to support that. So, I'm going to think more about it as an additional option.

Ironically this week, a church youth group and high school friend of mine from years ago, reached out to tell me about a clinical trial that her pharma research company is doing. It's for non-small cell lung cancer folks who did not have success with chemotherapy and have low PD-L1 and TIL scores. It combines Opdivo with a heat protein test drug, called HS-110. There are currently 35 people in the trial and preliminary results are indicating that a third of the group's tumors are going from "cold" to "hot" and successfully responding to the combination therapy vs. those taking Opdivo alone.

This is very encouraging! The issue is that the closest center to me hosting the study is in La Jolla, CA outside of San Diego. I'd have to fly to San Diego every week for 16 weeks and drive 15 minutes to the clinic to get my treatment. I have some more research to do and folks to talk to about it, but I'm hoping there might be a way to participate here in Vegas and have Dr. Gollard and his team administer the program. We'll have to see.

So, I'm feeling a bit overwhelmed with information and what to do next, but I'm definitely leaning toward doing the clinical trial in some way, shape or form. I just want to know that what I choose to do next is going to make a real difference and help extend my life.

Trying to remain #PetzingStrong!, but struggling.

MAY 14 2018

Approved for a "Test"!

I'm in my hydration chair this morning getting my "Fun Bag" of goodies. It should give me a nice "pick me up" for the next 1 1/2 days or so. Overall, I had a good weekend of energy and was able to play a lot of poker, culminating in a 7th place finish for $1154 last night in the $20K Guarantee $200 NLH Rebuy tourney at the Venetian. Hopefully, I'm getting back on track with my winning ways.

This past Friday, I finally got some "good news." I spoke with the head of research, Lori, for the pharma company that is currently testing the new HS-110 heat protein drug with Opdivo in a clinical trial. We discussed my entire situation and found that I qualify for the trial, but that it would require flying to San Diego every week for four months and then driving 15-20 minutes to La Jolla, CA to participate in the study. Without knowing the side effects that I'd experience from receiving both of these drugs in combination, it's not clear whether I'd even be able to make those trips if I was in a lot of pain, nauseous, or completely drained of energy.

I asked Lori if there was a way the "test" could be administered here in Vegas by Dr. Gollard and his team of amazing nurses. To my surprise, she said, "Yes, through a program called Expanded/Compassionate Use." Think of it like a charity donation to someone in need of help who could potentially benefit from the new drug, but for whatever reason can't physically participate in the study at an approved testing center.

Lori explained to me that only because of my good relationship with Janice, my church youth group and high school friend who works for the same pharma company, would they even consider allowing me to receive the drug in Las Vegas. I was ecstatic and felt so blessed that they are going to make this special arrangement for me.

So this week will be spent filling out paperwork, getting Dr. Gollard on board with Lori, and making sure the test protocol can be implemented properly here in Vegas. I'm really excited and hopeful that the test drug will enhance Opdivo's efficacy and actually work for me.

The plan is to get started within the next two weeks. I will receive Opdivo as an infusion every other week (8 times) over four months and be administered the test drug via an intra-dermal injection every week (16 times), alternating the injection sight between my upper left and right thighs and left and right shoulder blades. Apparently, it's common for there to be a lot of inflammation, pain, and soreness around the injection area, along with some body aches. But I'm told that it's actually a good thing to have those side effects, as it's an indicator that the drug is working, and the body/tumor is responding. We'll have to wait and see what will happen with me.

So, finally, I've got some renewed hope and optimism. It's no coincidence that Janice reached out to let me know about this study at the same time I was going to be put on Opdivo anyway. I really believe this is a "message" from my Higher Power or heavenly angels who are watching over and protecting me. I know I'm supposed to do this "test" and the fact that an exception is being made for me is incredible!

I'm re-energized and ready to get things going again! I remain #PetzingStrong!

MAY 17 2018

Words with So Much Meaning To Me

Dr. Gollard is on vacation this week, so I've been gathering all of the information and FDA/Confidentiality/Protocol paperwork he will need to sign to administer the Opdivo/Test Drug combo clinical trial for me here in Vegas. I have an appointment with him on Monday morning to confirm that he will participate and then I'll set him up with Lori, the Research Director at Heat Biologics, to get the ball rolling. I'm hopeful that I can get started right after Memorial Day Weekend, as I continue to hear the "tick tock" of a clock in my head and worry about wasting time, which is of the essence right now.

Since I stopped receiving chemo about a month ago and radiation a week ago, I've been feeling better than usual. The chemo is almost out of my system, while the radiation will still be working for another few weeks. Dr. Dean said that we'll know the radiation is doing its job if I see a reduction in my wheezing and a lessening of my hacking cough. So far so good, as both are starting to happen! I also continue to receive my hydration "fun bag" every Monday, Wednesday and Friday. It's helping me stay energized and more functional than usual. So, overall, I can't complain!

Spiritually, I've been reaching out more to my Higher Power and asking for his guidance and help. I'm working hard at trying to stay in the present and embracing my lack of control over what is and isn't happening at any given moment. This is really difficult for me as I've always had a PLAN for getting to where I want to be in my life. And this plan has worked beautifully, until Cancer interrupted it for the second time. Now I can't really plan for anything in the future because of all the current variables I'm faced with today. I'm learning to grow more comfortable with just having a plan for each day that I'm fortunate to still be here on this great Earth. For me, it's all about living fully in the moment and maximizing the opportunities each day brings...doing what makes me happy, while hopefully impacting others in a positive, inspirational way.

Interestingly, this was reinforced for me with a Facebook Messenger note I received last night from someone I don't even really know. Here's what Marcy said:

«Hi! We only met the one time at Art and Tom's wedding, but I've been following you on Facebook and just wanted to reach out to let you know I'm rooting for you all the time and sending positive energy every day. I remember you telling Jed, my husband, and me your story and feeling in awe that you took life by the reigns and made poker your job. You suck the marrow out of life, and you know how to live! It's inspirational and always will be. I have no doubt that you will continue your journey with the same amount of energy and resolve to 'do more of what makes you happy.' Just wanted to let you know how you touch people, even the ones who you've only met once. WE are all better for knowing you."

I have to admit that I have tears rolling down my face as I'm writing this. Marcy's note has touched me at my core. It's so meaningful to know that I can have a positive impact on people I don't even know, while experiencing and openly sharing an extremely difficult and negative situation in my life. I hope I'm blessed to continue to have the opportunity to do this now and in the future. I feel like it's my calling or a greater purpose that

I'm supposed to fulfill down the road. I'm excited for that and want to do whatever I can to be a strong role model for others. This will give my life more meaning.

Thank you, Marcy! You have no idea how much your note and encouraging words have meant to me.

MAY 21 2018

It's All Coming Together!

I had a great weekend of exciting news, feeling good, and winning at poker! It's the best I've felt since last October. Finally, some encouraging things are starting to happen that are giving me renewed hope and inspiration to keep on fighting my cancer battle.

On Friday, I spoke with Dr. Gollard via phone to tell him about the clinical trial opportunity that had been presented to me, combining Opdivo with a new test drug. He was conceptually on board with it and I told him I'd gather more information while he was on vacation last week. After our call, I immediately spoke with Lori at Heat Biologics, the company doing the trial, and learned that through a program called, Compassionate/Expanded Use, I can have the clinical trial administered by Dr. Gollard and his team here in Vegas versus me having to travel weekly to San Diego/La Jolla, CA to get treated. This was awesome news!

Later in the day, Janice emailed me to tell me about a new idea that her CEO, Jeff, at Heat Biologics had talked to her about relating to my situation. Apparently, there has been a lot of research going on in the area of oxygen therapy, looking at how it can suppress and kill cancer cells. Jeff believes that if they overlay intense oxygen 24/7 to the treatment combo of Opdivo and the "test" drug, that the overall efficacy and effectiveness of the trial will significantly increase.

So, Janice suggested that we learn more about the research going on and set up a conference call for us on Saturday morning with Natasa from the University of Miami. Natasa has been researching the impact of oxygen on reducing cancerous tumors in mice for over 15 years. She was very informative and truly believes that the work she has been doing is directly applicable and translatable to humans. In fact, in many instances, the cancerous tumors have completely disappeared in the mice.

As a result of our learning, I have agreed to now be a clinical trial of one. I will be hooked up to mobile oxygen everyday 24/7 for 18 weeks, while I receive the test drug injection weekly and the Opdivo infusion bi-weekly. It's a bit hard to picture having tubes in my nose and rolling/portable oxygen tanks with me all the time, but I know I can do it. The way I look at it is that I'll be committing 4 1/2 months doing this to hopefully expand my life expectancy well beyond five years.

As icing on the cake, Heat Biologics will pay for all of the test drug vaccines and the oxygen I'll be using. I couldn't be more blessed right now.

I know this is my calling. It's what I'm supposed to do. I'm excited to be the trailblazer in this uncharted territory, as it has never been done before. And, if this test model works, it could become the lifesaving treatment for so many others like me suffering with late stage lung cancer. What a miracle that would be!

On Friday, Janice also prodded me to start the process of getting a second opinion. She has a good friend from high school, also a Lori, who just happens to work at Memorial Sloan Kettering in New York City. Janice researched all of the doctors who specialize in lung cancer and are actively involved with clinical trials. She found a Dr. Gregory Reilly who fits the bill. After checking in with Lori and getting feedback from others, Dr. Reilly appears to be the best!

So, I've now got an appointment with him on Tuesday, May 29 at 10:30am. I'll be taking my first red-eye since September 2017, departing Vegas at 11:55pm on May 28 and arriving at Newark, NJ (just outside NYC) at 7:45am. Janice has graciously offered to join me in the meeting. I'm so excited to reconnect in person and give her a big hug for everything she has done for me.

Dr. Reilly will look at all of my records and scans and provide his thoughts on my situation. I expect we'll talk about clinical trials that I might qualify for at Sloan Kettering and/or others that he may be aware of at other elite cancer centers. I'm a bit gun shy about joining a trial there right now, as there is the possibility that I could be put in a placebo group where I'm not receiving any kind of treatment. I can't take that risk. Regardless, I'm very interested to learn more about what's going on in the area of cancer research from an expert, like Dr. Reilly, at a renowned institution, like Sloan Kettering.

Lastly, I met with Dr. Gollard this morning to update him on everything that has transpired since our phone call ten days ago. He is totally on board with helping me out and administering the clinical trial here. There is a lot of paperwork that needs to be filed with the FDA and local IRB (Internal Review Board), but he is more than willing to do it and Lori at Heat Biologics will help facilitate that process. My guess is that it will take a couple of weeks to pull everything together, so I expect to get started on the new treatment the first week of June.

Finally, I see a glimmering light at the end of the tunnel. I have renewed hope. I believe that this is going to work and provide a breakthrough in the area of cancer research. I continue to be #PetzingStrong!

MAY 28 2018

Feeling Good, But Missing Chris

It has been a week since my last journal entry. I've been feeling really good, both physically and mentally. The chemo and radiation I've received over the past few months has finally worked its way out of my system and I feel like I have a clinical trial plan that just might work in helping extend my life.

Chris arrived this past Tuesday night for our "monthly" visit and headed back to Grand Rapids, MI yesterday afternoon. The time flew by. We always have such a great time together, even when we're doing nothing!

I always try to plan a fun night out seeing a concert or Vegas show when Chris is here. This visit we saw Ricky Martin at the Park Theater. His show was entertaining enough and featured a great stage production, but Ricky's voice really isn't that good. He clearly enjoys and prefers singing in Spanish versus English. It's too bad the whole concert wasn't in Spanish, as those songs were much better overall. "She Bangs," his breakout song, was a disappointment as he just went through the motions. Ricky was 'over the top' dramatic in his delivery of ballads sung in English. However, to his credit, at 46, he is still sexy as ever and certainly knows how to command the stage with his dance moves. He'd be a nice addition to *Dancing With The Stars*. Chris and I gave the show a B- and sadly would not recommend it.

Chris and I also saw the movie, *Life Of The Party*, with Melissa McCarthy as a recently divorced Mom who ends up going back to her daughter's college to complete her archaeology degree. It was silly fun with a few good laughs, but predictable, slow moving, and a bit farfetched. Our rating: 2-2.5 stars.

On Saturday morning, we celebrated my bestie Ardys' 57th birthday with ten friends at a breakfast. I was excited that Chris got to meet and spend time getting to know some of my other friends here in Vegas.

After dropping Chris off at the airport at 1:30pm yesterday, I drove to my bestie Jackie's house for a surprise birthday BBQ for our friend, Tammy. It was a gorgeous day and Jackie & Mike had quite the spread for all of us to enjoy, including homemade cupcakes AND vanilla ice cream that were "out of this world." I wish Chris could have joined me and I miss him already.

I got home at 5pm, took an hour nap, and then played a 7pm poker tourney at the Venetian, but did not cash. Today, I'll be playing in a tourney at Aria starting at 11am.

Unfortunately, I was supposed to be flying out to New York City tonight for my second opinion consult with Dr. Reilly at Memorial Sloan Kettering, but I had to cancel the appointment and flight. Not surprisingly, my primary care physician's administrative staff did not file the proper referral documentation to my insurance company, so I was unable to get authorization and payment coverage in time. The appointment is going to cost between $3K-$4K, so once I get authorization I will re-schedule with Dr. Reilly.

In the meantime, progress is being made on setting up my clinical trial. There are a lot of variables involved and I'm hoping that I'll be starting treatment two weeks from today. Tomorrow morning, I'm having a CT scan to get starting measurements of the tumor in my right lung and to see how extensive the cancerous lymph nodes are in the middle of my chest. The clinical trial company is going to send Dr. Gollard a special minus 80 degree Farenheit freezer to store the test drug vaccine and review all of the test protocol with him. Dr. Gollard is referring me to a respiratory therapist, who will be part of our team, to help manage the 24/7 oxygen therapy and he's also working to recruit a local hospital, where I'll be tested and evaluated throughout the 18 weeks of the trial.

It has been nice being on hiatus from treatment for the past couple of weeks, but I'm ready to get the ball rolling again and beat this bastard. In the meantime, I'll be playing in the World Series of Poker starting on Wednesday. My first event is the $10K Bounty Super Turbo No Limit Hold'em tourney, where I'll earn $3K for each person I knock out. I feel like I'm going to catch fire this Summer and have an amazing run!

Continuing to be #PetzingStrong

JUN 2 2018

A Few Bumps in The Road

I met with Dr. Gollard on Wednesday to review the results of the CT scan I had on Tuesday. It appears that the 12 radiation treatments, pursuant to the 14 chemotherapy drips I had, helped shrink the tumor in my right lung by almost 50%. It's still quite large, but small enough so that I no longer am experiencing the constant wheezing and hacking cough that consumed me for almost five weeks just before and during my radiation treatments. In addition, the CT scan did not show any additional cancer spots, so this all great news!

During my appointment, we also discussed next steps for the clinical trial. Dr. Gollard told me that he had been in touch with Lori from Heat Biologics and confirmed that progress is slowly being made. He has to get a representative from a National Review Board to present my case and get approval. Additionally, we're waiting on an okay from the FDA. There are a lot of variables involved in making a clinical trial happen.

In our meeting, Dr. Gollard expressed his concern over the oxygen therapy component of the treatment. After reading the protocol, he saw that I would be receiving 10 liters of pure 60% oxygen (which is a drug) per minute pumped through my nose. He compared it to sitting in front of a high-powered air-conditioning unit with my mouth wide open 24/7 for 18 weeks. Given the mild case of COPD (Chronic Obstructive Pulmonary Disease) I also have, he thinks that my body, especially the kidneys, may have to work too hard to process all of the oxygen. This could result in my development of respiratory acidosis, an acidic state throughout the body that could cause a myriad of additional problems. So, Dr. Gollard asked me to set up an appointment with Dr. Tavares to review the situation and get a second opinion. It is scheduled for this coming Tuesday morning.

Simultaneously to all of this, Lori from Heat Biologics contacted me to ask how many hours a day I am generally out of the house. I told her about 12-14. This may pose a problem with the oxygen therapy because the portable oxygen units only pump a maximum of 3 liters per minute. The protocol requires 10L/minute and only the large compressor units can provide that flow. So, basically, I'd be homebound and hooked up to oxygen for 4 1/2 months. Unfortunately, that just won't work for me. I think that would kill me before the lung cancer! Both of these issues, along with the concern over respiratory acidosis, could be deal breakers for the oxygen therapy component of the clinical trial.

In the meantime, I asked Lori to contact Natasa at the University of Miami to see if there might be a way to adjust the protocol and still get anticipated good results. We'll have to see what she says.

So, it's not looking good for the oxygen therapy. I'm still hopeful that I can do the original clinical trial combining Opdivo with Heat Biologic's new test drug. Dr. Gollard wants me to start the Opdivo, so I'm scheduled for that infusion on Wednesday. He is going to meet Lori this weekend at a cancer conference, so they will talk more about my possible options. Needless to say, I'm feeling a bit deflated but am optimistic that something else will present itself down the road as a viable option. I just need to be patient and continue my prayers.

On the positive side of things, I cashed in two poker tournaments this past week and am physically feeling good. Additionally, our Vegas Golden Knights hockey team is battling to win The Stanley Cup versus the Washington Capitols and the World Series of Poker is underway, so I'm hoping for a big win(s) over the next six weeks!

#PetzingStrong

JUN 6 2018

Oxygen Therapy is Possible, But Impractical

I met with Dr. Tavares yesterday to get a second opinion on the 60% pure oxygen therapy as an overlay to the clinical trial that combines Opdivo and the test drug, HS-110. Dr. Gollard was concerned about the intensity of 10 liters/minute of oxygen being pumped into my nose 24/7 for 18 weeks and it potentially causing a negative reaction called respiratory acidosis, where my body is unable to process it effectively and, in turn, discharge the accumulating carbon dioxide.

I brought Dr. Tavares up to speed on my 14 chemo and 12 radiation treatments that "didn't work" and the background info on the clinical trial with and without the oxygen overlay. He also reviewed my recent PET scan. Interestingly, he had no issues whatsoever in my ability to handle the oxygen therapy. He indicated that since I was never a smoker, was not overweight, and was in good physical health (outside of the cancer) that he believed my brain would be activated properly by the excess oxygen and inform my kidneys to process it and get it out of my body. He gave the trial with the oxygen overlay a "thumbs up" and said I should do it.

I then brought up the issue that apparently there are no portable oxygen units that pump more than 3 liters/min and that having to be home bound 24/7 for 18 weeks with a large compressor unit seemed impractical and too difficult for me to handle. It would completely affect my positive attitude and bring me down. I think I'd feel differently about doing the oxygen therapy if it was guaranteed to work, but it's not. Dr. Tavares and I talked about proposing a change to the current protocol whereby for twelve hours/day I'd do the at home oxygen at 10L/min and the other twelve hours, when I'm away from home, I'd use the portable pack at 3L/min. He didn't think it would fly with Heat Biologics, but I said I'd call them and explore the possibilities. There has to be a better option out there and I will find it!

Today I had an appointment with Dr. Gollard to catch up on the status of things and fill him in on my meeting with Dr. Tavares. I told him that Dr. Tavares had no issues and was totally fine with moving forward with the oxygen therapy. However, after Dr. Gollard met with Lori and her staff in Chicago at a cancer conference this past weekend, he learned that I would need to use 45 tanks of oxygen per day at home with the large compressor to get 10L/minute. That's ridiculous! Shipping and storage coordination would be a nightmare with 45 tanks needed per day. Even worse, I'd have to wake up hourly to replace the tanks. How would I sleep?! It just seems so impractical. Clearly, the protocol was not written with logistical aspects in mind. I'm hoping there is some flexibility and shared Dr. Tavares' and my idea to change the protocol with Dr. Gollard.

Dr. Gollard indicated that he didn't think Heat Biologics would change the protocol because it would take too much time and effort to get the necessary approvals from the FDA, IRB and others. I told him that I'd call Lori to see if they'd give it a shot and will do so by the end of the week.

After my meeting with Dr. Gollard, I received my Opdivo immunotherapy infusion, along with an anti-nausea drug and steroids to help lessen any unpleasant side effects. It's 11:55pm and I'm a bit wired, so the steroids are definitely working, and I feel good. We'll have to see if I bottom out tomorrow or Friday. The good news is that I receive hydration on Friday, so I'm hopeful that it will help me get through the weekend with solid energy and few negative issues. Only time will tell.

Unfortunately, poker hasn't gone so well the past week or so. I'm definitely due for a cash and/or a BIG win! I know it's coming and will continue to fight hard for it, just like I will battle this cancer until IT dies and leaves my body. That's how it's going to be!

I continue to be #PetzingStrong.

JUN 16 2018

A Tough Ten Days!

Well, it has been ten days since I've done a journal update. I apologize for that and hope I haven't worried anyone. I've been having a tough time with things, needed a bit of a break, and was just feeling a bit overwhelmed. Let me bring you up to date.

I received my first Opdivo immunotherapy infusion a week ago on Wednesday. It was given to me with steroids to counteract any potential side effects. Dr. Gollard is still working with Heat Biologics to get the HS-110 test drug that will improve the efficacy of the Opdivo, but the process is moving slowly. We're still waiting for FDA and local IRB approval, as only 35 people nationwide are currently getting the Opdivo/HS-110 treatment combo in a clinical trial. Since I'm a Compassionate Use candidate and getting the trial administered outside of the primary site, there are extra hurdles to overcome. My guess is that I will start receiving the HS-110 injection in 10 to 14 days.

I also learned last week that my insurance company, Health Plan of Nevada (HPN), denied my request for coverage of a second opinion by Memorial Sloan Kettering Cancer Center in NYC. I'm very disappointed about this, as the cost for a consult is between $3-4K, excluding travel expenses. I want my second and third opinions to come from the most renown lung cancer facilities, where they are actively involved in conducting clinical trials and know the latest and greatest techniques for battling late stage lung cancer. HPN did throw me a bone and said they'd cover a consult at Keck Hospital of USC in Los Angeles-Department of Hematology Oncology. I likely will give this a shot, however I'm going to appeal the denial and take it to a higher level.

Ironically, I ran into my friend, Marty, at the World Series of Poker (WSOP), who has been a big supporter of mine. I mentioned my insurance coverage struggle and he told me about a friend of his, Jill, who used to be the person at health insurance companies who stamped, "DENIED," on coverage requests. She knows all the "ins and outs" of the system and actually left her job because of all the bureaucratic bull shit she saw and the denials she was required to make. Marty has hooked me up with her and we plan to chat this weekend. Jill said she'd help me with my appeal and I'm really excited to talk with her.

Since my chemo and radiation treatments stopped over seven weeks ago, I have been generally feeling great! Most of the poison and toxins have worked their way out of my system. I've had good energy and no coughing or wheezing. Oddly, this past Sunday, while I was playing Day 2 of the WSOP $1500 8-Game Mix event, I felt like my heart was beating out of my chest. We were already in the money and there were 35 of 481 runners left in the tourney playing for the $148K first prize. I was calm, cool and collected and had an above average chip stack but was becoming quite concerned about the pain that was piercing my upper back, shoulders, and neck, and also shooting up and over my head. It was hard to concentrate. Luckily, my friend, April, was railing me and I went over and told her what was happening. She got me some Advil, which helped a little, and then I got a 60-minute massage at dinner break, thinking that would alleviate some of the pain.

We started playing again after dinner break and I felt a slight bit better. My chest was tightening up directly under my neck, the heart was still beating fast and the pain started coming back. I got into a big pot in the game, Razz, and lost a heart breaker along with all of my chips finishing in 31st of 481 players for $3344. I was really happy with my play, especially because the tournament consists of eight different poker games and I'm really just a No Limit Hold'em specialist. I got my money and walked out to my car at 2am. I was huffing and puffing by the time I got to it. Fortunately, I only live seven minutes from the Rio Convention Center, so I arrived home quickly. I took some Tylenol and a Xanax to calm myself down and help me sleep. I got in bed, still feeling pained (7 of 10), and sat for a while. I couldn't fall asleep sitting up, so I laid down and the pain level shot up to a 9.5 out of 10. I was really worried that I might pass out and that no one would know, so I threw on some clothes, packed my backpack, fed the cats and drove myself to the Sunrise Hospital Emergency Room which was only eight minutes away from my condo complex.

Yes, I know it was a bad decision to get in the car and drive myself, but I wasn't thinking properly. I should have called Uber or a friend, but it was 2:45am.

I arrived at the emergency room and there were 15 people ahead of me in the waiting area. I checked in and mentioned that I thought I might be having heart attack. Fortunately, my name was called within ten minutes and I was escorted into the actual emergency room where there had to be at least 40 people strewn all over it. There weren't even enough chairs for everyone. There were people on the floor crying and rolling around. I felt like I was in a third world country.

I found a chair in the corner and waited. Again, I was lucky, and my name was called within 15 minutes. I went through the standard interview and admitting process and off I went to my own examining room.

Quickly, they took my vitals, an EKG and blood work for testing. The results came back that I was borderline for a mild heart attack. The cardiologist was called in and decided to do an angiogram to see if I might have artery blockage. Since I would be unconscious during the procedure, we had to make a decision then on how I would be treated if he discovered over 70% blockage. The concern was that he'd need to treat me with Heparin and blood thinners that might cause me to bleed out because of all the chemo treatments I've had, but he wasn't sure. I agreed that if I was 90% or more clogged, that he could go ahead and do what he needed to do. So, the cardiologist put me out and inserted a long needle with a camera up my groin to evaluate the situation. He found that one of my arteries had 50% blockage, so nothing needed to be done at that time. He also wasn't sure that it was enough to cause a heart attack.

So I was kept for more tests and observation. Given the pain I was having in my head, I was concerned that maybe the lung cancer had spread to my brain. They administered an ultrasound, more blood tests, a chest x-ray, and a CT scan of my brain and chest. The EKG monitor continued to indicate an "out of normal range" situation. My nurse, Joanne, was amazing! She took such great care of me and I felt like a King. And then the case manager came in and said that my insurance was not taken at Sunrise Hospital and that I'd have to be transferred to a hospital that did accept it. Really!? I'm sure the costs I had incurred up to that point were ridiculously high. The attending physician came into see me and I expressed my concern. He said he'd do what he could to make sure that my costs were covered. It appears that on my transfer papers he said I had an acute heart attack that, in turn, would be reason for my insurance to cover me in a dire situation. We'll see what happens.

At 11pm on Monday night, I was transferred to Desert Springs Hospital, which is only five minutes from Sunrise. The difference between the two was night and day. Desert Springs Hospital was Las Vegas' first hospital and is known as the "Heart" hospital. It is old and not updated. Basically, it's a dump with bad energy. I was transported there via ambulance and immediately taken to my room, where I had a roommate on the other side of the curtain. I finally was in my bed at 11:30pm and not one person came in to see me until 2am. I had been on morphine and Percocet for pain at Sunrise and needed something badly. It took them an hour to get me a pain pill. Horrible! I woke up every hour until 7am when "breakfast" arrived. It consisted of a dried up cinnamon apple pancake, a thick slice of cold white mystery meat (which I learned was processed turkey), and a hardboiled egg plopped on top of the pancake. Disgusting! Everything went downhill from there.

The attending physician assigned to my case didn't come by until 10am. He had not read my case file from Sunrise, so I had to explain my whole cancer background and what had happened to me for the fifth time in 36 hours. I told him I was disappointed that he hadn't read up on me, the tests I had undergone, and what the doctors at Sunrise thought about my situation. He said he liked to "hear it from the patient's mouth first."

My translation of that is, "No, I'm a lazy SOB and don't really give a damn about you because your one of 25 patients I have in this hospital."

Anyway, he said he'd have the cardiologist look at my file and get a determination from him. I also asked him to call Dr. Gollard to share all of my test results with him and determine if perhaps I had a negative reaction to the Opdivo infusion I received only five days earlier. He said he would. Interestingly, my nurse overheard our conversation and told me that he is known for not responding in a timely manner.

Argh.

The nurses and aides at Desert Springs were so bad. No one would come for thirty minutes or more after I pressed the call button. My roommate, Richard, warned me about how awful the hospital and care were. He was right. It was a shit show.

Late in the afternoon, the cardiologist blew into my room and announced that, "Your heart is perfectly fine. I don't even know why they bothered to transfer you here. You did not have a heart attack. You shouldn't even be here, so I'm recommending that you be discharged."

That one way "conversation" lasted three minutes. I asked what he thought happened to me.

He said, "I don't know, but it's not your heart." And off he went.

My roommate, Richard, was very bizarre and quite the chatterbox. Basically, I found out that he was from Hawaii but living in Vegas, had been left a lot of money when his Mom died, loved his old Camaro, was a big drinker, had friends sneak beers into the hospital for him, and that he had killed a man by shooting him in the back when he tried to steal his Camaro and never got prosecuted. I decided that I'd be friends with Richard.

My attending physician never appeared again until 3:30pm. He told me had left Dr. Gollard a message, but that he hadn't returned the call. He said that he thought I should remain in the hospital overnight for observation until he spoke with Dr. Gollard. I wanted out of there but agreed to stay because no one really knew what was wrong with me. My pain had subsided a lot and I was feeling better.

I called Dr. Gollard's office and asked why he hadn't returned the message. They scoured all their answering machines and said they had nothing from my attending physician. The nurse was right. He never called. Dr. Gollard asked me to get his phone number so he could call him directly, but they would not give it to me because they don't belong in the same practice. I demanded it and said that this was a "shit show" and needed them to speak immediately. The nurse said that he'd come back to see me between 7-8pm.

At 8:45pm, my lazy attending physician rolled in and said he finally spoke with Dr. Gollard and that although he didn't think my "attack" was a result of the Opdivo infusion, it could still be a possibility and I'd need to follow up with him directly the next day. I was discharged with a "vascular spasm" diagnosis, prescribed medicine to manage the potential heart issue/blockage, and Jackie drove me home at 10:30pm.

I finally got a great night of sleep and felt pretty good the next morning. I went to see Dr. Gollard and we agreed to continue the Opdivo treatment, but with the addition of more steroids and Prednisone that I will be taking every day for five days after the infusion. Hopefully, that will limit any negative side effects coming from the Opdivo. So that's where we stand.

It has been a tough ten days, but I'm feeling back on track. Louise gave me an authentic Las Vegas Golden Nights hockey jersey as a gift and on the back, where the player's name goes, it says PetzingStrong! She also put number 54 on the jersey, which was the number on my high school varsity basketball uniform. It was such a thoughtful gift and I wore it yesterday.

I want to give a special thanks to all of my friends that came to visit me in the hospitals: Louise, Jackie, Nicole, Lynnore, Nancy, and Tammy & Jerry. You cheered me up and it was very much appreciated!

Now back to the poker tables. It's time to take down a big one! I remain #PetzingStrong.

JUN 30 2018

Hanging in There

I decided to take a two week break from writing in my journal, as there really hasn't been much change in my situation and I wanted to focus on poker. I've really been enjoying the World Series of Poker (WSOP) and all of the other tournament series. For the past 14 days, I have a 20% cash rate in tournaments and Sit N Go's (1 table tourneys). It's good, but not great. Overall, I've been very card and flop dead, and have had to put my bluffing skills to the test to accumulate chips. I'm definitely due to catch on fire and hopefully that will happen soon. There are still two big weeks of poker left to play, including the WSOP $10K Main Event, which I did well in last year.

I had my second Opdivo immunotherapy infusion 10 days ago. The addition of extra steroids given to me with it and the Prednisone I took for a week after it helped alleviate any side effects. I've been feeling really good physically and have lots of energy. I'm still waiting for the clinical trial HS-110 test drug to be approved by the FDA and IRB locally here in Vegas. I know that the applications are completed and filed and that the IRB met recently, so I should get a status update this coming Tuesday when I meet with Dr. Gollard and get my third Opdivo infusion.

Emotionally, I've been on a bit of a roller coaster ride. Waiting to move forward fully with the clinical trial has been difficult. I feel like I'm losing valuable time and there is no guarantee that it will work. It will be an 18-week program once I start receiving the HS-110 injections in combination with the Opdivo immunotherapy. At the end of November, I will have another PET scan to see what impact the combo treatment has made on the tumor and cancerous nodes. From those results, my doctors will be better able to give me a sense of where I stand with life expectancy. I will also move forward with getting a second, and possibly a third, opinion at that time.

My biggest fear right now is that the cancer might metastasize somewhere else in my body: brain, liver, bones, etc. If that happens, I'm in big trouble. It's very hard not to think about this because it's such a common occurrence with cancer victims. All I can do is hope and pray for the best outcome possible.

On top of all of this, I'm just feeling very lonely. Poker has been a saving grace as it gives me a purpose for getting out every day, while keeping my mind occupied and challenged. It's also my socialization outlet. But when I come home at night and wake up in the morning, it's just me. Not physically having someone else there, just to be with me and share my feelings and concerns with, is difficult. I'm not and never have been a needy person, but sometimes I just wish I had that regular 'in person' support.

This is not to say that I don't have an amazing group of friends, who I know truly care about me and would do whatever I needed, but it's different. And, Chris, who lives with his family in Michigan, does his best to be supportive long distance. However, it's just not the same as having someone there with and next to you on a regular basis when you're going through a difficult time every single day.

I hope this isn't coming off as "whiny" because that's not my intention. I'm just expressing how I feel emotionally and am doing my best to be strong and manage through it. Of course, some days are better than others, but overall I think I'm doing pretty well.

That about covers it for now. I hope you all enjoy your July 4th holiday weekend!

Continuing to work hard at being #PetzingStrong!

JUL 8 2018

A Disappointing Week

The past eight days have been full of poker. I haven't had a tournament cash since last Sunday, so I'm feeling very frustrated that I've been running so badly. I haven't hit my sets or straight and flush draws when I needed to the most, and I've missed almost every important flip. Sometimes poker is like that. It just hurts when it happens. My biggest disappointment of the week was only getting through Day 2 of the $10K Main Event and busting out early in Day 3. Last year I cashed in the Main and had hoped to better my performance this time around, but sadly it wasn't "in the cards." Hopefully, all of the bad juju is gone now and my outcomes will improve this week.

I had my third Opdivo immunotherapy infusion the other day. All went fine and I haven't had any negative side effects. I believe this is due to Dr. Gollard continuing the addition of steroids to my treatment and to me taking Prednisone twice a day for a week after each infusion.

Unfortunately, progress came to a halt this week on getting the clinical trial drug, HS-110, which I desperately need to help improve the efficacy of the Opdivo treatment. Right now, given my cancer cell profile, I only have a 5% chance of the Opdivo working alone to shrink and/or kill the right lung tumor. But with the combo treatment of HS-110 and Opdivo together, my chances increase to 33%.

The reason for the slowdown is that there are so many protocol requirements involved with the shipping, receiving, storing, management of the injection itself, and disposal of the hazardous waste materials. The FDA and IRB here in Las Vegas require that each step of the process have someone in charge and responsible, which will mean that a number of different people need to be trained and brought into my treatment loop. In my appointment with Dr. Gollard on Wednesday, he indicated that his staff could not do all of this work and that other folks from OptumCare Cancer Care would need to get involved to make this happen. He also recommended that Lori, my contact from Heat Biologics, coordinate all of the players and come to Las Vegas to train them.

I expressed my frustration to Dr. Gollard and asked him to please do what he could to get the right people in his organization on board as soon as possible. I said that I would call Lori and see what she could do to help. My concern is that I'm losing valuable time. Once everything is approved, I will receive the HS-110 vaccine injection once a week for 18 weeks and the Opdivo infusion every other week during that time. We just need to get this going! I'm also at the point where, starting at the end of July, I may just decide to fly to San Diego every week and join the actual clinical trial in Carlsbad, CA., if that's an option.

The potential problem with that is if I have negative side effects, like fever, body aches, severe soreness at the injection site, or something unexpected, I may not be able to make the trip alone. I've discussed this with my closest circle of friends and they said they would do whatever it takes to get me there and back, even if it means driving me roundtrip in a day each week. Louise also offered me her San Clemente home as a place to stay if I need to. I feel so blessed to have such an amazing support group!

I finally got a chance to speak with Lori directly this past Thursday. She explained to me that she had made contact with the head of Research for OptumCare Cancer Care here in Vegas and made some good progress with him. It looks like he's now ready to support the effort. So, I'm hopeful that the right people are now being recruited from the organization to help manage the process. I should know more a week from Tuesday when I go back to see Dr. Gollard for my fourth Opdivo infusion. My fingers are crossed for a "green light" to move forward.

Finally, on a sad and disappointing note, I had to "divorce" a friend of mine yesterday. We've known each other for over ten years and have had some fun times together, but I don't like the selfish and insincere person that she has become. When a friendship is one-sided and that person only reaches out when they need something or it's convenient for them, they aren't really a true friend. As we go through life, we start to understand that it's not important to have a lot of friends. What truly matters is that we have real friends!

JUL 30 2018

Fever & Frustration

I apologize for being so delinquent in keeping you up to date on my status. It has been three weeks since my last journal entry and I just haven't had the motivation to write. I've really felt down and out as nothing seems to be moving forward in the way I had hoped. I'm trying to stay positive, but it's hard. I feel like time is not on my side and constantly hear the "tick tock" of a clock in my head.

My biggest frustration has been the lack of significant forward movement in getting the HS-110 trial drug approved for use with me here in Vegas. This drug, in combination with the Opdivo immunotherapy treatments I've been receiving over the past two months, has the potential to significantly improve my overall chances of the combo treatment working. I just want to get it going!

The hold up right now is getting OptumCare Cancer Care, my cancer treatment center, to provide the IBC (a drug safety organization) with exactly how they are going to handle all of the steps of the process from receipt of the drug to storage, administration, and disposal of the hazardous waste. It sounds simple, but it's not. The VP of Operations is handling this now and must have responsible parties assigned for each step who will follow specific protocols. I have two phone calls in to him requesting an update on where things are, but haven't heard back from him yet. Tomorrow I get my fifth Opdivo infusion and have an appointment with Dr. Gollard, so hopefully he'll have more information for me.

Oddly, for the past five days, I've been getting a fever that starts in the early afternoon and peaks in the evening around 102. Then it's magically gone in the morning, except for today when I woke up with a 99.6 fever. It comes with fatigue, body aches and chills and I've had to nap for 2 to 3 1/2 hours each day. The research I've done indicates that these side effects do occur for some Opdivo patients. Hopefully, my blood work tomorrow will identify more of what's really going on.

On a positive note, I was able to travel to Michigan for six days to visit Chris and his family. It was just what I needed after a long two months of poker. It was so nice to live a "normal" life with him and his kids during that week. It had been ten months since I had seen them, and they have really grown up. He has all girls: 11, 14, 17 and 19. I was able to spend some individual time with each of them and I feel like our bonds grew even stronger. The youngest two are very attached to me and I just love talking to and spending time with them. We went out to lunch and to the movies to see Skyscraper and all enjoyed it.

While in Michigan, we took a weekend trip to Traverse City to see Chris' Mom and his sister, Anne, and her family. They have a cottage on the lake, and it was so refreshing to just hang out there for a couple of days, taking in the gorgeous views and being with his family. Chris' Mom, Joan, and I also got to spend some great quality time together. She is very religious and blessed me with Holy water twice during our visit. Joan also gave me a beautiful rosary and some prayer cards to use. She is so sweet and told me that she thinks of me as one of her sons. I was so touched!

I was hoping to go to Los Angeles on Thursday to play poker there for a long weekend, but given this bothersome fever I've had for the past five days I'm not sure that's a good idea. I'll decide tomorrow if that makes sense or not.

I remain optimistic that things will get better for me and continue to be #PetzingStrong!

AUG 7 2018

Feeling Out of Control

It has been eight days since my last journal entry. I'm in a pretty foul mood today, however I'm going to start with something that really touched me yesterday.

I received a text from my ex-wife's best friend, and a friend of mine, Faye. Sadly, her Dad is also fighting lung cancer. This is what she wrote:

> "Hi Jim,
>
> I wanted to reach out to you because I wanted to let you know that your CaringBridge posts have been very instrumental with my dad's treatment. As you know, my dad has been diagnosed with lung cancer and by reading your CaringBridge I was able to talk to the doctors with a little more knowledge. We were able to get a feeding tube inserted before he started any treatments. We also were able to get a hydration bag request approved for two times a week. Thank you so much for sharing your journey with us. If it wasn't for you, I don't know that he would have been able to get everything we needed for my dad. I have and will

continue to pray for you for a full recovery. I know you've got this, Jim!

Best, Faye"

It's notes like these that really keep me going. I want to know that I'm making a difference in others' lives with my story. If I can just help a handful of people, it makes me feel good!

Sadly, I didn't have the benefit of knowing anything about Cancer, especially neck cancer when I was first diagnosed with it back in 2014: treatment options, side effects, the need to be your own advocate, and the physical, mental and emotional turmoil I'd be faced with. I know my book has helped many as I continue to receive Facebook messages, emails and texts from many who have read it. This gives me great satisfaction! I will also be making this blog into my second book to continue to try to make a difference.

On another positive note, last Wednesday, I cashed for $6,200 finishing in 2nd place in the Wynn NLH Seniors Tournament. So hopefully that will get me back on track and in the win column more often than I have been lately.

Other than those two "good news" items, I continue to have daily fevers ranging from 99.5-102. When I met with Dr. Gollard last week, he confirmed that they are likely a side effect of my Opdivo immunotherapy treatment and that they will occur the entire time I'm on this drug. So it looks like I will have a fever, chills and mild body aches every day for the next five months or so. Great! I have to learn to manage through and live with this. I'm not going to let it get the best of me or keep me isolated in my apartment. The only thing I can do for it is to take Tylenol. So, I will figure out a system that works for me.

In general, I wake up with a mild fever and then it dissipates by late morning. Around 3pm, it starts back up again and peaks between 6pm and 8pm. That's when I feel the worst. I usually fall asleep watching TV around 10:30pm, wake up, take a Xanax and only get up to pee once or twice. Additionally,

I'm getting severe night sweats and have to change my t-shirt frequently. I guess I should be thankful that I'm not nauseous and that it's not any worse than this.

Then there is the continuing saga of not being able to get my HS-110 test drug here in Vegas under the Compassionate Use statute. The problem centers on the VP of Operations at OptumCare Cancer Care who just can't seem to find the time to get his shit together and get the local IBC safety submission filed. He has lied to Dr Gollard and the clinical trial folks to try to cover his ass.

Well, he has been caught in those lies and I'm on the warpath to get him exposed. I plan to take my case all the way to the CEO, if necessary, and I'm even going to pursue legal action. I should have been receiving this drug, which increases the efficacy of the Opdivo I'm already taking from 5% to 33%, over a month ago. Now, at best, I have to wait at least another four weeks. It's total bullshit and no one is going to fuck around with my life! This guy has no idea who he is dealing with. He didn't even have the courtesy to return two pleasant voice mail messages I left for him over three weeks ago, where I wanted to introduce myself and check on status of the IBC submission. Well, of course he didn't return my calls because he hadn't done anything!!!

I'm seething.....

Due to this delay, I now am pursuing a full time trial with the HS-110 drug in La Jolla, CA, Tuscon, AZ, or Portland, OR and am waiting to hear if I will be accepted. This will likely require me to physically move to one of those areas and live there until the end of the year. I'm stressing out a bit about it, but I really have no choice. My clock is ticking and I'm very concerned. This is my last hope in modern medicine. If it doesn't work, I likely will have to pursue alternative medicine. So, yes, I'm freaking out just a bit and have lots of negative emotions enveloping me.

That's it for now. I'll provide an update when I have something good to report on, but don't hold your breath. Virtually nothing has gone right for me medically since October.

Trying to remain #PetzingStrong but becoming incredibly difficult. It's as if everything is out of my control! I just don't want to live this way anymore.

SEP 14 2018

I'm Back!

I've been quite delinquent for not giving you all an update during the past 5 1/2 weeks. Honestly, I just wasn't up to it and needed to take a break from writing. I was frustrated, sad and depressed from battling two weeks of fever and not making any significant progress on getting my HS-110 clinical trial test drug. It was like being in a "black hole," just floundering around not having any direction and wondering where and how I am going to end up. I didn't have anything positive to say, so I decided not to burden everyone with my somber mood and dark thoughts.

Sometimes I don't think anyone really understands how tiring it is to act okay and always be strong, when in reality you're close to the edge. A strong person is not the one who doesn't cry. A strong person is the one who is quiet, and sheds tears for a moment, and then picks up the sword and fights again. This clearly describes where I was and where I am now. I'm definitely re-energized and ready to fully take on this bastard called Cancer!

During my hiatus from journaling, I took a long weekend trip to Flagstaff, AZ to see Steve & Cory. They were my ex-wife, Charlene, and my best friends when we were married. We always had so much fun together when we lived in Chicago and had a second home in the seasonal resort area of Long Beach,

IN on Lake Michigan. I have fond memories that will always be with me. I hadn't seen Steve & Cory in over a year, and they invited me to visit them for a much needed get away. It was so nice to be out of the hot Vegas desert and find myself in a beautiful, natural environment with trees, mountains and wildlife.

Even though I was still having my daily fevers, I forced myself to take this trip and am so glad that I did. It was just the rejuvenating break from my reality that I needed. Steve & Cory custom-built their gorgeous home that sits on the side of a mountain and has the most incredible, scenic views. Each morning, we would sit on their back patio and have our coffee while watching the colorful array of birds and squirrels playing in the trees and wildflowers. It was so peaceful and calming. We had great conversations and enjoyed just hanging out together. It felt so good.

After returning to Vegas, my fevers suddenly disappeared. I haven't had one in over 3 1/2 weeks and have been feeling really good! Additionally, my poker game is back on track and I've cashed in six events since August 14, making the final table in five of them. Currently, I'm in Los Angeles at the Commerce Hotel & Casino preparing to play in their $1100 No Limit Hold'em Main Event today through Sunday. I was here last week and won my entry in a $175 satellite and then won another one last night, so I have two bullets to fire at this one. The guaranteed prize pool is $500K, so I plan to get a big part of that!

As I've mentioned before, poker has been a saving grace for me. It gives me purpose each day, keeps my mind focused on something other than having cancer, and provides a stimulating socialization outlet.

On another positive note, Chris came to visit me for a week over the Labor Day holiday. I miss him so much and always love when we can spend quality time together. We had a busy schedule during his visit. We saw two shows, "Hitsville, the Motown Review" and David Copperfield, along with two movies, "Operation Finale" and "Crazy Rich Asians." They were all great! We also had a lunch and dinner with different groups of my friends. Everything is so easy with Chris and I always look forward to being together.

And finally, after being my own patient advocate and writing a strong, passionate letter to OptumCare Cancer Care about their lack of urgency in getting the necessary paperwork filed with local health and safety organizations so that my clinical test drug could get approved for my use in Vegas, I have some GREAT news! I will start receiving the HS-110 test drug injections next week in combination with the Opdivo immunotherapy treatments I'm already receiving. I am hopefully optimistic and my fingers are crossed.

So I think that brings us up to date on where things are with me currently. I very much appreciate all of your caring and ongoing support. It means so much to me. I know I'm not fighting this battle alone and having you in my corner makes all the difference!

SEP 19 2018

Finally...I Got My Test Drug Injection!

So before I could actually start receiving the HS-110 clinical trial test drug, I had to get an EKG, heart blood work and a CT scan completed to make sure everything was in order. My EKG and heart blood work were "perfect." And even better news was that my CT scan, per Dr. Gollard, showed "a stable disease that might even be a little better" after enduring eight Opdivo immunotherapy treatments over the past four months. I expected these results and am happy with them. I'm also very relieved that my situation is not any worse!

This afternoon I received my first five injections of the HS-110 test drug. Ardys met me at OptumCare Cancer Care for moral support as I was a bit anxious and not quite sure what to expect.

After briefly sitting in the lobby, we were brought into the treatment area. Janet, one of my chemo nurses, sat with us while I read ten pages of a consent form outlining all of the trial specifics, possible side effects and potential dangers associated with receiving the test drug. After signing off, we were taken back to one of Dr. Gollard's patient rooms and on the door was a large, red plastic sign that said, "Danger Biohazard." Janet, who was trained a little over a week ago by Heat Biologics, explained that she needed to go "gown up and get her mask on" with another nurse, who would administer the injections with her.

Ardys and I waited for about 20 minutes until Janet and the other nurse arrived dressed head to toe in their gowns and masks. They asked Ardys to leave the room for safety and privacy reasons. Janet explained that she would be giving me five injections in a circle just under the skin of my upper right thigh and that we should be looking for raised bumps, like a mosquito bite, on at least four of the injection sites. The assisting nurse laid out all five of the syringes and handed them to Janet one at a time.

On the first attempt, Janet went a little too deep and we didn't get the raised bump. However, the other four injections were all successful! The shots themselves really didn't hurt that much and just felt like small bee stings. I think Janet was as nervous as I was and we were both relieved when we saw the four bumps appear, which was the goal.

It took about five minutes for Janet and the assisting nurse to clean up everything and properly dispose of the hazardous materials. Janet told me that I'd need to sit for 30 minutes to make sure I didn't have an immediate negative reaction. She went back out to the lobby and told Ardys she could come back and hang with me. The whole process went as I expected, and I felt fine after the half hour wait. Mission accomplished! I am so happy we finally got this going and that Week 1 of 18 is in the books.

Ardys and I had made plans to have a late lunch at an Asian restaurant and then go see the movie, *A Simple Favor*. It was so nice spending extended quality time with her, as we don't get a chance to do so very often. Lunch was great and the movie was very good and quite thought provoking. I highly recommend it!

I just watched the *America's Got Talent Finale Results* show and am really excited about its winner, who I will not reveal here. I'm not the spoiler type. The top two will definitely get to star in the November headline show here in Vegas. Now, I'm glued to Cuomo Prime Time on CNN and am catching up on the current controversial issues of the week. I'm quite tired, which I believe is a result of today's injection, and am ready to head to bed.

Thanks to all of you for being there in spirit and supporting me. It means so much...more than you know!

SEP 20 2018

Beating the Odds

It has been 33 hours since I had my first set of the five trial drug injections. So far, I feel just fine and am not experiencing any side effects. I expect that my reaction to the HS-110 drug will be similar to when I was receiving chemo and that I'll start feeling fatigued after the third or fourth week of treatments. I know this will sound strange to most of you, but I hope that I actually do get sick.

Why? Because those folks in the clinical trial, who share a similar lung cancer profile to me and whose tumors are responding to the combination of Opdivo immunotherapy and the HS-110 test drug, are feeling quite ill. So...it would be a good sign that "things" are working if I get sick, too!

Sometimes I'm asked by friends and acquaintances, in a roundabout way, what my prognosis is. What they are really asking is, "How long do you have to live?" I don't have a problem with this question.

I know most people are asking because they truly care about me and have their own need to know.

I, of course, also desperately want to know the answer to this difficult question. And, I've asked both Dr. Gollard and Dr. Dean the same question because I want to put a plan together for whatever future remains for me.

Interestingly, both doctors have told me that they can't and won't answer this question right now. They want to see how I do with the Opdivo/HS-110 combination treatment over the next 4 1/2 months, at which point, after a CT scan, Dr. Dean has promised that he will give me his opinion on this topic. I expect to receive the same from Dr. Gollard, too.

Ironically, Elizabeth just texted the following September 17th daily devotion. It says:

"You will not find My Peace by engaging in excessive planning: attempting to control what will happen to you in the future. That is a commonly practiced form of unbelief. When your mind spins with multiple plans, Peace may sometimes seem to be within your grasp; yet it always eludes you. Just when you think you have prepared for all possibilities, something unexpected pops up and throws things into confusion.

I did not design the human mind to figure out the future. That is beyond your capability. I crafted your mind for continual communication with Me. Bring Me all your needs, your hopes, and fears. Commit everything into My care. Turn from the path of planning to the path of Peace."

Peter 5:6-7; Proverbs 16:9; Psalm 37:5 (NKJV)

I can't tell you how hard it is to "let go" and follow this sentiment, as statistics don't bode well for me. I constantly feel the nagging need to do everything I can before my time is up, that includes fighting as hard as I can to NOT succumb to this ugly, horrific disease. It's just not in my nature to lose, but I do have to be realistic about the situation.

On Facebook today, I read an excellent article on LungCancer.net entitled, "Stage 4 Lung Cancer Stats Beginning Upward Climb," written by a Stage 4 lung cancer patient. Here are some excerpts that really struck me:

"I knew going in that a Stage 4 diagnosis meant a rough ride that would probably end at the pearly gates. And when I learned that the one-year median survival was only 8-12 months and the five year survival rate hovered between 1-2%, well that pretty much confirmed the reactions I was receiving from most people. That is, most people other than my oncologist.

"You see, I wanted my doctor to give me a prognosis so I would have a clear sense of whether I should start living it up and spending my retirement set-aside money immediately, while I was still fit enough to enjoy it. But he would not offer a prognosis. He just told me we would have to treat the disease and see how things proceed, especially since I was in good physical condition overall."

"This lead in is simply to say that even though we have well known statistics, they are both a large scale average and cannot predict the future of any single individual. In essence, they're a lagging indicator. The 5-year survival statistics, for instance, must be compiled using data from patients taken a minimum of five years prior to the latest publications. Meanwhile, in the past five years, massive changes have occurred in treatment modalities that I believe will have a significant impact on future 5-year stats. We just won't know about that for another five years or so."

"Lung cancer hope for the future comes in many forms--friends who are continuing to live for years and not months, FDA approval of new drug treatments, dedicated researchers tirelessly working on our behalf and yes, improving survival statistics, too."

Of course, like the writer of this article, I researched "my" statistics immediately after being diagnosed. They aren't good. The prognosis of "5% of individuals will still be living five years from their diagnosis" weighs heavily on my mind EVERYDAY. It never goes away. However, based upon the article I read today, I'm hopefully optimistic that with all of the new advances in technology and treatments, like I'm currently receiving, I can beat whatever odds are stacked against me. I hate losing and I'm not going down without a fight to the finish!

SEP 26 2018

Living in the Present

I'm sitting in my treatment chair at Dr. Gollard's office receiving my ninth infusion of Opdivo immunotherapy. When I arrived this morning, I was immediately taken into the "Biohazard" designated room where my vitals were taken, and I received my second round of the HS-110 test drug via five injections in my right shoulder blade. It hurt a bit more today than last week, when the shots were given in my right thigh, because there isn't as much excess tissue in the shoulder blade area. Next week, I'll get the injections in my left shoulder blade and then the following week in my left thigh. The injections will rotate like this for a total of 18 weeks.

Interestingly, I did not have any negative reactions to the HS-110 test drug last week. The raised spots from the injections disappeared after 2 1/2 days and I did not have any redness, soreness, fever, nausea or aches. My guess is that, like chemo, there will be a cumulative effect and I'll start not feeling so good in the next few weeks or so. We want this to happen because that means the combination treatment is working and that my immune system is responding! Fingers crossed that at some point I'm complaining about my symptoms and how horrible I feel. That seems kind of contradictory, doesn't it?!

I've earmarked a few recent passages from my book of daily devotions that have been meaningful to me as of late. I'd like to share one with you about the importance of living in the present and not wasting time and energy on obsessing about the future:

"Trust Me and refuse to worry, for I am your Strength and Song. You are feeling wobbly this morning, looking at difficult times looming ahead, measuring them against your own strength. However, they are not today's tasks--or even tomorrow's. So, leave them in the future and come home to the present, where you will find Me waiting for you. Since I am your Strength, I can empower you to handle each task as it comes. Because I am your Song, I can give you Joy as you work alongside Me.

Keep bringing your mind back to the present moment. Among all My creatures, only humans can anticipate future events. This ability is a blessing, but it becomes a curse whenever it is misused. If you use your magnificent mind to worry about tomorrow, you cloak yourself in dark unbelief. However, when the hope of heaven fills your thoughts, the Light of My Presence envelops you. Though heaven is future, it is also present tense. As you walk in the Light with Me, you have one foot on earth and one foot in heaven."

Exodus 15:2; 2 Corinthians 10:5; Hebrews 10:23

I used to live for the future and always had a plan. As a cancer patient in ongoing treatment, having any kind of plan is virtually impossible because you just don't know if or how your disease is going to progress. Frankly, I wake up each day just happy to be alive and grateful that I can get out of bed to live as fully as possible for the next 24 hours. This is not a bad thing. It helps me appreciate everything I experience in that day, just a little bit more. I don't take things for granted like I used to, especially because there is no guarantee for a tomorrow. I've come to terms and an inner peace with this. I try to live each day like I'm not "sick." Some days I don't even think about having chronic lung cancer, until the day comes to an end and I fall into bed.

Often my mind races then, so I take a Xanax to relax and help me fall asleep. It's all good.

Sometimes life will kick you around, but sooner or later you realize you're not just a survivor. You're a warrior and you're stronger than anything life throws your way. This is my life now and I've learned to embrace it on a day-to-day basis. For me, the Future is a very distant concept. It will be what it's supposed to be. I have absolutely no control over that right now, so why even think about it?

OCT 6 2018

One Year Later from Diagnosis

This past week was the one-year anniversary of me getting the news from my primary care doctor that I have Stage 3B lung cancer. I remember getting the call from him on my cell phone while I was playing poker at the Venetian. I saw his name come up on the screen and quickly left the table so I could take his call.

Dr. Tahir said, "Jim, I need you to come in to see me as soon as possible."

This can't be. I said, "This doesn't sound good, Dr. Tahir. Just tell me right now. I'm a big boy and can take it. Do I have Cancer AGAIN?!"

He paused and there was uncomfortable silence for a moment. My heart was beating out of my chest. He then softly said, "I'm so sorry, Jim, yes you do."

I remember shouting back at him on the phone, "No, this can't be! Are you fucking kidding me? AGAIN?! Are you sure?"

Thankfully, I had gone into a side area of the poker room to take his call and only a few people saw and heard my outburst. He repeated that I needed to come into see him immediately and we agreed that I'd be at his office first thing the next morning.

As I sit here writing this journal entry, it's amazing to me how vivid and pronounced that particular moment in time is imprinted in my memory. I remember everything.

After getting the horrifying news, I recall pulling myself together and going back to the poker table to continue playing in the tournament. There were tears rolling down my face. People at the table were staring at me. I didn't want to be there anymore, so I decided to go "All In" on the next hand hoping to get busted by someone with a better hand. I did. The next thing I remember is being in Dr. Tahir's office the following morning and discussing his thoughts on what I needed to do next. And so, my second cancer fight in four years had begun.

Over the past year, I've endured 90+ hours of high-powered chemotherapy, 12 intensive radiation treatments (over 4 hours), and nine Opdivo immunotherapy infusions (18 hours.) In addition, I've received three sets of five injections of the clinical trial test drug, which hopefully will improve the efficacy of the Opdivo in stimulating my immune system to fight harder against the cancer cells. This will be an 18-week program. If it's working, I should start feeling sick in the next couple of weeks (around Week 5 or 6) and then not feel well until Week 12 or 13. The last four or five weeks, I should start feeling a little better each week. I'm told everyone responds a bit differently, so it's hard to say what will happen with me.

I guess the good news is that I'm not worse off than a year ago. My tumor is still the same size and some infected nodes still remain in the middle of my chest, which is why I'm classified as Stage 3B. If the cancer spreads anywhere else in my body, I will be at Stage 4. The purpose of the current combo therapy I'm receiving (Opdivo and test drug) is to prevent that from happening. Ironically, I've been feeling great for the past three months, except for the two weeks when I had daily fevers of 100-103 as a reaction to the Opdivo. Now my hope is that I start getting sick soon. Then I know the treatment is working.

I've been in my head a lot lately. Life expectancy statistics for Stage 3B lung cancer patients aren't good, but they're improving a bit as new treatment options, like the one I'm on now, are coming into play.

Basically, only 5% of people with Stage 3B lung cancer are still living five years from their initial diagnosis. I've just completed Year 1. My fear is not knowing when things start getting worse.

It's different for everyone. I just want to be sure that I'm able to do all the things I want to do BEFORE the cancer spreads somewhere else and I'm too sick to do them.

Tick tock tick tock tick tock.

How much time do I really have? Not a day goes by when I don't think about this. Fortunately, I'm very good at compartmentalizing, so I'm not obsessing about it. Of course, I've pointedly asked Dr. Gollard and Dr. Dean about their thoughts on my life expectancy, but they don't want to talk about it. They said it's still a bit too early to tell. Dr. Dean promised me that when I finish the 18-week Opdivo/test drug combo and he gets the results from my January PET scan, that he will have this conversation with me. I'm assuming Dr. Gollard will do the same.

I just need to know, so I can plan. That's one of the most frustrating aspects of this journey. You can't really plan anything because there is so much that is unknown. Will the cancer spread? Will I get so sick from the treatments that I can't function normally? If the current treatment doesn't work, then what? Do I look for another clinical trial or try alternative medicine options, like THC, and be on a hallucinogenic high for three months? Where will I live if I get so sick that I can't take care of myself?

Questions like these are constantly haunting me. I fight them off as best as I can. Some days I'm better at it than others.

I've decided that I'm a Cancer Thriver, not a cancer victim. I could definitely be classified as a victim, since I'm now battling the bastard for the second time. But, that's not who I am. I'm embracing and living each day I have as fully as I can. In fact, I often "pretend" that I don't have Cancer and that I'm "normal." I think that's a good thing. It keeps my attitude much more positive. I don't dwell in self-pity or sadness. There is no benefit to that. That's not to say I don't sometimes ask myself, "Why ME?" But there's nothing I can do to change that. It has happened and I need to embrace it. What I can do is live in the present and be the best me I can be each day! This gives me purpose and satisfaction. As for the future, I also have no control over that. So, I try not to think too much about it. However, I do wish I could have more of a plan. It's just who I am.

I recently read a daily devotion that speaks to this:

"I am perpetually with you, taking care of you. That is the most important fact of your existence. I am not limited by time or space; My Presence with you is a forever-promise. You need not fear the future, for I am already there. When you make that quantum leap into eternity, you will find Me awaiting you in heaven. Your future is in My hands; I release it to you day by day, moment by moment. Therefore, do not worry about tomorrow.

I want you to live this day abundantly, seeing all there is to see, doing all there is to do. Don't be distracted by future concerns. Leave them to Me! Each day of life is a glorious gift, but so few people know how to live within the confines of today. Much of their energy for abundant living spills over the timeline into tomorrow's worries or past regrets. Their remaining energy is sufficient only for limping through the day, not for living it to the full. I am training you to keep your focus on My Presence in the present. This is how to receive abundant Life, which flows freely from My throne of grace."

Matthew 6:34; John 10:10; James 4:13-15

So, YES... this is what I aspire to achieve each day I continue to be on this great earth!

NOV 21 2018

All is Good

WOW! I can't believe it has been six weeks since my last journal entry. Apparently, I just needed a break from writing. And, if I'm being totally honest, I think the one-year anniversary of my lung cancer diagnosis threw me into a bit of a spiral. Even though I've been feeling really good physically and emotionally, I've been in a bit of a funk.

I so want to believe that I will be one of those lucky few that make it to the five year mark, but I also hope to be very functional and still able to enjoy life at that point. The scary realization that "getting sick" could start any day now OR perhaps not for two to three years is difficult to grasp. It makes planning for anything almost impossible, which is why I work so hard at living fully in the present.

For the past six weeks, I've continued the combo treatment of Opdivo, which I get by infusion every other week, and the HS-110 heat protein test drug that I receive weekly through a set of five injections alternating clockwise from my upper right thigh to right shoulder blade to left shoulder blade and finally to upper left thigh. Originally, the clinical trial folks thought that those patients showing ongoing regular reactions to the shots (soreness at injection site, general pain, aches, rash, etc) would be benefitting the most.

Now they believe that as long as there is an initial reaction of five "wheels" (raised white bumps) upon receiving the shots, it is a good sign that the drug is doing what it should for the patient. However, the real verdict will come from the results of my PET scan, which likely will happen the week between Christmas and New Years. We'll all be praying that the tumor in my right lung has shrunk a little or, at worst, stayed the same in size and location and that the cancerous lymph nodes in my chest are fewer or non-existent.

If the combo treatment has maintained or improved my status quo, we will continue on with it. Likely, my visit frequency will be reduced from weekly to monthly when I will receive both the Opdivo infusion simultaneously with the test drug shots. This would be awesome and free me up to travel more and/or move to Puerto Vallarta, MX. If I make the move, I will travel back to Las Vegas for a long weekend each month to get my treatment, play poker and see friends. It's a tentative plan for now, but I am serious about it. I've always wanted to live in a foreign country and on or near a beach. Puerto Vallarta (Old Town/Zona Romantico) has been a vacation destination of mine for many years and I absolutely love it there. I would fill my mornings with volunteer work, likely teaching English, spend afternoons on the beach, and play poker online at night. Living a simple life is very appealing to me and I think I'd really like it there! Plus, I know that Chris and other friends would come visit, so I wouldn't be too lonely. And, yes, Zing & Zang, my two cats, would make the trip with me.

As I mentioned previously, I've been feeling really good over the past six weeks and have had a ton of energy. So, I've been playing a lot of poker, but don't have the results I'd like for the effort I've put in. I've cashed in four or five tourneys over this timeframe, but nothing too big to be that excited about. I've taken a lot of bad beats and suck outs, which is part of the game, but feel like I've had way more than my fair share of them. Poker is a game of wide variances, so that is to be expected especially when you play every day. It's just hard to weather the ups and downs sometimes. Hopefully, things will get a bit better from now until the end of the year. The "good news" is that, per The Hendon Mob poker database I'm still ranked 10th in the World and 4th in the USA (out of over 565K tracked players) in number of major tournament cashes this year with 41. So, at times, I think I'm a bit hard on myself.

Finally, I'm very happy that Chris is here visiting me for a week. We've kept busy with binge-watching some Netflix shows, like *The Bodyguard* (soooooo good!), going to the movies (*Boy Erased* and *Halloween*), eating out, and distributing clothes to the homeless last Sunday with a group of my poker friends. It was our second annual "Help the Homeless" event and we supplied over 150 homeless folks in Tent City with underwear, t-shirts, socks, shoes, jeans, pants, sweaters, hoodies, sweatshirts, dress shirts, workout gear, blankets, pillows, gloves, wipes, sanitary napkins, etc. It was such a rewarding experience! We had so much stuff that we could have opened our own thrift shop. I can't wait to do it again next year.

That's it for now. I'm sorry I haven't been more consistent with my writing. I will certainly try to do better! Tomorrow is Thanksgiving and we all have so much to be thankful for. I'm just happy and blessed to be alive!

#BackToBeingPetzingStrong

DEC 15 2018

Holidays Can Be Tough

I've been physically feeling great the past few weeks. My energy, attitude and outlook have been really good until yesterday. For a number of reasons, the holidays have always been a bit difficult for me. I don't generally feel the joy and Christmas spirit that others do, but I do my best to play along. This holiday season I'm in a very introspective place to the point where I finally had to let it out. Facebook was my vessel for doing so and here's what I posted yesterday:

"For many of us fighting cancer during the holidays is especially tough. As others are celebrating the joys of Christmas and planning their 2019 New Years' resolutions, we constantly have in the back of our minds whether we will be around for the holidays next year. I know that I'm doing my best to put on a happy face and get into the spirit of the season, but I'm scared about what's in store for me. I want to believe that all will be fine, but there's a good possibility that I could get sicker and not be able to function like I am now. Attitude is everything and I will continue to live each day fully with hope, optimism and positivity. But deep down inside, I can't help but be concerned about my future.

I'm quite sure that many folks in my situation feel the same, so please understand that we're doing our best to embrace this special time of year and be present each day for our families, friends and loved ones during this holiday season."

So there you have it. I've put it out there and feel a bit better. It is what it is.

On a more uplifting note, I did manage to buy some Christmas cards yesterday for family and close friends, along with some wrapping paper. Need to get some gifts wrapped this weekend, too. I've also been listening to a 24/7 Christmas music radio station (106.5 FM) in my car to get myself into the Christmas spirit. I'll be flying to Michigan on Tuesday afternoon to be with Chris and I'm so looking forward to a traditional family Christmas with them.

I'll be back in touch soon. Thanks for being there for me!

JAN 3 2019

Best News Ever!

Happy New Year!

I made it through the holidays feeling really good, both physically and mentally. Christmas with Chris and his family was just what I needed. We also traveled to Traverse City to see his Mom, Joan, who I just love. On Christmas Eve, I made dinner for everyone: cheesy chicken stuffed shells, shrimp teriyaki, mandarin orange and Craisins salad, green beans with bacon, and M&M dream bars for dessert. There was even a little snow, so we did have a white Christmas.

Upon my return to Vegas, my high school buddy, Mike, and his wife, Kelly, came to visit and stayed with me until yesterday. They came and went as they liked and got the full flavor of Vegas during their visit. Together, we played a lot of Black Jack (successfully), participated in a small poker tourney at MGM (unsuccessfully), experienced downtown Fremont Street (always interesting), had some nice meals, watched and bet on NFL Football (successfully) at the Westgate Sports Book (largest in World) and saw Boyz2Men and Bruno Mars in concert (amazing!) at the T-Mobile Arena. I really enjoyed having them.

The icing on the cake was the great news I received on December 31st during my appointment with Dr. Gollard to review my PET scan results! Here's what I learned and posted on Facebook that day:

"To all of my friends who have been praying for and supporting me through my second cancer fight, Thank You! God has heard us all. I met with my chemo oncologist today. Results from the PET scan I had late last week could not have been better! It appears that the combo therapy of Opdivo and clinical trial test drug is doing its job. I am so relieved. I'm showing what's called a partial response to the treatment. In other words...a very slight shrinkage of the tumor in my right lung. There is currently no sign of growth or movement, and the cancerous lymph nodes in mid-chest cavity are gone! We're continuing with bi-weekly Opdivo infusions and going monthly on the test drug injections. All good! I feel so blessed to be starting off 2019 with this awesome news!"

Truly, I couldn't have expected to hear anything better. I was confident that I would receive a good report because I've been feeling so good during the past four months but was worried at the same time about hearing something bad. Cancer plays with your head that way. I'm in such a good head and body place now as I embark on my plans for 2019 which include a lot of travel, adventure and checking off my bucket list!

On January 16th, I'll be flying to Sydney, Australia with Ardys to see her daughter, Rachel, and then we're off to Melbourne to play poker in the world-famous Aussie Millions poker series. Hopefully, we'll both hit it big there and start off 2019 with a bang! I return to Vegas on February 5th, so it will be a nice three-week getaway where I can enjoy Summer in Australia, too.

Here's wishing all of my readers a very happy, healthy and prosperous 2019!

NOV 19 2019

The Last Chapter… At Least For Now

It has been 10 1/2 months since my last entry. I stopped writing because I developed writer's block and just wasn't feeling up to it. It's hard to explain, but I didn't want to share my thoughts about my fight with cancer anymore. It was draining me.

However, not completing this last chapter has been hanging over my head for too long now. I've even had bad dreams about it. It's so NOT ME to start something and not finish it. I just haven't had the motivation to wrap up my story. What the hell is wrong with me!?

Perhaps the issue has been that this story never really ends. The fact is that I'm chronically ill and incurable. I will always have lung cancer. It will not go away. No surgeon will operate on me because I'm so high risk. Currently, there are no treatments that will eradicate it. And at some point, it will get the best of me.

Knowing this has become a struggle. Even though I've physically been on top of my game and don't look or act sick, I'm emotionally exhausted. What many don't recognize is that just because I carry it all so well, doesn't mean it's not heavy. I often feel like a paperweight is pressing down upon me, squeezing out every last bit of oxygen so I can't breathe. When I see myself going there, I work hard to snap out of it. I can't allow myself to be a victim of the devil called Cancer.

I like to refer to cancer as a "disability." Disabilities can be overcome. No one needs to or should be defined by their disability. Having a disability does not necessarily mean that one can't live fully. We figure out a way to make it work for us, not against us.

Each day that I wake up and roll out of bed, I feel blessed. I'm grateful to have another opportunity to live fully in the moment and be the best person I can be. Clearly, I have many flaws, but I want to be a real inspiration to others and try to make a difference in some way.

On that note, I've spent the past year checking off my "bucket list" items, while I'm feeling well and can travel. I've enjoyed amazing trips to Australia, Spain, Florida, Connecticut, Michigan and California to see family & friends and play poker. In February, I went on a Caribbean cruise with Chris and was fortunate to win another cruise for two when I took down the onboard poker tournament! I'll be enjoying that cruise in December with Elizabeth. So, life is pretty good right now, and I really have nothing to complain about.

However, for the past six months or so, I've been flailing around in a "black hole" with no clear direction or plan. This is a result of having an undefined prognosis for longevity and survival.

I'm also burned out on Vegas, miss being with Chris on a regular basis, and don't feel fulfilled. Additionally, playing poker has become more of a job than a hobby. It's also a very selfish game.

But that's not who I am or what I'm about. I know I'm supposed to be doing something more and it has to do with helping others. My Higher Power has kept me going for a purpose. I need to deliver on that for Him and for myself.

Now, with this final blog entry, the content for my second book is a wrap. I'll be contacting my publisher shortly to get the ball rolling. I'm so hopeful that those who read it will take away something valuable for themselves.

I also hope to embark on another project that I'm very excited about! It's a YouTube video series called, "Don't Stop Believing: Thriving with Lung Cancer." Its mission will be to provide hope, inspiration and support for lung cancer fighters, thrivers and those who love them. The series will consist of a dozen or so five to ten minute informational and uplifting segments. These themed episodes will encompass the physical, emotional and spiritual challenges faced during one's journey toward wellness. It will be fun working on this with a few of my talented friends. Together, WE will make a positive impact on the lives of others!

Since I can't fix the world's problems or cure cancer, I can at least do my best to make a difference where I CAN! I'm very optimistic that my new book and video series will help do that, while re-energizing me in a much-needed way.

And now that I've told you about these endeavors, there's no turning back. I must and will make them happen!

I will live with intention. Shouldn't we all?

EPILOGUE

March 31, 2020

Fast forward 4 1/2 months since my last entry. It's hard to believe what has happened both to me and all of us during this short timeframe.

We'll start with the good things. On November 26, I placed second in a very large and significant World Series of Poker Circuit (WSOPC) event ($1700 No Limit Holdem Main with 778 players) at Planet Hollywood here in Las Vegas. It was my largest cash ever in a poker tournament, taking home $133,462! I played a total of 30 hours over three days, but it was well worth it. Clearly, this was the ultimate highlight of my professional poker career so far. So exciting!

Then, in early December, I went on a Caribbean cruise (Harmony of the Seas) with my angel, Elizabeth. She was my rock during my battle with neck cancer in late 2014/early 2015 and is like a sister to me. We had an awesome time in St. Maarten, San Juan, and Haiti and thoroughly enjoyed the ship's onboard activities, like the ice skating, water, comedy and Broadway-type shows. We ate and ate and ate our way through the cruise and were lucky to have some amazing weather!

After spending an awesome week before Christmas with Chris, my boyfriend, and his family, I went to Durant, OK to play in the WSOPC tournament series at the Choctaw Casino & Resort. I had one nice cash for $2K+ and a couple of smaller ones. Upon my return to Vegas, I played in a few tourneys at the Wynn and placed third of 50 players in a $400 Pot Limit Omaha event for a win of $3000. So it was a pretty good start to the year.

At the end of January, I saw my friend, Ryan, in Fort Lauderdale, and then went on another Caribbean cruise, this time with Card Player Cruises. Joining me was my bestie, April, along with other good friends (Bill, Jim, Marty and Sandy.) We're all avid poker players, so this trip was just perfect for us. Every evening, and during all days at sea, we had the opportunity to play cash games and tournaments. Most of my friends won future cruises or had some nice cashes in the tournaments. My girl, April, actually won the first tournament on the cruise! Even though I bricked (struck out) everything I played, I had an amazing time and never laughed so much in a week as I did on that trip. It was also the first time I ever did gummies. We'd enjoy a few each evening and boy did they hype my appetite. I always had a plate of food or cookies in hand, ate non-stop, and ran my mouth incessantly while giggling. If you're a poker player and enjoy cruising, I highly recommend a Card Player Cruises cruise.

February wasn't a great poker month, so I took a break and flew to St. Petersburg, FL to meet up with Chris for a long weekend. The weather was surprisingly cool, so we never made it the beach. We did, however, do a lot of walking, bar hopping and eating. The highlight was going to a huge local craft fair in the park just across the street from the very nice, quaint old downtown hotel we stayed at. We had an awesome time together, as always!

Now for the not so good news. Prior to going to St. Pete, I had a CT scan on February 4 and then a PET Scan on February 19. The CT scan showed that the cancer in my right lung had spread from the main tumor to the outer edges and to the area at the top of my stomach and bottom of my esophagus. It also unveiled some new additional spots on my diaphragm. Getting the news from Dr. Gollard that I now had Stage 4 lung cancer and that the cancer was actively progressing, came as a horrific shock as I had been feeling great. He was also very concerned that the cancer may have spread to my liver, so that's why I had the PET scan a few days later. Thankfully, the results came back with no cancer in the liver.

Given the progression of the cancer, Dr. Gollard put me on a new power-packed chemo regimen designed to work in parallel with the Opdivo immunotherapy and test drug shots I was already receiving monthly. I was so worried that that going back on chemotherapy would disqualify me from the clinical trial program, but it didn't and now I'm the only person in the World receiving what we call, The Quad. It includes two chemotherapy drugs, Taxotere and Cyramza, that I will receive every three weeks for nine weeks, along with monthly Opdivo immunotherapy infusions and the five trial drug injections. The purpose of this intensive approach is to attack the cancer so it becomes overwhelmed and stops moving through my body.

Today, I'm receiving my second treatment of the chemotherapy. I handled the first treatment quite well and only had a mild fever and body aches during the first week after the initial treatment. I've still had an appetite and been able to function normally over the past three weeks. Hopefully, my reaction will be similar after today's treatment, but I've been told that the side effects often differ after each treatment. So fingers crossed that I don't get really sick.

The last live poker tournament I played was on March 8 at the Wynn. Why? The COVID-19 virus pandemic has hit us all. It causes a pneumonia that fills the lungs with water and chokes off the ability to breathe. Since I'm in the highest risk group of dying from this disease (almost 60 years old, have Stage 4 lung cancer, am receiving chemo, and have a very compromised immune system), I have been self-isolating and quarantined in my apartment since March 11. Today is Day 20 and the pandemic is running rampant through New York, especially NYC, and the states of New Jersey, California, Michigan, Massachusetts, Florida, and Louisiana. Current estimates of potential deaths in the USA are now at 100,000 to 200,000 people. This is a hugely transmittable and fatal virus, that is most dangerous to older folks and those with underlying medical conditions. I am so scared that if I contract COVID-19, I will die. There is a huge shortage of personal protection equipment (PPE) for our healthcare workers and first responders, along with masks, ventilators, ICU units and hospital beds. This is the biggest disaster, both health-wise and economically, that we well see in our lifetime. All non-essential businesses, schools, gyms, bars and restaurants, malls, etc. are closed. There aren't enough test kits available to determine who is and isn't carrying the virus, which is a big problem because many carriers are asymptomatic and don't even know they have the disease. All we can do is stay at home to try to prevent the spread of the virus and not get infected ourselves. Currently, April 30 has been set as the date by President Trump to evaluate whether or not the USA can open back up for business. My guess is that social distancing, self-isolation and quarantining will continue through at least mid-May. Today, over 165,000 Americans have tested positive for COVID-19 in America and there have been over 3,000 deaths.

My biggest fear is that this awful COVID-19 is going to take me out after I've worked so hard at beating neck cancer in late 2014/early 2015 and fighting lung cancer for the past 2 1/2 years. Given the severe ventilator shortage that currently exists, I have nightmares of lying on a makeshift bed, in an overcrowded hospital emergency room, next to a younger man or woman with two young kids at home. We both have COVID-19 and are in desperate need of oxygen. Two doctors are conferring privately with each other and I overhear them talking about the fact that they only have one ventilator to keep one of us breathing. Who are they are going to choose? I don't think it's going to be me because of my older age and the fact that I have Stage 4 lung cancer. The young man has a wife and family to support. He has a better fighting chance. OMG, they're rolling out the ventilator. Who are they going to pick?

I'm still breathing.

Made in the USA
Columbia, SC
26 August 2020

17710005R00214